# The Lesser Banishing Ritual of the Pentagram:

## A 21st Century Grimoire

# The Lessser Banishing Ritual of the Pentagram:

## A 21st Century Grimoire

## Michael Benjamin

Megalithica Books

**Stafford England**

The Lesser Banishing Ritual of the Pentagram:
A 21st Century Grimoire
by Michael Benjamin
© 2014 First edition

Cover Art: Danielle Lainton
Editor: Marianne Braendlin
Layout: Taylor Ellwood

Set in Book Antiqua
MB0169

ISBN 978-1-905713-95-0

Megalithica Books Edition 2014

A Megalithica Books Publication
An imprint of Immanion Press
http://www.immanion-press.com
info@immanion-press.com

# DEDICATION

To the original scholarly genius behind
the Hermetic Order of the Golden Dawn,
the Master Mentor whom the Great Beast 666 betrayed;
for as the Mysteries teach
(and as reflected in Frazier's *The Golden Bough*):

**"The initiate must kill the initiator."**

*S' Rhioghail Mo Dream;
Deo Duce Comite Ferro.*

". . .the laborer is worthy of his rewards."
-1 *Timothy* 5:18.

"My business is circumference."
-Emily Dickinson

# ✪Table of Contents✪

## Deo Duce Comite Ferro

Enflame me in thy light
Of golden spirit,
Mighty Lord!
With Aaron's staff as my guide
And my companion, Michael's sword.

# Chapter 1: Introduction

*"Magic, after all, is but the absolute science of nature and its laws.*
*So the Star of Hope shines for us truly as when,*
*like a magnet, it drew the Wise Men to Bethlehem.*
*You will seek the Holy Doctrine – the Blazing Star of Truth, the Royal*
*Secret of creation. So do we slowly climb toward the final goal, the*
*state of perfection."*

**-Brother Henry C. Clausen, 33° (1976)**
(former Sovereign Grand Commander of the Supreme Scottish
Rite Council of Ancient and Accepted Freemasonry; Mother
Supreme Council of the World).

# The Lesser Banishing Ritual of the Pentagram

## Opening Qabalistic Cross

Facing East, take a steel dagger in thy right hand, touch thy forehead with its blade and declare, "Ateh."

Touch the dagger blade to thy heart and declare, "Malkuth."

Touch the blade to thy right shoulder and declare, "Ve-Geburah."

Touch the blade to thy left shoulder and declare, "Ve-Gedulah."

Grasp dagger between thy hands and declare, "Le-Olahm."

Raise dagger skyward and sing, "Amen."

## Main Ritual

Facing East, trace the earth pentagram with thy dagger from hips to forehead, and then point its tip to the center of the star traced, vibrate YHVH.

Trace a horizontal arc of visualized light or flame from the star's center with thy dagger while rotating a quarter turn deosil. Facing South, trace the earth pentagram with thy dagger from hips to forehead, and then point its tip to the center of the star traced and vibrate ADNI.

Trace a horizontal arc of visualized light or flame from the star's center with thy dagger while rotating a quarter turn deosil. Facing West, trace the earth pentagram with thy dagger from hips to forehead, and then point its tip to the center of the star traced and vibrate EHIH.

Trace a horizontal arc of visualized light or flame from the star's center with thy dagger while rotating a quarter turn deosil. Facing North, trace the earth pentagram with thy dagger from hips to forehead, and then point its tip to the center of the star traced and vibrate AGLA.

Trace a horizontal arc of visualized light or flame from the star's center with thy dagger while rotating a quarter turn deosil, thus returning to the East and completing the flaming circle around thee. Keep in thy mind's eye the stars and their proper elements and the flaming circle connecting them and encircling thee. Extend thy arms in the form of the Cross.

Then, while still in the posture of the cross declare, "Before me stands Raphael." (Visualize the proper Archangel before thee as a giant lighted figure whose wings stretch across the expanse of the East quarter).

"Behind me Gabriel." (Visualize the proper Archangel as before to the West).

"To my right hand Michael." (Visualize the proper Archangel as before to the South).

"To my left hand Auriel." (Visualize the proper Archangel as before to the North).

"For around me flames the pentagram."

"As in the column shines the six-rayed star." (Visualize the Hexagram enwrapped around thine own body, parallel to the ground, with its front and rear points aligned with the centers of the East and West pentagrams. Maintain the visualization of the entire scene: stars and circle aflame; angels in countenances of fiercely warding and guarding).

# Conclude with the Qabalisitic Cross.

# Foreword

We live in a time unparalleled in human history, in a time unmatched in Gaia's entire existence. Our potential as a species for either positive, progressive ascension, or conversely, for negative demonic reversion exceeds immensity, is above and beyond any quantitative measure. Ramana Maharshi and John Wayne Gacy would be obvious, respective examples of the stark, paradoxical potentials that exist in humanity's nature. As these real examples illustrate, our duality represents both the sage and the monster, the angel and the beast. With one open hand we create medicines and therapies that heal the multitudes. With the other fist we foster nuclear missiles and neutron bombs that threaten our very futures. Regardless of the rugged individualism that was necessary at a previous stage of our social evolution, a stage required to break us from the bonds of dogma, tribalism, and tyranny, we have now entered a New Age, from Pices to Aquarius, in our development as a species. We have entered an age in which it has become our responsibility, in which it has become a dire need for our own planetary survival, to choose a collective path that will lead to a greater good for the whole. In the past, oppressive dogmas and ideologies have attempted to forcibly guide us towards what was proclaimed by such proponents as the "greater good." Historical retrospection has proven that such measures were most often conspired deceit. Both governments and religions, ideally meant to be the purveyors of security and truth, have more often been motivated by the selfish interests of their own aristocratic elite and not by the common needs of the subjects for whose care their authority was responsible. In our future, if there is to be one, humanity shall not be dependent upon external, corporeal sources of control to guide us in what is true and right, for such mechanisms (like prisons and priests) have already proven themselves sadly inadequate. It is up to us as sovereign individuals to seek a higher consciousness, to seek the next step of the evolutionary impulse within ourselves that will someday permit us to only do what is loving, right, and true. As the

Christos admonished us, "Be ye therefore perfect even as thy father in heaven is perfect." (*Matthew* 5:48, KJV). Or perhaps to the 19th century hymn, *These Things Shall Be*, by J. Addington Symond, should we steadfastly aspire:

> These things shall be: a loftier race
> Than e'er the world hath known shall rise
> With flame of freedom in their souls
> And light of knowledge in their eyes.
> They shall be gentle, brave, and strong
> To spill no drop of blood, but dare
> All that may plant man's lordship firm
> On earth, and fire, and sea, and air.
>
> Nation with nation, land with land,
> In armed shall live as comrades free;
> In every heart and brain shall throb
> The pulse of one fraternity.
> Man shall love man with heart as pure
> And fervent as the young-eyed throng
> Who chant their heavenly psalms before
> God's face with undiscordant song.
>
> New arts shall bloom of loftier mould,
> And mightier music thrill the skies,
> And every life shall be a song,
> when all the earth is paradise.
> There shall be no more sin, nor shame,
> Though pain and passion may not die;
> For man shall be at one with God. . .

The previous century, and well as this one, has seen an explosion, an absolute exponential expansion, in all intellectual realms as far-reaching as philosophy to technology. It could be rightfully argued that the knowledge attained in the 20th century surpassed the sum-total of knowledge achieved by our species prior to this time. I specifically use the word "knowledge" here, meaning facts and information, for while we have excelled in this quest, our growth in wisdom and understanding has been critically negligible. Humanity does not know how to correctly utilize the knowledge it has obtained. In our pitiful lack of wisdom, bridled with our inherent hubris, the only thing that our precious knowledge has achieved is to carry us to the precarious brink of eco-suicide and bio-genocide.

Despite our incredible advances in learning, the great sorrows of the human condition (known as far back as the pre-Christian era and extrapolated by the Buddha), such as physical death, old age, sickness, poverty, loneliness, hatred, avarice, and so on, not only still exist, but rage as a wild fire and advance as a plague upon the planet. Our enormous advances in information and machinery, instead of instilling a greater peace and order to our world, have proven a terrible nemesis. This nemesis of knowledge, without the temperance of wisdom, has proven the single most monumental contributor to an increasing inner sense of spiritual confusion and outer state of socio-political instability. Religion, science, and government, despite their many obvious successes, have also been responsible for innumerable failures. Such global crises as economic marginalization of peoples, despicable planetary pollution, destruction of habitat and biodiversity, and the increasing barbarity of warfare provide some basic examples of such pervasive yet common catastrophes.

If we do not wish for our species, and most others under our human sway, to go the way predicted in the various apocalyptic prophecies – from John of Patmos, to the Vedic Kali Yuga, to the Norse Ragnarok, to the end of the Mayan calendar – we must pursue a higher wisdom through the betterment of change, through self-evolution to a higher consciousness. Not the so-called external, materialistic progress that has birthed so many forms of destruction and unhappiness today. On the contrary, we must seek an internal and spiritual progress characterized by a profound insight into ourselves, coupled with an unyielding empathy and compassion for all forms of life. We must become our own Messiachs, our own Mahdis, our own Matreiyas. The vow of the Bodhisattva must be taken by all. In short, as the Golden Dawn's own creed avowed, we must become *more than human.*

If we are to survive as a species, and not take most of the magnificent and beautiful life-forms upon Gaia with us into the oblivion of extinction, we must, as Christ told us, be **reborn**. This rebirth is not to be mistaken for the paltry, erroneous view held by the infantile factions of "born again" Christian fundamentalists who espouse a retrogression into infantile states of consciousness and petty tribalism, but a progression into a *truly* universal and evolved state of being. Such fundamentalist factions, sadly and tragically, deny that evolution even exists. They ignorantly fail to realize the true lessons of their Savior, and in worshiping the messenger have completely and utterly missed His message; a message more akin to the teachings of Krishna, Buddha, and Lao Tzu; to Meister Eckhart, Jacob Boehme, and Eckhart Tolle; to Ramana Maharshi, Adyushanti, and Ken Wilber; than that of any pope, bishop, church council, priest, pastor, or minister. It takes more than verbally pledging one's allegiance to a Palestinian carpenter who was hung upon a Tau to gain the rebirth Jesus Christ illuminated. This rebirth is in fact the most profound change to be experienced and witnessed in humanity's biological and cultural history, and it is in our own hands, not His, to accomplish. From *homo sapiens* must be born, must evolve, the *homo novus*, the *homo spiritus;* what Jesus called *the new creature.*

This lofty goal cannot be accomplished by reason *or* faith. Nor can it be accomplished by their respective disciplines of science *or* religion. Our progress and our survival will only be possible by their fusion, by the integral, perennial synthesis of these seemingly competing and conflicting intellectual approaches of faith *and* reason; religion *and* science. It is the essence of this synthesis which forms the philosophy and practice of all true White Magick. It is this essence which guides all aspirants on the Right Hand Path, upon the Road of Return, to cross the ocean to the Other Shore.

Despite the prehistoric origins of Magickal practice hidden in the dawn of humanity's first shamans, Magick's philosophy holds profound significance for this new millennium as we rapidly draw closer to the full circle of our history. Magick, as properly understood today, is not a belief in superstitions, nor a systemization of dogmatism and metaphysics. It is rather, the correlation and hybridization of all forms of knowledge *and* wisdom pursued; or to express it more colloquially. . .of all "truth." When Pontius Pilate asked the Christos, *"Quo vadis?"* the scriptures are unfortunately reticent in providing an explicit answer. The Divine has left this quest for each and every one of us and no one person may impose a complete explanation. Christ, however, did accurately report that in the last days all that was secret (*occulto* in Latin) would be known. Magick is this conscious and artful quest for the *vadis occulto* in ourselves, in the universe, and in the Divine. Without Magick we may never as a species be able to unveil the mystery of a higher state of being; to create a link to another order of energy; to sustain the emergence of a new level of consciousness.

It is high time for the establishment of this link! It is time for new paradigms and modes of thought! Not, however, by replacing the ancient ideas, knowledge, and traditions upon which our civilization has been raised, but rather by reinterpreting the founding mysteries and furthering the understanding of our ancestral origins in the light of our current conditions. It is time for a higher level of consciousness in humanity; for an evolutionary step forward and upward, selflessly directed towards our Divine Source. Without this aspiration, which is the ultimate goal of all true White Magickal schools and hierarchies, we will fall far short of being spiritually reborn, of establishing the New Jerusalem, of uniting Heaven and Earth, of reconciling the Samsara with the Nirvana, of metaphorically casting the myth of Satan to Hell, and of unlocking the Kingdom of God that is within us. As the Magus Crowley stated, *Magick is for all*, but it is perhaps most needed for us today than at any other juncture in the epochs. At this apex of our history it is needed as no less than a crucial panacae for our collective critical illness.

It is my Will that this modest thesis should provide a quaint window into the world and meaning of the Magi. But be warned. . .please take heed. This treatise is meant as a potent and specialized grimoire of my own design. **It is not to be taken lightly.** You need but turn the page to begin the way. May only the serious, reverent, and thoughtful be the ones to do so.

-MB (Rockford, Illinois – February 2013).

# The Duality Paradigm of Magick

> We assert a secret source of energy which
> explains the phenomenon of genius. . . This
> source may be reached by the following out of
> definite rules, by the degree of success
> depending upon the capacity of the seeker...
> We assert that the critical phenomenon which
> determines success is an occurrence in the brain
> characterized essentially by the uniting of
> subject and object.
> -Aleister Crowley, *Book Four.*

Before proceeding any further, it is necessary to provide a construct upon which our examination may be based. To do so, two definitions are necessary at this beginning point. Regardless of the plethora of ancient and modern models constructed to frame the myriad of schools of occultism, the proponent of Magick can most inclusively and simplistically interpret its workings by the dual theorems hereby explained by the terms *figurative* and *literal*.

The **figurative theory** denotes that all Magickal workings and exercises are merely emblematic and theatric analogies; that they are but symbolic poetry and dramatic practices[1] designed to affect the practitioner's psychological and emotional processes. Figurative Magick could therefore be considered Jungian in its strictest sense, stimulating and utilizing the subconscious mind and its archetypal "programming" or "hardwiring" (to use modern computer analogies) by use of purposeful, systematic artistic ritual and symbolism. As in any

---

[1] All drama began in religion, specifically of the pagan variety, in ancient Greece, and in Egypt before her. The Egyptian Priests, and Greek Priests and Priestesses, invented theatrical drama as a means of relating their mythos and cosmologies and as a way to invoke the presence and powers of their gods. This was the historical beginning of the Mystery cults; the usage of their dramatic theater also being the vehicle for the initiation of Neophytes. "Historical" beginning is specified here, as the true roots of such practices predate written record in the mists of Shamanic tribal prehistory.

other religious or philosophical system, the figurative Magician's purpose resides in the transformation of their inner mind, soul, or self. The heightening of the mind's faculties, such as thought control, memory, organizational skills, creativity, analysis, synthesis, along with what Crowley (1970) has termed, "The broadening of the horizon of the mind," (p. 375) are expected outcomes of disciplined dedication. Magick's effects, therefore, beyond influencing the individual's own behavior or actions, are not expected to have external repercussions, but simply internal subjective results.

In contrast, the **literal theory** accepts Magick at its original face value, assuming that it can and will, like a scientific technology, cause effects upon objective, external reality by its secret workings upon cosmic mechanisms. Literalist Magick is thus not intended as a means of mystical introspection, self-mastery, or psychological development per se, though these qualities may be prerequisites for the efficacy of certain practices. It is, rather, the Magickal mastery and control of nature and aspects of the external environment that are the literalist's intentions and aspirations. The eminent occult scholar Richard Cavendish (1983) explained this stance when he wrote,

> When a magician masters the full power of his will and acts in a certain way, he believes that he causes the forces of the universe outside him to act in the same way. This is an extension. . .of "As above, so below." (p. 17).

Together, these two perspectives intermingle to form what I term the **Duality Paradigm of Magick**. I postulate no opinion as to which is proper, but rather, opine that all workings, causes, and effects of Magick reside within one, the other, or a combination of both these theorems. In regard to the Lesser Banishing Ritual of the Pentagram (hereafter abbreviated as LPR for Lesser Pentagram Ritual), as we proceed we shall examine how such a practice's analysis lends itself to both of these definitions.

# Fundamental Advice

To correctly pursue the discipline of any Magickal system or ritual, like the LPR, the student must arduously incorporate the two-fold path of learning. This two-fold path contains both the road of scholastic discipline, that of the academic, and the road of practical experience, that of the journeyman. These are the only two keys to the mastery of any skill, Magick being no different. Intensive study and persevering practice are the only secrets to expertise.

Likewise, since Magick in part consists of the scientific method, certain scientific principles must be maintained in all Magickal practices such as the LPR. The student must strictly follow the discipline of replicable experimentation and quantifiable evidence in their practices. Such practice must thus be recorded in journal form for the purpose of retrospection, the gleaning of patterns, and review of results. For the LPR it is suggested that the student keep an on-going diary recording their daily practice of the ritual, the time performed, any results noted in the interior of the psyche, emotions, etc., as well as any paranormal phenomenon noted. Such a record cannot be too detailed, even the slightest of notes could perhaps bear future fruit upon re-reading and ensuing contemplation.

Beyond this scientific approach, the student must, in addition, through their own personal evolution, learn how to reconcile the internal paradox needed to be a Magician. This paradox is the need to harmonize the opposing factors of the scientist and the monk. That is, the Magician must possess the logic, skepticism, and critical judgment of the scientist while still maintaining the passionate faith and fervent devotional ecstasy of the cleric. All great masters of the occult have possessed and espoused this personal formula, both Aleister Crowley and Eliphas Levi[2] being no exceptions.

With regard to the former quality, remember the Buddha's words,

---

[2] For an extended examination of the paradoxes between reason and faith that must be reconciled in the practitioner of the Magickal arts see Eliphas Levi <u>Paradoxes of the Highest Science</u>.

> Believe nothing, O monks, merely because you have been told it or because it is tradition, or because you yourselves have imagined it. Do not believe what your teacher tells you merely out of respect for the teacher. But whatsoever, after due examination and analysis, you find to be conducive to the good, the benefit, the welfare of all beings – that doctrine believe and cling to, and take it as your guide. (Kalama Sutta).

In addition to the Buddha's words, we must also turn to another master of the East for further solid guidance in spiritual instruction. The following lessons are taken from one of the Buddha's spiritual descendants, the great Padmasambhava, who is credited with bringing the Mahayana (or greater vehicle) doctrine of Buddhism to Tibet. While not specific to the topic of the LPR, these general guidelines are worthwhile knowledge for any spiritual seeker regardless of time, locale, personality, or system. The following advice is quoted from the great Parisian adventurer (and Lama in her own right), the eminent Tibetan translator and Buddhist scholar Alexandra David-Neel (1971).[3]

> Padmasambhava is said to have described the stages of the mystic path in the following way.
> 1). To read a large number of books on the various religions and philosophies. To listen to many learned doctors professing the different doctrines. To experiment oneself with a number of methods.
> 2). To choose a doctrine among the many one has studied and discard the other ones, as the eagle carries off only one sheep from the flock.
> 3). To remain in a lowly condition, humble in one's demeanour, not seeking to be

---

[3] Her works represent some of the most vital pioneering studies and foundational literature regarding both Tibet and Buddhism in the early 20th century. She was an accomplished disciple of Lamism and a longtime resident in the "Land of the Snows" when few in the West had even heard of the Dalai Lama!

conspicuous or important in the eyes of the world, but behind apparent insignificance, to let one's mind soar high above all worldly power and glory.

4). To be indifferent to all. Behaving like the dog or pig that eats what chance brings them. Not making any choice among the things which one meets. Abstaining from any effort to acquire or avoid anything. Accepting with an equal indifference whatever comes: riches or poverty, praise or contempt, giving up the distinction between virtue and vice, honourable and shameful, good and evil. Being neither afflicted, nor repenting whatever one may have done and, on the other hand, never being elated nor proud on account of what one has accomplished.

5). To consider with perfect equanimity and detachment the conflicting opinions and the various manifestations of the activity of beings. To understand that such is the nature of things, the inevitable mode of action of each entity and to remain always serene. To look as a man standing on the highest mountain of the country looks at the valleys and the lesser summits spread out about him.[4]

6). It is said that the sixth stage cannot be described in words. It corresponds to the realization of the 'Void' which, in Lamaist terminology, means the inexpressible reality. (pp. 268-269).

To briefly comment on these crucial injunctions. . .

In 1 we see the very injunction of the two-fold path of learning advised in the opening paragraphs of this section: study and practice!

---

[4] Or to add a Western correlative to this truth, as the great Roman Stoic philosopher-emperor Marcus Aurelius Antoninus said, "Live as on a mountain" (cited in Eliot,1969, p. 279).

In 2 we see a decisiveness and focus that must be exercised should the aspirant wish to make any real progress and not be stuck "spinning their wheels" throughout this incarnation.

In 3 and 4 we see the example provided by the very life of S.L. MacGregor Mathers, a man of both supreme occult and martial erudition who often did not know where his next meal would come from. Like the Buddha, he sacrificed a life of ease to be a devout student of the Mysteries, for both his own evolution and the betterment of the world. As a result, poverty, as well as the sword, were often his companions.

In the last sentence of number 5 we see the very essence and imagery of the lesson contained in Key 9 of the Greater Arcana (The Hermit), to be examined later in Chapter Three.

In 6 we see the Lamaist conception of Divinity, expressed as "the Void," despite the popular misconception that Buddhism is an atheistic philosophy! As the impeccable scholar of both Celtic and Tibetan religion, the late great W.Y. Evans-Wentz (1968) has so poetically explained in his edition of *The Tibetan Book of the Great Liberation*:

> . . .the Voidness (known in Sanskrit as Shunyata). . .is the Unbecome, the Unborn, the Unmade, the Unformed, the predicate-less Primordial Essence, the abstract Cosmic Source whence all concrete or manifest things come and into which they vanish in latency. Being without form, quality, or phenomenal existence, it is the Formless, the Qualityless, the Non-Existent. As such, it is the Imperishable, the Transcendent Fullness of the Emptiness, the Dissolver of Space and of Time and of sangsaric (or mundane) mind, the Brahman of the Rishis, the dreamer of the Maya, the Weaver of the Web of Appearances, the Outbreather and the Inbreather of infinite universes throughout the endlessness of Duration. (p. 1).

Or by Western terminology, simply, God.

Perhaps the most astute advice to be heeded in practicing the LPR or any Magickal ritual comes from the Master Eliphas Levi (2010). As he wrote in his monumental *Threshold of Magical Science*, the Magi must possess the following qualities of character:

> They are without fears and without desires, dominated by no falsehood, sharing no error, loving without illusion, suffering without impatience, reposing in the quietude of eternal thought..... a Magus cannot be ignorant, for magic implies superiority, mastership, majority, and majority signifies emancipation by knowledge. The Magus welcomes pleasure, accepts wealth, deserves honour, but is never the slave of one of them; he knows how to be poor, to abstain, and to suffer; he endures oblivion willingly because he is lord of his own happiness, and expects or fears nothing from the caprice of fortune. He can love without being beloved; he can create imperishable treasures, and exalt himself above the level of honours or the prizes of the lottery. He possesses that which he seeks, namely, profound peace. He regrets nothing which must end, but remembers with satisfaction that he has met with good in all. His hope is a certitude, for he knows that good is eternal and evil transitory. He enjoys solitude, but does not fly the society of man; he is a child with children, joyous with the young, staid with the old, patient with the foolish, happy with the wise. He smiles with all who smile, and mourns with all who weep; applauding strength, he is yet indulgent to weakness; offending no one, he has himself no need to pardon, for he never thinks himself offended; he pities those who misconceive him, and seeks an opportunity to serve them; by the force of kindness only does he avenge himself on the ungrateful (p.75).

And elsewhere, Levi (1997) expounds this brief but vital advice:

> To attain the Sanctum Regnum, in other words, the knowledge and power of the Magi, there are four indispensable conditions – an intelligence illuminated by study, an intrepidity which nothing can check, a will which nothing can break, and a discretion which nothing can corrupt and nothing intoxicate. TO KNOW, TO DARE, TO WILL, TO KEEP SILENCE – such are the four words of the Magus.

**NOW, TO WORK!**

# Introductory Comments on the LPR

"Every man and every woman is a star."-Aleister Crowley, M.I.T.A.P.

While seemingly simple upon cursory examination, the root form of the LPR as perpetuated in the original Golden Dawn tradition and expounded here is undeniably one of the most profound Magickal rituals extant in the literature of 20th century occultism. While properly performed in roughly 5 minutes, give or take, no other exercise designed for solitary practice synthesizes such important archetypes, symbolism, esoteric lessons, and sublime goals into one ritual act of such utter brevity. The Golden Dawn tradition teaches that the formal purpose of the LPR is the induction and conduction of Divine energy. This usage is directed towards the purification and banishment of malignant elemental forces through the invocation of personified angelic beings. As will also be examined, the LPR is likewise a perfect dramatic expression in ritual form of the Magickal formula FIAT LVX.[5]

Beyond its Magickal functions, however, the LPR is also a weighty intellectual tool and powerful spiritual calisthenic. Through both its form and content, as expressed in its creative visualizations, the ritual imbues within the dedicated practitioner greater psychological and organizational skills, the ability to cognate in association blocks like an accomplished poet, and mental focus akin to a martial arts expert. Most impressively, as we shall see, the LPR encompasses all the processes of Yoga and reflects a universal cosmology of the Secret Traditions stylistically embodied within the framework of the three primary Western esoteric schools: Hermeticism, Rosicrucianism, and the Qabalah.

As will be exemplified, the LPR is the fundamental basis of all Western Magickal workings. Its movements, intentions, and formulae express a balance, equilibrium, and harmony from which all modern Magickal ritual originates and to which

---

[5] Flatus (air), Ignus (fire), Aqua (water), Terra (earth) – Light in Extension.

it must return, like an orbit or circuit. It is the assumption of the center within the void; or to Thelemically express it, Hadit becomes self-aware within Nuit. It is the creation of the universal mandala; Ezekiel's wheel rolling on; Key 10 of the Major Arcana turning smooth. In its ideal and perfected form the LPR does nothing less than unveil and catalyze the fulfillment of the Great Work, the 5 = 6, the reconciliation of the Microcosm with the Macrocosm, the Pentagram with the Hexagram. It is the Squaring of the Wheel, the harmonizing of the subjective perspective with an objective yet super-mundane reality; of the Samsara with Nirvana. It is the realization of Divinity unlocked through the transformation of human consciousness. In Eastern terms it holds the key to Samadhi, Moksha, and Kensho/Satori. In Western terms it is Atonement, Gnosis, and the confection of the Philosopher's Stone.

In the pages to follow we will explore the history, contents, and theory of this ritual, analyzing its components to explicitly illustrate and prove these assertions. Students of exceptional insight will come to realize why Aleister Crowley said of the LPR, "Those who regard this ritual as a mere device to invoke or banish spirits, are unworthy to possess it. Properly understood, it is the Medicine of Metals and the Stone of the Wise" (Regardie, 2004, p. 241). Or to put this avowal in Eastern terms, the LPR upholds itself to be the ultimate Seva-Sadhana – the supreme sacred act of religious reverence and devotion.

# Speculation on the History of the Ritual

The history surrounding the origin of the LPR, like the founding of the Golden Dawn itself, is illuminated by a few facts while still being shrouded in much apocryphal legend. We know for certain that the LPR is one of the few fundamental, practical Magickal exercises taught by the pre-1900 (C.E.) schism of the original Hermetic Order of the Golden Dawn's outer order. It is extant throughout the Order's documents, is instructed in the first knowledge lecture of the Order, and is used extensively in the opening and closing of numerous complex Golden Dawn

**Aleister Crowley (10/12/1875 – 12/01/1947): "the Great Beast 666," in his 60's; founder of the A.A. Order, Thelema, and alleged successor to Theodore Reuss as head of the Ordo Templi Orientis.**

*"Perdurabo;" "Baphomet;" "V.V.V.V.V."*

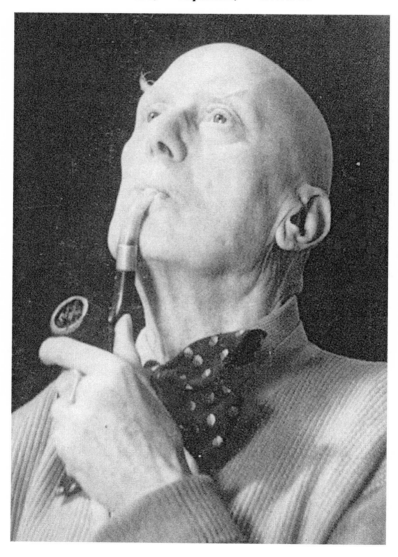

rituals. [6] However, who (or what) can rightfully claim its authorship cannot be absolutely substantiated by primary sources despite some few occult scholars who allege otherwise. Nevertheless, creative contemplation and historical pondering has yielded some interesting possibilities on the origin of the LPR that we shall now survey.

1). One, some, or maybe all of the Golden Dawn's founders (i.e. W. Wynn Westcott, S.L. MacGregor Mathers, Dr. W.R. Woodman, and Rev. A.F.A. Woodford)[7] authored the LPR themselves, either by their own original creativity and learning, or based upon other occult resources known or researched by them, perhaps in the British Museum or the Bibliothèque de l'Arsenal, some time prior to or shortly after their Order's official founding under the English charter of 1888 that birthed London's Isis-Urania Temple. All were high grade Masons as well. In addition, Westcott was head (Ipsissimus) of the Rosicrucian Society in England, the SRIA (Societa Rosicrucia in Anglia). Thus, they may have drawn upon these secret societies for their material.

2). The LPR may have been contained in the original and infamous "Cypher Manuscripts." These papers were reportedly given to Westcott by Woodford to decode (Colquhoun, 1975). Woodford had, in turn, obtained them out of old documents left to him in the estate and will of the mystic/clairvoyant Fred Hockley after his death in 1885. (Some sources, in contrast, report these papers were found in the cupboard of Freemason Kenneth Mackenzie by Woodford). These manuscripts, as now publically available, are extensive skeleton notes in code of Magickal teachings and rituals as observed on the European continent at that time. Westcott also decoded references to the defrocked Catholic priest turned magician, the Frenchman Louis Alphonse-Constance, known now by his initiate name, Eliphas Levi. Likewise there were references to, and the address of, the possibly legendary Fraulein Sprengel, an allegedly high-grade German Rosicrucian with whom Westcott supposedly

---

[6] Primary examples include the Neophyte Ritual, the Bornless Ritual, the Ritual of the Equinox, and many others.

[7] For outstanding historical accounts on the biographies of these individuals see Francis King's *Ritual Magic of the Golden Dawn* and Ethel Colquhoun's *The Sword of Wisdom.*

corresponded and through whom he purportedly obtained permission for the first Golden Dawn temple charters. Whether these Cypher Manuscripts were, and are, authentic is not a matter that can be substantiated in the historical or scholarly sense. There is a real possibility that they are forgeries. Additionally, we can never know for certain whether Sprengel truly existed or not, and if she did, if she was actually who she claimed to be. What we do know for sure is that the Golden Dawn was ostensibly born in this genesis and its effects upon Western occultism are incalculable. However, whether such an influential Order could be spawned in deception and perpetuated by myth is certainly open for debate.

3). If such reports are true and authentic, Westcott contacted Sprengel in Germany and started a voluminous correspondence with her until her death 1891. It is this correspondence alone that suggests there truly was someone at least posing as a high-grade Rosicrucian named Sprengel, if not completely true at face value. It is doubtful that Westcott would have faked such correspondences being a man of no small societal standing in England or if he even could have done so without being discovered by his Order cohorts as a mere liar and charlatan. It is unknown specifically which of the Golden Dawn materials came directly from these correspondences, if any, but it is entirely possible that much of it did. Thus the LPR could have originated from this source as well.

4). If the validity of MacGregor Mathers' communications with the Golden Dawn's alleged "Secret Chiefs" (beginning in 1892) is accepted, then spiritual intelligences could be considered a possible source for much of the Order's material (Colquhoun, 1975). The LPR may have thus been born from such paranormal hierarchical origins.

5). It is documented that Mathers and his wife Moina "brought through" much of the Golden Dawn's teachings and rituals by use of the clairvoyant divinatory method of the pendulum – a Ouija board-like practice of attaining spelled-out messages from alleged spiritual origin (King, 1997, pp. 14-19). Whether this spiritual explanation of the pendulum be accepted, or whether one takes a more Jungian interpretation of

**A sample page from Woodford's copy of the "Cypher Manuscripts," circa 19ᵗʰ century C.E.**

**A sample page from Woodford's copy of the "Cypher Manuscripts," circa 19th century C.E.**

## A further page from Woodford's copy of the "Cypher Manuscripts."

**Another sample page from Woodford's copy of the "Cypher Manuscripts."**

this method (with such messages simply arising from the practitioner's own subconscious) is irrelevant, as either source, external or internal, may prove fruitful in unearthing praeternatural lessons. In either case, the LPR could have been authored by this means as well.

6). It is also documented that Eliphas Levi, years prior to the Golden Dawn's founding, was aware of a ritual, that if not identical, was very similar to the LPR (King 1997, pg. 37). This ritual may have been taught to him, or discovered by his own intense occult scholarship. In either case, this could evidence such a ritual originating prior to the 19th century when one considers the antiquated age of the medieval grimoires Levi was known to study, translate, and popularize for the occult revival occurring in the 1800's. On the other hand, when considering Levi's literary intelligence and poetic creativity, it is also a distinct possibility he authored such a ritual himself. Evidence that he was aware of a ritual similar or identical to the LPR is taken from Levi's own notes. He wrote:

> The sign of the cross used by Christians does not belong to them exclusively. It is also Qabalistic and there are two ways of making it, the one reserved for priests and initiates, the other set apart for neophytes and the profane. Thus for example, the initiate, raising his hand to his brow said: "Thine is." Then brought his hand to his breast, "The Kingdom," then transferred his hand to the left shoulder, "The Power," and finally to the right shoulder, "And the Glory;" then joining his hands he added, *"Tibi sunt Malkuth et Geburah et Chesed per Aeonas"* – the sign of the Cross which is splendidly Qabalisitc, and which the profanation of the Gnosis has completely lost to the official Church militant. The sign in this manner should proceed and conclude the Conjuration of the Four. (as cited in Regardie, 2004, p. 245).

**Eliphas Levi (02/08/1810 – 05/31/1875).**

**Crowley claimed to be his incarnation due to sharing the same birth year as Levi's death year.**

Here we see a description of what appears to be a practice extremely similar, but not exact, to the LPR's opening and closing "Qabalistic Cross". Likewise, Levi states that the making of such a Qabalistic Cross proceeds and concludes the "Conjuration of the Four," which seems again to be incredibly similar in description to what is executed in the LPR: the utilization of the four cardinal directions, the invocation of the four elements, the use of the four names of God in tetraform, the invocation of the four archangels, etc. In this quote from Levi it is entirely possible, if not probable, that we have an example of an earlier version of the LPR being described prior to its slight alteration and dissemination via the Golden Dawn, if this is indeed what it is. If so, however, it does not provide clarification of the LPR's origin, but simply relates that Levi was in knowledge of it some decades before the Golden Dawn's birth. Since the founding members of the Golden Dawn were all familiar with Levi's work, they may have adapted and adopted it from him.

The eminent Reichian psychologist, Dr. Israel Regardie, former secretary to Aleister Crowley and a practitioner of the Golden Dawn offshoot order, the Stella Matutina, makes a bit of an unsubstantiated claim regarding this issue (but due to his historical significance and credentials, it is worth noting). Over this quote from Levi about the Qabalistic Cross and Conjuration of the Four, Regardie writes in his classic Magickal treatise *The Tree of Life* (2004) the following opinion. He begins by rightly stating, "The history of this ritual is somewhat obscured. I have seen no instance like it which devolves from antiquity. . .In Levi may be found the first references to the particular ritual in question" (pp. 244-245).

He then quotes our sampling from Levi printed above and states the following harangue which he takes as fact and not speculation about Levi's quote. He writes,

> It goes without saying that (Levi's) method is but a part of (the LPR). . .It is to the Ritual of the Pentagram indubitably that Levi makes reference. . .Previous to this reprinting, I have been unable to trace any authoritative reference

> to anything which bears the resemblance to this
> ritual. (Regardie, 2004, p. 245).

Even so, to reiterate, this does not explain where Levi acquired the ritual or if he was its sole author.

When considering a pre-nineteenth century origin to the LPR, I conclude this section with the following speculations:

If it were Gnostic in origin, it could date as far back as the 2nd or 3rd centuries C.E. However, it appears nowhere in the known Gnostic scriptures (Layton, 1987) and when considering the cosmological and mythic content of these writings, when compared to that contained within the LPR, a Gnostic origin seems unlikely.

Pythagorean sources are just as improbable as a Gnostic one, for though the Pentagram (called the Pentalpha by Pythagoras) was a primary symbol of this school,[8] most of what has been left to posterity by this system are not Magickal practices or ritual teachings, but are of a philosophical, metaphysical, and mathematical nature.

The Qabalah (Hebrew for "receiving" and "tradition"), though of undoubted antiquity, is legendarily attributed to Moses and Abraham; the latter purportedly bringing it back for the Semites after acquiring the wisdom of the Chaldean Magi. Like most myths however, this story differs from the actual historical facts. As the eminent Jewish scholar Gershom Scholem (1965) has extensively researched, the Qabalah (or Kabbalah, or Cabala) did not emerge as a written, organized system of mysticism until the authoring of certain other primary texts. These are the *Sepher Yetzirah* (Book of Creation), written in Palestine or Babylonia between the 3rd and 6th centuries C.E., and later the *Zohar* (Book of Splendors) authored by Rabbi Moses De Leon of Guadalajara, Spain in the 13th or 14th century C.E. (Scholem, 1977). In addition to these, the works of Medieval Spanish Rabbi Simeon Ben-Jochai is likewise cited as a primary Qabalistic source (Scholem, 1974). That being said, in none of these works is there any ritual or practice even remotely approximating the LPR. This does not completely discount

---

[8] According to the Masonic genius Albert Mackey, the Pentalpha was invented by the Pythagoreans (Mackey & Clegg, 1929, pp. 762-763).

**Dr. Israel Regardie (11/17/1907 – 3/10/1985): Aleister Crowley's personal secretary, member of the Golden Dawn offshoot the Stella Maututina, and Reichian psychologist.**

other Qabalistic sources, whether of the Jewish, Christian, or Gnostic varieties, as sources for the LPR. Whoever its author was, he or she pays blatant homage or even allegiance to this philosophy by the very presence of the opening (and closing) "Qabalistic Cross."

If born of the vast eclectic system known as Hermetic, it could come from nearly any source in this evolving conglomerate. I say conglomerate, for as Dr. Stephen Edred Flowers (1995) has rightfully argued, Hermeticism is a syncretic school drawing from such varied sources as Egyptian mythos, Christian Gnosticism, Jewish Qabalah, Greek Neo-Platonism, Paganism, and Indo-Iranian Zoroastrianism. If the LPR is attributable to Hermeticism, it would most likely be of a more modern Hermetic origin than an ancient one, as nowhere in the classical writings attributable to Hermeticism's legendary founder (Hermes Mercurius Trismegistus) is there any record of a ritual resembling the LPR. However, he does allude to the formula of the Tetragrammaton and the manipulation of the Great Magickal Agent (i.e. the astral light or azoth) in the possibly apocryphal, but most ancient *Emerald Tablet of Hermes*.[9]

If Rosicrucian in origin, beyond Fraulein Sprengel, the LPR's authorship would most likely not pre-date the publication of this system's source essay, the famous *Fama Fraternitatis* of 1614[10] (Yates, 1996).

In the final analysis, the LPR may simply prove to be the invention of an anonymous and ingenious adept from nearly any time period or locale, perhaps decades or centuries before the great occult revival of the 19th century, or perhaps born right within it.

Every one of these points, of course, is pure speculation based on what scarce facts exist over which we may postulate. We can only hope that hitherto unknown primary resources may someday come to light and reveal incontrovertible historical proof of the LPR's origin. Regardless of this issue, the genesis of the LPR, a seemingly simple ritual and profound brief Magickal exercise, is truly irrelevant.

---

[9] While numerous translations of *Hermes' Emerald Tablet* are extant, the reader is referred to Flowers' translation (1995) and to this work's appendix of this text.

[10] The author is not in agreement with Yates' thesis that the eminent Elizabethan sorcerer and astrologer, Dr. John Dee, original source of the Enochian system of Magick, was the author of the Rosicrucian manifestos under the pseudonym of Christian Rosencreutz. While an interesting hypothesis, it remains unproven who Brother C.R. really was.

**W. Wynn Westcott (12/17/1848 – 7/30/1925): founding member of the Golden Dawn, high-grade Freemason, head of the Rosicrucian Society in England, and official coroner of London.**

*"Sapere Aude."*

Mike Benjamin

**Samuel Liddel MacGregor Mathers (01/11/1854 – 11/05/1918):
founding member of the Golden Dawn and Crowley's early occult
mentor.**

*"S' Rhioghail Mo Dream;" "Deo Duce Comite Ferro."*

**Moina Mathers (2/28/1865 – 7/25/1928): MacGregor Mathers'
wife, charter member of the Golden Dawn, and accomplished
artist in her own right.**
*"Vestigia Nulla Restrorsum"*

**Dr. William Robert Woodman (1828 – 1921): founding member of the Golden Dawn, high-grade Freemason, and Rosicrucian.**
*"Magna Est Veritas Et Praevalebit."*

**The clairvoyant Frederick Hockley (1808 – 1885).**

# The Pentagram as Symbol, Hieroglyph, and Pantacle

"Symbolism is the science of the relationship between different levels of reality." -Huston Smith (as cited in Wilber, 1996).

"(The) mechanism that transforms energy is the symbol." -C.G. Jung (1970).

To investigate the importance of the LPR as a spiritual exercise, it is first necessary to understand the archetypal meanings inherent in the ritual's main symbol, the pentagram or five pointed star. However, to even begin to comprehend the significance of the pentagram we must initially analyze the use of symbolism within occult studies. Written language, as taught within the Hermetic and Egyptian traditions, was the gift of Thoth (also called Tahuti). Thoth was the lunar messenger of the gods, as well as god of Magick and language, whose Greek and Roman counterparts later appear as Hermes and Mercury. It is from Thoth that symbolism is said to have originated.

Before the historically late development of phonetic alphabets, written language consisted of only symbols (first hieroglyphics then ideograms) which were understood only by the educated elite of ancient societies, such as the priesthood and royalty. These hieroglyphics and ideograms were the linguistically compounded evolution of basic cultural symbols. Just as deities eventually evolved into the anthropomorphic personifications of the forces of nature, [11] symbols, simply defined, became the visual representations of universal ideas and motifs. As is said colloquially, "a picture is worth a thousand words." [12] This theory is, in fact, the basic premise behind the quintessential system of universal symbols, known to some as *The Book of Thoth*, and to most as the Tarot.

---

[11] "The gods are the forces of nature themselves" (Crowley, 1970, p. 120).
[12] Likewise apropos, as Miyamoto Musashi said, "From one thing know ten thousand things" (cited in Harris, 1974).

While some foundational analysis surrounding the application of the Major Arcana of the Tarot in regard to the LPR will be covered later, the scope of Tarot studies far surpasses the focus of this work. Occult students, however, are encouraged to dive deep within its study, as it represents the

**Thoth – the ibis-headed Egyptian god of Magick and language.**

**The Greek god Hermes (or the Roman Mercury) holding the Caduceus.**

most important and profound set of symbols encompassing the whole of the Mysteries. Within the twenty two cards of its set are hidden the art and language of symbolism; it holds the deepest esoteric teachings contained within all of the world's great religions as well as the secrets to all truth regarding humanity, the universe, and God. It is the author's opinion and bias that the best system of study in this regard is that set forth by the Golden Dawn descendent, the Los Angeles headquartered Builders of the Adytum. This system is based upon the teachings of its founder, the late great Dr. Paul Foster Case and his spiritual heir Rev. Ann Davies. The system is, as tradition states, guided by the Ascended Master R. (Rakoczy), whom Case was reportedly tutored by in New York City in the early 20th century after having been approached previously by one of the Master's helpers years before in Chicago (Builders of the Adytum [BOTA], 1963). Seekers of the Light are *strongly* encouraged to pursue this challenging, yet fruitful course of study whose Arcana Keys are similar in artistry, but not identical to the Rider-Waite Tarot.

Furthermore, as a point of pertinent relevance, while the widely popular Thoth Tarot of Aleister Crowley conveys an artistry unprecedented in Tarot decks (as wonderfully conceived and beautifully painted under Crowley's patronage by Lady Frieda Harris), his attributions within the Major Arcana are not correct. Supposedly acting under the guidance of his channeled intelligence Aiwass, Crowley's infamous *Book of the Law* erroneously juxtaposes Keys 8 and 11, Adjustment and Lust (more widely called Justice and Strength in other Tarot systems). It is irrelevant whether or not this is an intentional occult blind committed by Crowley (as likewise done by Eliphas Levi with other keys in his Tarot attributions). For those seeking an accurate interpretation of the Major Arcana's keys, Case's is the sequence to which an honest aspirant must turn.

Returning to our current topic, namely symbolism, many schools of esotericism teach that symbolism is one of the most efficacious ways to instruct or relate the Arcane Wisdom. In the Orient, for example, it is considered one of the best ways of imparting secret acumen to the student. As the scholarly genius of Tibetan Buddhism, Dr. W.Y. Evans-Wentz of Jesus College, Oxford relates in his introduction to *The Tibetan Book of*

**Dr. Paul Foster Case: Golden Dawn member and founder of
Builders of the Adytum.
(October 3, 1884 – March 2, 1954).**

**Rev. Ann Davies (October 28, 1912 – 1975): successor to Paul Foster Case as head of BOTA.**

*the Great Liberation* (1968) there are four ways by which the Oriental Sages approach instruction to their acolytes, in order of the most effective to the least:

> 1). through telepathy or psychic osmosis; 2). through abstract symbols, such as mudras made by the various members of the body, and mandalas inscribed on the earth or painted on paper, cloth, or wood; and also through concrete symbols, which may be geometrical forms, images, living animals and their effigies, the celestial bodies, and magically produced forms; 3). through sound as in music or audibly expressed mantras, or spoken words which are often whispered into the ear of the neophyte during initiations; 4). through written words, setting forth the secret doctrines, usually in symbolical and very abstruse technical and metaphorical style. The first method is the highest, the fourth is the lowest method of imparting the higher learning. (p. 24).

While admittedly this very tome fulfills but the lowest of the methods as related above, it will become further illuminated as we proceed in this exposition that upon deeper understanding the actual practice of the LPR, as imparted by this volume, fulfills the second and third categories outlined. It is the method of Western Magickal instruction and Occidental Arcane teaching *par excellence*.

We now turn to an extensive and eloquent definition of symbolism as related by one of the 19th century's great occult scholars, Albert G. Mackey, 33° of the Ancient and Accepted Scottish Rite of Freemasonry. Brother Mackey (1929) writes:

> A symbol is defined to be a visible sign with which a spiritual feeling, emotion, or idea is connected. It was in this sense that the early Christians gave the name of symbols to all rites, ceremonies and outward forms which bore a

religious meaning; such for instance as the cross, and other pictures and images, and even the sacraments and sacramental elements. At a still earlier period, the Egyptians communicated the knowledge of their esoteric philosophy in mystic symbols. In fact, man's earliest instruction was by means of symbols. "The first learning of the world," says Dr. Stukely, "consisted chiefly of symbols. The wisdom of the Chaldeans, Phoenicians, Egyptians, Jews, of Zoroaster Sanchoniathan, Pherecydes, Syrus, Pythagoras, Socrates, Plato, of all the ancients that is to come to our hand, is symbolic." And the learned Faber remarks that "allegory and personification were peculiarly agreeable to the genius of antiquity, and the simplicity of truth was continually sacrificed at the shrine of poetical decoration."

The word symbol is derived from a Greek verb which signifies to compare one thing with another; and hence a symbol or an emblem. . .is the expression of an idea derived from the comparison or contrast of some visible object with a moral conception or attribute. . .

The objective character of a symbol, which presents something material to the sight and touch, (is) explanatory of an internal idea... Hence, in the first ages of the world. . .all propositions, theological, political, or scientific, were expressed in the form of symbols. Thus, the first religions were eminently symbolical, because, as that great philosophical historian, Grote, has remarked, "At a time when language was yet in its infancy, visible symbols were the most vivid means of acting upon the minds. . ."

To the man of mature intellect, each letter of the alphabet is the symbol of a certain sound. When we instruct the child in the form and value of these letters, we make the picture of some familiar object the representation of the letter which aids. . .the memory. Thus, when the teacher says, "A was an Archer," the Archer becomes a symbol of the letter A, just as. . .the letter becomes the symbol of a sound.

Doctor Barlow (*Essays on Symbolism I*, page 1) says:

"Symbolical representations of things sacred were coeval with religion itself as a system of doctrine appealing to sense, and have accompanied transmission to ourselves from the earliest known period of monumental history. Egyptian tombs and stiles exhibit religious symbols still in use among Christians. Similar forms, with corresponding meanings, though under different names, are found among the Indians, and are seen on the monuments of the Assyrians, the Etruscans, and the Greeks. The Hebrews borrowed much of their early religious symbolism from the Egyptians, their later from the Babylonians, and through them this symbolical imagery, both verbal and objective, has descended to ourselves. The Egyptian priests were great proficients in symbolism, and so were the Chaldeans, and so were Moses and the Prophets, and the Jewish doctors generally – and so were many of the early fathers of the Church, especially the Greek fathers.

Philo of Alexandria was very learned in symbolism, and the Evangelist St. John has made much use of it. The early Christian architects, sculptors, and painters drank deep of symbolical lore and reproduced it in their works."

Squier gives in his *Serpent Symbolism in America* (page 19) a similar view of the antiquity and the subsequent growth of the use of symbols:

"In the absence of a written language or forms of expression conveying abstract ideas, we can readily comprehend the necessity. . .of a symbolic system. That symbolism in a great degree resulted from this necessity is very obvious. . .It thus came to constitute a kind of sacred language, and became vested with an esoteric significance understood only by the few."

. . .all the instructions in. . .mysteries are communicated in the forms of symbols. (pp. 1002-1003).

In Magick, the symbol is utilized in various scholastic and technical ways. Scholastically, the symbol can manifest as a secret or hidden means of conveying information and teachings, as in the display of lamens or pantacles. Symbols can be technically utilized in magickal operations in the forms of talismans, sigils, seals, and circles. As Crowley (1994) differentiates:

> The lamen is a sort of coat of arms. It expresses the character and the power of the wearer. A talisman is a storehouse of some particular kind of energy, the kind that is needed to accomplish the task for which you have constructed it. The pantacle is often confused with both the others; accurately it is a Minutum Mundum, 'the universe in little;' it is a map of all that exists, arranged in the order of nature. (p. 155).

And, again, returning to the learned Brother Mackey (1929):

> TALISMAN. From the Hebrew "tselem" and the Chaldaic "tsalma," meaning an image or idol. . .signifies an implement or instrument. . .The talisman. . .was supposed by the ancients. . .to be invested with supernatural powers and a capacity for protecting its wearer or possessor from evil influences, and for securing to him good fortune and success in his undertakings. .
> .

The use of talismans was introduced in the Middle Ages by the Gnostics. Of the Gnostic talismans none were more frequent than those which were inscribed with Divine Names. Of these the most common were IAO and SABAO, although we find also the TETRAGRAMMATON, and ELOHIM, ELOHI, ADONAI, and other Hebrew appellations of the Deity. Sometimes the talisman contained, not one of the names of God, but that of some mystical person, or the expression of some mystical idea. Thus, on some of the Gnostic talismanic gems, we find the names of the three mythical kings of Cologne, or the sacred ABRAXAS. The orthodox Christians of the early days of the Church were necessarily influenced by the popular belief in talismans, to adopt many of them; although of course, they sought to divest them of their magical signification, and to use them simply as symbols. Hence, we find among these Christians the Constantinian monogram, composed of the letters X and P, or the VESICA PISCIS, as a symbol of Christ, and the image of a little fish as a token of Christian recognition, and the anchor as a mark of Christian hope.

Many of the symbols and symbolic expressions which were in use by the alchemists, the astrologers, and by the Rosicrucians, are to be traced to the Gnostic talismans. The talisman was, it is true, converted from an instrument of incantation into a symbol; but the symbol was accompanied with a mystical signification which gave it a sacred character. . . (pp.1009-1010).

Besides the Hexagram, or *Magen David*, of all the emblems, lamens, talismans, pantacles, and hieroglyphs found throughout the centuries in occult literature, no single symbol is as fundamentally important in the pursuits of Magick as is the five pointed star, called both the Pentacle (not to be confused with the pantacle above) and Pentalpha, but more commonly known as the Pentagram.

Beginning with one more quote from Brother Mackey (1929), we will then complete a brief survey of what some of the most eminent occult scholars and practitioners from the past two centuries share regarding the supreme glyph called the Pentagram.

> Pentacle – the Pentaculum Salomonis, or magical Pentalpha, not to be confused with Solomon's Seal. The Pentacle is frequently used in Hermetic philosophy. . .
>
> Pentagram – From the Greek words "pente," meaning five, and "gramma," a letter. In the science of magic the pentalpha is called the holy and mysterious pentagram. Eliphas Levi says. . .that the pentagram is the star of the Magians; it is the sign of the word made flesh; and according to the directions of its rays, that is, as it points upward with one point or with two, it represents the good or the evil principle, order or disorder, the blessed lamb of Ormuzd and of Saint John, or the accursed god of Mendes; initiation or profanation; Lucifer or vesper; the morning or evening star; Mary or Lilith; victory or death; light or darkness. . .
>
> Pentalpha – The triple triangle or the pentalpha of Pythagoras, is so called from the Greek words. . .pente, meaning five, and. . .alpha, the letter A, because in its configuration it presents the form of that letter in five different positions. It was the doctrine of Pythagoras, that all things proceeded from numbers, and the number five, as being formed by the union of the first odd and first even, was deemed of peculiar value; and therefore Cornelius Agrippa says. . .of this figure, that "by virtue of the number five, it has great command over evil spirits because of its double triangles and its five acute angles within and its five obtuse angles

without so that its interior pentangle contains in it many great mysteries."

The disciples of Pythagoras, who were indeed its real inventors, placed within each of its interior angles one of the letters of the Greek word TTIEIA, or the Latin one SALUS, both which signify health; and thus it was made the talisman of health. They placed it at the beginning of their epistles as a greeting to invoke secure health to their correspondent. But it was not confined to the disciples of Pythagoras. As a talisman it was employed all over the east as a charm to resist evil spirits. Mone says that it has been found in Egypt on the statue of the god Anubis. Lord Brougham says, in his Italy  that it was issued by Antiochus Epiphanes, and a writer in Notes and Queries. . .says he has found it on the coins of Lysimachus. On old British and Gaulish coins it is often seen beneath the feet of the sacred and mythical horse, which was the ensign of the ancient Saxons.

The Druids wore it on their sandals as a symbol of Deity and hence the Germans call the figure "druttenfuss," a word originally signifying Druid's foot, but which, in the gradual corruption of the language, is now made to mean witch's foot. Even at the present day it retains its hold upon the minds of the common people of Germany, and is drawn on or affixed to cradles, thresholds of houses, and stable doors, to keep off witches and elves.

The early Christians referred to it as the five wounds of the Savior, because, when properly inscribed upon the representation of the human body, the five points will respectively extend and touch the side, the two hands, and the two feet. The medieval Freemasons considered it a symbol of deep wisdom, and it is found among the architectural ornaments of most of the ecclesiastical edifices of the Middle Ages. . . (pp. 762-763).

**Albert G. Mackey, 33°: Sovereign Grand Commander of International Freemasonry.**
**(March 12, 1807 – June 20, 1881)**

Before expanding our survey into other scholars' insights, it should be noted that in addition to Brother Mackey's extensive erudition regarding the history of the Pentagram, unbeknownst to him at the time, the five pointed star is also widely used amongst the traditions of the Tibetans (in both the Mahayana Buddhist-Lamaist religions such as the Madhyamika school of Nagarjuna, the Vajarayana/Dzogchen lineage, and the indigenous Tibetan shamanic religion of the Bonpos), the Native Americans of North America, and the Mesoamericans of

59

the Southern continent. Its widespread presence is even apparent to this day amongst the Pennsylvania Dutch of the Eastern United States who still utilize it as a charm upon their barns. In other contexts it is placed upon the U.S. Flag, "Old Glory," is the official regalia of the U.S. Air Force, and oddly enough, is also placed within the Republican party's elephant icon! (Upside down, that is).

From occult scholar Lewis Spence (1960):

> The Pentagram, the sign of the Microcosm, was held to be the most powerful means of conjuration in any rite. It may represent evil as well as good, for while with one point in the ascendant it was the sign of Christ, with two points in the ascendant it was the sign of Satan. By use of the Pentagram in these positions, the powers of light and of darkness were evoked. The Pentagram was said to be the star which led the Magi to the manger where the infant Christ was laid. . .It was believed to be of great efficacy in terrifying phantoms. . .and the magicians traced it upon their doorsteps to prevent evil spirits entering and the good from departing. . .This symbol has been used by all secret societies, by the Rosicrucians, the Illuminati, down to the Freemasons of today. Modern occultists translate the meaning of the Pentagram as symbolic of the human soul and its relation to God. The symbol is placed with one point ascendant. That point represents the Great Spirit, God. A line drawn from there to the left hand angle at the base is the descent of spirit into matter in its lowest form, whence it ascends to the right hand angle typifying matter in its highest form, the brain of man. From here a line is drawn across the figure to the left angle representing man's development into intellect, and progress in material civilization, the point of danger, from which all

nations have fallen into moral corruption, signified by the descent of the line to the right angle at the base. But the soul of man, being derived from God, cannot remain at this point, but must struggle upward, as is symbolized by the line reaching again to the apex, God, whence it issued. (pp. 261-262).

More from the pen of the Magus Eliphas Levi (1997):

The ancient magi were priests and kings, and the Savior's advent was proclaimed to them by a Star. This Star was the magical Pentagram, having a sacred letter at each point. It is the symbol of the intelligence which rules by unity of force over the four elementary potencies; it is the Pentagram of the magi, the Blazing Star of the Children of Hiram, the prototype of equilibriated light; to each of its points a ray of light ascends, and from each a ray goes forth; it represents the grand and supreme athanor of nature, which is the body of man. The magnetic influence issues in two beams from the head, from either hand, and either foot. The positive ray is balanced by the negative. The head corresponds with the two feet, each hand with a hand and foot, each of the two feet with the head and one hand. This ruling sign of equilibriated light represents the spirit of order and harmony; it is the sign of the omnipotence of the Magus, and hence, when broken or incorrectly drawn, it represents astral intoxication, abnormal and ill-regulated projections of the astral light, and therefore, bewitchments, perversity, madness, and it is what the Magi term the signature of Lucifer. (p. 194).

Levi (1996) further expounds,

> . . .mystic Kings. . .came from the East, led by a
> star, to adore the Savior of the world in His
> cradle. . .The star which conducted the pilgrims
> is the same Burning Star which is met with at
> all initiations. For Alchemists it is the sign of
> the Quintessence. For Magicians it is the Great
> Arcanum, for Kabbalists the sacred Pentagram
> ...The study of this Pentagram did itself lead
> the Magi to a Knowledge of that New Name
> which was to be exalted above all names and to
> bend the knee of all beings who were capable of
> adoration." (pp. 1-2).

And elsewhere Levi continues (1996),

> . . .great marvels can be shown by the
> Pentagram, which is the Seal of the Microcosm;
> for the Microcosm is the reflection of the
> Macrocosm; the Microcosm is Man and his
> human Will; he is the reflection of the universe,
> which is the macrocosm. The Man whose
> intelligence has received culture can by his Will
> Power, exerted through the Pentagram, control
> and command the powers and beings of the
> elements, and restrain evil elementaries from
> their perverse works. (pp. 19-20).

(Note to the advanced student – in this prior paragraph's final
sentence we see elucidated a strong correlation to the meaning
and teaching behind the Greater Arcana's Key 8 – "Strength" to
be examined later in Chapter 3).

Let us now look again to Regardie's masterpiece on
Magick, *The Tree of Life* (2004) from which he provides a superb
exposition on the powers of the Pentagram:

> To understand the meaning of the geometrical
> form of the Pentagram, and to realize why in it
> is the power to banish all inferior forces from a
> given sphere, and why it is 'the Word made
> flesh,' a hasty recapitulation of aspects of the

Qabalah is called for. One of the Divine names by which the Jews conceived the universal creative force was YHVH (‫י ה ר ה‬), which, denominated the Tetragrammaton, came to be considered the equivalent of the Four Elements in the Cosmos. It was also conceived to represent the ordinary unenlightened man in whom the light of spirit had not yet made its appearance; the unregenerate being of earth, air, fire, and water, given up to the things of the unredeemed self. By means of Magick it was considered that into these four elements on which the flesh is based, the Holy Spirit amidst fire and glory and flame descended. In Hebrew the element Spirit is typified by the letter Shin ‫ש‬ , with its three darting prongs of spiritual fire united under the form of one principle. Bursting asunder the fleshly being, and carrying with it the germs of enlightenment and inspiration and revelation, the Holy Spirit forms by its presence in the heart a new species of being, the Adept or Master YHShVH( ‫יהשרה‬ ). This word, in Hebrew, is the name Jesus, the symbol of the God-Man, a new type-species of spiritual being, greater than Whom there is nothing in all the heavens and planes of nature. Because of this fact, and the ideology summarized in the sign of the Pentagram, the symbol of the four elements surmounted by the crowning and conquering flame of the Holy Ghost, it owes its incomparable efficiency and power to subdue all astral opposition, and to cast out gross substance from the being of the Magus.

"Depending entirely on the direction towards or away from any of the five points in which this figure is traced by the Magician so will the result be. Proceeding from the topmost point and descending in a straight line to the lower right-hand point, the powers of Fire will be invoked. On the other hand, if the Magician traces with his wand the figure from the left-hand corner to the top, he will banish the elements of Earth. It may also be remarked that it is this latter type of Pentagram which is used in the Pentagram ritual, it usually sufficing to banish beings of whatsoever class. (pp. 239-240).

As Regardie's (2004) footnote to this excerpt also explains:

"Yeheshua. . .is also called the Pentagrammaton, a Greek word which means "five-lettered name." This refers to the Tetragrammaton or "four-lettered name". . . with the letter Shin ש placed in the center of the name. Thus the four elements of YHVH (Fire, Water, Air, and Earth) are completed, crowned, and governed by a fifth – Spirit (p. 250).

Reiterating ideas expounded by both Spence and Levi, Dr. Regardie (1994) also relates the following official Golden Dawn teachings that were perpetuated in the schism-offshoot faction to which he personally belonged, the Order of the Stella Matutina. He shares:

The Pentagram is a powerful symbol representing the operation of the Eternal Spirit and the Four Elements under the Divine Presidency of the letters of the name Yeheshua. The elements themselves in the symbol of the cross are governed by YHVH. But add the letter Shin, representing the RUACH ELOHIM, the Divine Spirit, being added thereto, the name becometh Yeheshua or Yehovasha – the latter when the Shin is placed between the ruling Earth and the other three letters of Tetragrammaton. From each reentering angle of the Pentagram, therefore, issueth a ray, representing a radiation from the Divine.

Therefore, it is called, the Flaming Pentagram, or Star of Great Light, in affirmation of the forces of Divine Light to be found therein. Traced as a symbol of good, it should be placed with the single point upward, representing the rule of Divine Spirit. For if thou shouldst write it with two points upward, it is an evil symbol, affirming the empire of matter over that Divine Spirit which should govern it. See that thou doest it not. . . (p. 280).

As our last resource to be reviewed in this modest survey of the Pentagram's meaning as a symbol we turn to the distinguished occult academic Richard Cavendish (1983). He writes,

"Before. . .(Magickal) ceremony. . . begins all irrelevant or disturbing forces must be banished from the circle. Pentagrams. . .are used for this and also act as additional defenses during the ceremony. . .the Pentagram is a barrier against evil forces. . .The stock medieval explanation of its power is that the five points of the star stand for the five wounds inflicted on the body of Christ and for this reason devils are terrified of it. In modern theory, the pentagram represents God or man [1] added to the physical universe [4– solidity, the elements] and is a symbol of the Divine power which man has over the physical universe. It is also an emblem of man, because a man with his arms and legs stretched out is a living pentagram, the points of the star being his head, hands, and feet. . .The pentagram with one point upwards repels evil, but a reversed pentagram, with two points upwards, is a symbol of the Devil and attracts sinister forces because it is upside down and. . .stands for the number 2. It represents the great Goat of the witches' Sabbath and the two upward points are the Goat's horns. (p. 242).

In summary, as we have seen, both classical sources and modern theories interpret the Pentagram as one of, if not the most, potent and meaningful of symbols in all of occultism. Paracelsus (cited in Jacobi, 1988) considered it no less than the supreme and most powerful of sigils and signs. In addition to the analysis provided above, it is also worth noting that traditional sources explain that in regards to the upright Pentagram, or sign of the good, the uppermost triangle of the star represents the Holy Trinity of father, Son, and Holy Spirit. While the attributions of the Sephiroth (or spheres of being) are far beyond the scope of this treatise, know that Qabalistically, the top triangle of the Pentagram also represents the Three Supernals upon the Tree of Life; Kether (The Crown), Chokmah (Wisdom), and Binah (Understanding); as well as the three divisions of the human soul:

1). **Nephesh** – the lower soul residing in Yesod upon the Tree of life, composed of primal instincts, fundamental drives, and animal vitality; comparable to the Jungian unconscious; the Freudian libido and id.

2). **Ruach** – the mid-level of soul representing the cognition, logic, and reasoning faculties of the mind; comparable to the Freudian ego.

3). **Neshamah** – the highest aspiration of the soul residing in Kether, Chokmah, and Binah upon the Tree of Life; in the barest sense comparable to Freud's super-ego. It is better attributed to the Mahayana precept of "Buddha Nature" automatically and intrinsically possessed by all sentient beings, though in the majority, is simply unrealized. By this same schematic, the lower triangle created by the infernal, evil inverted Pentagram can, from a fundamentalist framework, represent the diabolical trinity of Satan, Antichrist, and False Prophet. Qabalistically, it can also represent the Dark God of Rabbi Ben-Simeon.[13]

Taken together, the upright (fire) and downward (water) triangles thus created, and then superimposed on each other create the Hexagram; sign of the Macrocosm, the universe, of God. It is this symbol which bears the same meaning as the

---

[13] See Levi's *Book of Splendours* (1973) regarding Rabbi Ben-Simeon's concept of God's dark side, a truly Advaitic idea reflective of not only Yahweh in the Old Testament (i.e. Isaiah 45), but also of Vedantic teachings regarding Brahman.

Taoist Yin-Yang. In its duality is reflected the Unity of All, Vedantically known as Advaita, the non-dual (or "not two") truth that All is One. In Taoism this is taught in the lesson of the Tai Chi or "Grand Ultimate;" the One Source from which the initial duality of Yin and Yang and all manifestation spring forth. To paraphrase Lao Tzu's *Tao Te Ching*: from the one comes two, from the two the four, and from four comes the million million changing things of our universe. This Advaitic truth is likewise reflected in Nagarjuna's Mahayana philosophy in which it is taught that the Nirvana and Samsara are not two but One, both existing in and from Shunyata; "the Void," "emptiness," the Buddhist Divine (as cited in Evans-Wentz, 1968, p.157). Thus are we brought back full circle to the Qabalah in which it is taught that the first Sephiroth, Kether (also called the Rashith Ha-Galgalim or "beginning of the whirlings"), spawns the duality of Chokmah and Binah which constitutes the matrix of all existence as created through the subsequent seven Sephiroth thereby formed.

Likewise, we have evaluated the Pentagram in its geometric form to see that it symbolically represents the shape of man and is thus a sign of the Microcosm. It is also emblematic of the five wounds of Christ; He being known Qabalistically as Yeheshua or Yehovahsha. He is thus also called the Pentagrammaton which is the four elements of the Tetragrammaton (fire, water, air, and earth respectively represented by the Hebrew letters Yod, He, Vau, He)[14] crowned by Shin (the Ruach Elohim, the Breath of God, the Fire of Spirit). It is by the formula of the Tetragrammaton, represented by the cross, and symbolizing the four Qabalistic worlds, that God created the Kosmos. These worlds or planes of existence are:

1). **Atziluth** – "the plane of nobility" and realm of Divine archetypes, attributable to the Sephiroth of Kether, and the element fire.

2). **Briah** – "the plane of creation" and realm of the archangels, attributable to the Sephiroth of Chokmah and Binah, and the element water.

---

[14] The Hebrew Ineffable Name of God, irregularly pronounced with two syllables in some cases, and with three or four in others, depending on the source and context (i.e. "Yah-way"; "Ya-hoo"; "Yah-ho-va"; "Yod-hay-vow-hay", etc.).

3). **Yetzirah** – "the plane of formation" and realm of the angels, attributable to the Sephiroth of Chesed, Tiphareth, Netzach, Hod, and Yesod, and the element air.

4). **Assiah** – "the material plane" and realm of physicality, action, and matter, attributable to the Sephiroth of Malkuth, and the element earth.

It is precisely this meaning implied by the Tetragrammaton that is in the same way related in the Magickal formula FIAT LVX, pictorially represented by the Rosy Cross and alchemically expressed by the Quadrature of the Circle.[15] Furthermore, it is by the Pentagrammaton that God created mankind and, in turn, became a man (the Messiach in Hebrew or Christos in Greek). As the *Book of Genesis* relates, God breathed His breath, or Spirit, into an inanimate doll of earth to make our primordial father Adam. Man is thus a being composed of the four elements of materiality, yet endowed with the Divine Spirit, as was Christ – also called the Adam Kadosh, or New Man.

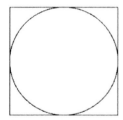 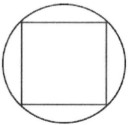

**Two Forms of the Quadrature (Squaring) of the Circle – Spirit in Matter; Matter in Spirit; or from another perspective, the Divine immanent within creation, and creation within the transcendent Divine.**

---

[15] The Quadrature (or Squaring) of the Circle denotes that matter is composed of the four elements (the square) which are but manifestations of the cyclical motion of energy or orbital paths of subatomic particles (the circle). This is the ancient understanding of the atom. The figure is empty in the middle, showing the great paradox of matter; that it is composed of atoms and that atoms are mostly empty space. Thus, solid matter is mostly empty space. It is mostly nothing or voidness; the Shunyata of the Mahayana Buddhists (a concept completely in agreement with modern physics). This also illustrates that Spirit (energy, the circle) is the intrinsic, prime component of all matter.

In such an interpretation we find the fundamental error of all exoteric Christianity. Christ did not represent the one and only Son of God. We all are the sons and daughters of the Divine. Christ was not the great exception, but rather, the grand rule. He thus becomes, as in the philosophy of the Catholic theologian turned evolutionary biologist Teillard De Chardin (1950), the "Omega Point" to which we are all compelled to ascend. Or as the Vedas teach, He catalyzes the Sarvodaya, the uplift of all. "And I, if lifted up. . .will draw all men unto me" (*John* 12:32, King James Version).

Christ, esoterically interpreted as such, just like all the great Avatars[16], Arhats,[17] Buddhas,[18] demi-gods,[19] Tathagatas,[20] and Bodhisattvas[21] of the world, represents the next stage in human evolution as catalyzed by God-realization, as formulated by attaining Cosmic Consciousness. He reminds us, "I and the

---

[16] An incarnation of a god into human form as taught in Hinduism.

[17] Per Evans-Wentz,

> . . .literally "Worthy One" is a Buddhist saint, often indistinguishable from a *Bodhisattva*, and comparable to a Hindu *Rishi*, who has attained the goal. . .and at death is befitted for *Nirvana*. If (he) renounces his right to enter *Nirvana*, in order to work for the salvation of the unenlightened, he automatically becomes a perfected *Bodhisattva*. (1968, p.122, footnote #1).

[18] Awakened ones, the enlightened, those who have achieved Nirvana like Prince Siddhartha Guatama of Buddhism or Mahavira of the Jains.

[19] The offspring of gods and men.

[20] As the Shakyamuni Buddha defined, a Tathagata is,

> . . .Fully Enlightened One, blessed and worthy, abounding is wisdom and goodness, happy, with knowledge of the world, unsurpassed as a guide to erring mortals, a teacher of gods and men, a blessed Budddha. He, by Himself, thoroughly understandeth and seeth as it were face to face, this Universe – the world below, with all its spiritual beings, and the worlds above, of Mara and Brahma, and all creatures, Samanas and Brahmins, gods and men; and He that maketh his knowledge known to others. The Truth doth he proclaim, both in its letter and in its spirit, beautiful in its origin, beautiful in its consummation; the higher life doth he reveal, in all its purity and in all its perfectness. (Tevigga Suttanta, I, 46).

[21] Those who have attained Buddhahood, but have chosen to not accept Nirvana, to not step off the wheel of Samsara (birth, life, death, transmigration, and rebirth – ad infinitum) until all other sentient beings have been freed from bondage and liberated from suffering.

Father are One" (*John* 10:30, King James Version) not as a proclamation of His own singular "only-begotten" uniqueness, but as a lesson and standard for every human being. In this brief, yet profound pronouncement we find echoed the great assertion of the Vedantic sages that preceded Jesus: "The Atman is one with the Brahman. . .Tat twam asi. . .Thou art That."

In closing this section, the advanced student is reminded that it is in the mystery of the Magickal formula IAO that these two central symbols, the cross and the star, are reconciled. For it is by IAO that the universe evolves and progresses. It is in IAO that the Christ exists within us all. And it is in IAO that every aspiring Magus must live and must die.[22]

# Postscript

Advanced students are advised to make an especial effort at studying the Squaring of the Circle formula of ALHIM (3.14... etc.). Levi's (1997) examination of the Tetrad and the Pentagram in Parts 1 and 2, Chapters 4 and 5 of *Transcendental Magic – Its Doctrine and Ritual* are of particular importance. Levi also touches upon the application of the Power Word ABRACADABRA as a key to the Pentagram elsewhere in that prodigious clavicle, but not as precisely and comprehensively as Crowley (1993) does, however, by application of GEMATRIA in the work "Sepher Sephiroth" of 777.[23] The student is directed to the entry for "418" in that volume for an analysis of Crowley's

---

[22] Within the universe, **Isis** represents the creative, fecundate birth force inherent in all of Nature; the growth process in all of life; Hegelian thesis. Alchemically speaking, it is the process of *coagula*, of coming together, of evolution. Vedantically it is Brahman-Vishnu. **Apophis** is the destructive force of Nature; systemic breakdown and dissolution; entropy; death; Hegelian antithesis. In alchemy it is represented by the concept of *solve*. Vedantically, it is Kali. **Osiris** is the new birth; the regeneration of life out of death; seeds from the soil; baby crows upon carrion. It is the resurrection of Christianity and the reincarnation of Hinduism and Buddhism. It is alchemical admixture and Hegelian synthesis. Vendantically it is represented by Krishna.

[23] A work known to have been plagiarized by Crowley from materials and notebooks shared with him by the Hermetic magus turned Buddhist bhiksu, Allen Bennet, Crowley's first teacher in Magick.

alternate rendering of this Power Word (into "ABRAHADABRA") as a key to the Pentagram.

This combination of letters, per Eliphas Levi (1996), is a key to the Pentagram per the Power Word ABRACADABRA. The initial A is repeated five times and reproduced thirty times, thus providing:

A B R A C A D A B R A
A B R A C A D A B R
A B R A C A D A B
A B R A C A D A
A B R A C A D
A B R A C A
A B R A C
A B R
A B
A

Furthermore, the elements and numbers of the following two figures are likewise representative of the Pentagram and Hexagram, the 5 = 6, the reconciliation of the Microcosm with the Macrocosm.

Mike Benjamin

## The Holy Pentagram – Sign of the Microcosm

## Man as the Pentagram

Mike Benjamin

## The Magickal Pentagram of Eliphas Levi

## The Elemental Pentagram of Yeheshua

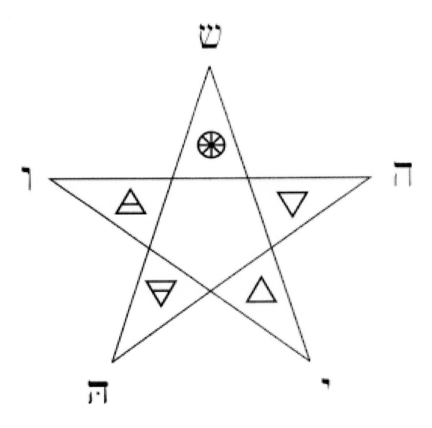

## The Sigillum Dei Aemeth of Dr. John Dee (founder of the Enochian system)

**The Pentagram of Solomon from the Lemegeton**

**The Infernal Pentagram– Sign of Baphomet, Satan, & Disharmony**

**The Sacred Hexagram – Sign of the Macrocosm**

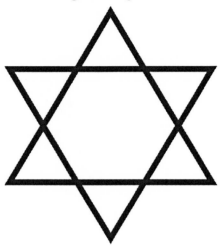

**Crowley's Unicursal Hexagram – Symbol of Thelema**

THE GREAT SYMBOL OF SOLOMON

Mike Benjamin

## The Taoist Yin-Yang, Symbol of the Tai Chi (The "Grand Ultimate")

## Taoist Elemental Pentagram

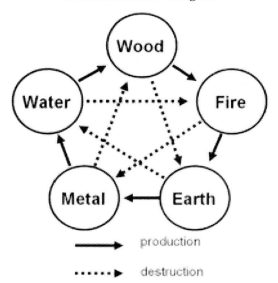

# Chapter 2: Instruction & Execution of the Ritual

"In this book it is spoken of the Sephiroth and the Paths; of Spirits and Conjurations; of Gods, Spheres, and Planes, and many other things which may or may not exist. It is immaterial whether these exist or not. By doing certain things certain results will follow; students are most earnestly warned against attributing objective reality or philosophic validity to any of them."

**-Aleister Crowley,** *M.I.T.A.P.*

# Preliminaries

1). Before exercise of the LPR, the practitioner must take necessary measures to be as calm of mind[24], free of distraction from the external, superfluous matters of life, [25] focused in

---

[24] Crowley (1976), in the true Libertine and Bohemian fashion for which he was famous, would have argued, ". . .take wine and strange drugs. . .and be drunk thereof" (II:22). While it may be true, to a limited and risky extent, that the use of psychedelics can be an aid in opening the mind and temporarily expanding consciousness, they likewise pose serious danger to the aspirant, not the least of which is the real potential for acquiring addiction – to which Crowley (and his notorious heroin, ether, hashish, and brandy abuse) proves a major example. To paraphrase the marvelous beatnik writer and author of *One Flew Over the Cuckoo's Nest*, Ken Kesey, in regards to the use of drugs for spiritual gain, once you've gotten the message, you need to hang up the phone.

In contrast to this Bacchanalian viewpoint, the student must note the emphasis placed in so many systems upon utter sobriety as a means of spiritual advancement, as such abstinence proves an important tool for the development of self-control; an indispensable weapon in the arsenal of the Magician. Beyond the Buddhist advocacy for such a path, note also that Levi admonished against inebriation and intoxication in many writings. Note also the strict rules for sobriety provided in such Magickal operations as those espoused in the *Clavicula Salomonis* (Mathers, 1989) and the Abramelin system (Mathers, 1975).

One is also reminded of John of Patmos and his *Book of Revelations*, regarding the last days in which we find ourselves (the Kali Yuga of Hinduism) that, ". . .by sorcery were all deceived." (*Revelations* 18:23, King James Version). What is now translated in English Bibles as "sorcery" is derived from the original Greek "pharmakeia," the word from which we now linguistically derive the term "pharmaceutical." It could be interpreted that John was warning us about a pattern of control and oppression by the forces of evil through the mass use of drugs; not only the street variety, but even more alarmingly and arguably dangerous, the overwhelming A.M.A./allopathic doctors' propensity to prescribe psychotropic "medicines," transforming society into an ever more Huxley-like *Brave New World* where the citizenry be controlled through the use of anesthetizing, "feel-good" drugs. This is easily reflected in the rise of accidental overdose via the use of prescription drugs like Oxycontin and Vicodin. It is likewise illustrated in the alarming trend of medicating our children with risky substances like Ritalin, Adderall, and others, for being in a normal state of childhood consciousness (i.e. low attention span and high energy), all the while erroneously dubbing such typical youthful mentality as ADD/ADHD. My final example of this point is the suppression of the natural process of sadness or grief in both adults and adolescents through the epidemic use of antidepressants (serotonin re-uptake inhibitors), with more than 25 types on the market today; not to mention that the side-effects of these drugs (i.e. homicidal and suicidal ideation) can be worse than the conditions for which they are prescribed!

[25] This is the real purpose behind the priestly vows of chastity, poverty, and

concentration, and intent in Will as possible. The student should feel "clean," even if physical bathing is necessary.[26] Note that upon the completion of the ritual, the bodily feeling is distinctly different from such corporeal washing, as it should leave the student feeling *cleansed* – "clean" being an external physical condition free of soil and grime; "cleansed" being the internal soulful counterpart. In this regards, one of the outcomes of a successful execution of the LPR should be this feeling of being cleansed. As Regardie (2004) explains,

> There should be a clear sense, unmistakable in its manifestations, as of cleanliness, even of holiness and sanctity, as though the whole being were gently but thoroughly purged, and that every impure and unclean element had been dispersed and annihilated. Just as a plunge into a cool running stream on a hot midsummer day leaves one blessed with the sense of refreshment and purification, so also should be (a result) of this ritual. (p. 244).

Also, classical sources warn that the practitioner should be of healthy body, and more importantly, healthy mind before undertaking any Magickal practice. While the details of this will be discussed later under the chapter on "Warnings," Dr. Regardie, for example, suggested students undergo at least one year of psychoanalysis before attempting to learn Magick.

---

obedience, which few priests today are actually required to take in the False Church of Rome (or in Luther's protest-schism branches, of equal invalidity). The true purpose of these vows is not to morally appease the hypocritical wishes of some pissed-off Semitic volcano god in the sky. They are, rather, intended to remove all external sources of superfluous stimuli in one's life and environment that divert the attention away from the pursuit and achievement of the Great Work. Such vows assist in removing all erroneous and extraneous sources antithetical to the spiritual path that can arouse internal conflict, deviation of focus, mental confusion, physical temptations, and the like.

[26] Crowley (1970) says, "The bath signifies the removal of all things extraneous or antagonistic to the one thought (i.e. the Magickal intention or purpose)" (pp. 101-105). This bathing process is also integral to the banishing and purifying preliminaries of the Abramelin Magick (Mathers, 1975, p. 45) and the operations of the *The Key of Solomon* (Mathers, 1989, pp. 90-91).

Mike Benjamin

2). The student should don their ceremonial robes or garments[27] reserved for such work, or may in contrast, perform the ritual naked. Regarding the former, Crowley (1970) instructs,

> It is ceremoniously desirable to seal and affirm this mental purity by ritual and accordingly[28] the first operation in any actual ceremony is bathing and robing. . .The bath signifies removing all things extraneous or antagonistic to the one thought (the Magickal goal). The putting on of the robe is the positive side of the same operation. It is the assumption of the frame of mind suitable to that one thought. (p. 103).

3). The ritual should be performed in a place set aside from the affairs of daily life. This directive is meant to place you in an environment free from distracting stimuli and thus conducive to fostering mental focus and emotional calm. This personal space is also necessary to separate the practitioner from the interfering, depleting, or distracting auras of others. A formal altar room is obviously the best location.[29] However, a den, home library, or similar room is also acceptable. Whatever the spot, the balance of the furnishings of the room, what the Chinese call *Feng Shui*,[30] must be kept in mind.

4). Differing classical instructions advise that any Magickal ritual must be performed within a consecrated circle (Mathers, 1989; Crowley, 1996). This is not necessary with the LPR as the LPR achieves just this very function. The LPR's utility is to consecrate, purify, intensify, and expand the Magician's *essential circle*, their aura or Body of Light. "The

---

[27] Examples of stylized robes corresponding to the days of the week on which they are to be donned can be found in Levi (1996, pp. 9-11). For Golden Dawn examples see Regardie (1994, pp. 252-253, 254, 257, 332-333, 468, 471, 473, 545).
[28] Nakedness suggests a symbolic expression of the state of our primordial, mythic parents, Adam and Eve, before their allegorical Fall from Eden; a state of purity, innocence, and harmony in the direct presence of Divinity.
[29] For construction of the altar see Crowley (1996, pp. 61-63).
[30] Feng Shui is the Taoist art of properly placing environmental objects (such as furniture in a home or shrubbery in a landscape) based on their shape and color in order to foster a healthy, balanced flow of Qi (universal life energy).

habitual use of the Lesser Pentagram Ritual (say thrice daily) for months and years. . .should make the real circle, i.e. aura of the magus, impregnable" (Crowley, 1970, p. 99). Thus, the LPR forms its own consecrated circle astrally by the outline of the visualized symbols, protected by the imagery of the Archangels, and empowered by the vibration of the Divine Names.

5). Classical instructions also state the utilization of the Air Dagger (per Regardie), or variably, the Fire Wand (per Crowley) in the ritual performance and the tracing of the Pentagrams, flaming circle, and so forth. I have always used a steel Dagger set aside specifically for this purpose, but this is simply a personal bias. I would add, however, that the bare hand can be just as effective and appropriate. If the bare hand is used the practitioner needs to extend and use the proper finger corresponding to the direction/element being faced. [31]

6). Ardent study is an essential for development with this ritual. The Magician must have a thorough understanding of all pronunciations, definitions, symbolism, and correspondences of all words and visualizations therein. Study of this tome's concluding appendixes will assist in fulfilling this condition.

7). "As a form of prayer, the invoking (LPR) ritual should be performed in the morning, and the banishing (LPR) in the evening" (Regardie, 1994, p. 54). Ideally, these should be timed with the respective rising and setting of the sun. The primacy of this solar correspondence, beyond the obvious pantheistic and pagan undertones, is also a monotheistic metaphor; Sol being to Gaia what God is to humanity. The harnessing of positive energies, dispelling of the negative, and other uses will be critiqued in later chapters.

8). A journal detailing any and all effects and results, no matter how seemingly trivial or tangential, must be kept and recorded immediately following every performance of the ritual. Insights will be gained in the recording of such and also in re-reading the entries coupled with contemplative reflection. I personally disagree with the Stella Matutina's injunction of practicing the LPR for one year without reflecting upon it. The quest for spiritual truth cannot, regardless of the charges made

---

[31] Per Regardie (1994): thumb = spirit; index finger = water; middle finger = earth; ring finger = fire; pinky = air (pp. 100-108).

by exoteric religion, be carried out in blind faith, nor can the scientific method (the paradigm of all Magick) be unaccompanied by strict, unwavering, and critical analysis. To truly have, as Christ advised, the faith of a little child applied to one's spiritual quest does not denote unquestioning belief, but rather advises curiosity, inquiry, incredulity, and skepticism. When have you ever met a child who did not pester their elders with the demand "Show me!" or the questions "Why?" and "How come?"

9). The practitioner must remain earnestly silent in this and every Magickal practice. It is not for water cooler discussion at work or in the lunch line. Discussion with no one, in no way, save your Guru or Frater Superior, is essential and part of Magick's discipline. In the not-so-distant past, as in the Dark Ages and the Burning Times (and to a much lesser extent, the fundamentalist resurgence of the 1980's) silence and secrecy were necessary to protect Brethren and Sorores from persecution. But there are deeper spiritual reasons for such communicative reticence (Crowley, 1995, pp. 120-122). As the Philosophers of Nature (1997) have also pointed out,

> By practicing silence we learn to conserve our energies and to direct them to other creative enterprises. . .those you succeed in this undertaking (Magick) keep silent about it until it is manifest. Those who fail seemingly waste their energy in verbal outlets. . ." (p. 19).

10). In regard to the Magician's diet, this next directive may cause some consternation amongst carnivore-omnivore Western occultists, especially those still imprisoned to the myth of human dominion over Nature and the usage of such for any and all of our own selfish desires. Regardless of this risk, for the good of the planet and all upon it, this assertion must be made. It is in this topic, in my opinion, that the Eastern Masters of Wisdom must be heeded over those of the West. (But, as we shall see, the West too holds its own proponents of the argument to hereby be extended). It is earnestly advised that any devotee on the Path of Return; that any student of the occult mysteries of the Right Hand Path, of the Way of Light and Love; if they are to achieve the goals of the Great Work; if they are to becomes true Qabalistic Hasidim (Masters of Compassion); if they are to achieve progression into the next stage of human evolution – then they must become devout practitioners of at least a vegetarian, if not a completely vegan, lifestyle as exemplified by no less than the Tathagatas and Bodhisattvas, such as Mahavira and Buddha. In Eastern terms, such as that outlined in theYogic system (which we will see later is closely related to Western Magick in its functions and purposes), one may not ascend past the Manipura chakra[32] in spiritual development while still exercising a diet that partakes in dead animals (Avalon, 1974, p. 119). As the incomparable Indian Sage, Sri Ramana Maharshi rightly advised,

> Of all (physical) disciplines (for spiritual development), food discrimination, i.e. partaking of only sattvic (or pure, vegetarian food) and in moderate quantities, is the most important. By means of this, the mind is rendered more sattvic (or pure), and atma-vichara (right inquiry into the nature of Reality) more and more effective (as cited in Evans-Wentz, 1968, p.72).

Echoing this Hindu precept, as the Buddhist Lankavatara Sutra states,

> The Bodhisattva. . .desirous of cultivating the virtue of love, should not eat meat, lest he cause terror to living beings. When dogs see, even at a distance, an outcaste. . .who likes eating meat, they are terrified and think: "These are dealers of death and will kill us!" Even the minute beings living in earth, air and water have a very keen sense of smell and detect at a distance the odor of the demons in meat-eaters, and they

---

[32] See Appendix B for further explanation and correspondences.

flee as fast as they can from the death which threatens them.

Likewise, the Magician is also encouraged to partake in regular bouts of fasting. This practice not only strengthens the Magician's Will through its action of self-discipline in denying oneself that which is regularly indulged in (i.e. eating food), it also increases one's compassion and empathy towards the downtrodden; for in this discipline we come to directly understand and feel the hunger pains and suffering incurred by the poor.

Pragmatically speaking, by lessening our intake of food we make more of it available for others; for the poor and for the hungry. In agricultural terms, more hunger can be alleviated by omitting animals from food production. By what is saved in both grain and fresh water usage to grow animals versus just growing fruits and vegetables for direct human consumption, more people can be fed. By changing to vegetarianism or veganism we also lessen the suffering of our sentient brethren, the animals, who are incredibly and terribly tortured in the modern factory farm industry process. Any visit to a factory farm or slaughter house will easily prove this assertion as will even the most cursory perusal of investigative videos on PETA's website. Such an herbivore lifestyle also lessens our negative environmental impact upon Gaia caused by the wasteful, filthy, and cruel factory farming of our fellow creatures.[33]

While it is not the purpose of this tome to be a thesis propounding such eating habits, it can be said that some of the greatest thinkers in all of humanity, both ancient and modern,

---

[33] Such factory farming committed by big agri-business is wrongfully dependent upon the deforestation of land to create grazing and stockyard space (especially, now, throughout the Amazon jungle) for livestock, especially cattle for America's red meat addiction; upon the use of growth hormones in animals to make them fatten faster (a major contributing factor in the current human obesity epidemic caused by ingestion of such tainted meat); and upon extensive injection of antibiotics into the animals (a major contributing factor to the increase in resistant bacterial infections like Staph and MRSA). Finally, such factory farming of animals is incredibly harmful to the ecosystem due to the need for excessive usage of limited grain and our lessening supply of fresh water needed for the upbringing of the livestock.

have espoused this lifestyle. Pythagoras taught, "For as long as men massacre animals, they will kill each other. Indeed, he who sows the seed of murder and pain cannot reap joy and love" (cited by Kon, 2000). Leonardo Da Vinci said, "The time will come when men such as I will look upon the murder of animals as they now look on the murder of men" (cited by Kon, 2000). Identically in sentiment, centuries later Albert Einstein wrote,

> Our task must be to free ourselves . . . by widening our circle of compassion to embrace all living creatures and the whole of nature and its beauty. . .Nothing will benefit human health and increase chances of survival for life on earth as much as the evolution to a vegetarian diet" (cited by Kon, 2000).

And as our own American Sage, the Philosophical genius and inspirer of Gandhi, Henry David Thoreau (1980) wrote In *Walden*,

> Is it not a reproach that man is a carnivorous animal? True, he can and does live, in a great measure, by preying on other animals; but this is a miserable way - as anyone who will go to snaring rabbits, or slaughtering lambs, may learn - and he will be regarded as a benefactor of his race who shall teach man to confine himself to a more innocent and wholesome diet. Whatever my own practice may be, I have no doubt that it is a part of the destiny of the human race, in its gradual improvement, to leave off eating animals, as surely as the savage tribes have left off eating each other when they came in contact with the more civilized. . . I believe that every man who has ever been earnest to preserve his higher or poetic faculties in the best condition has been particularly inclined to abstain from animal food. . .No humane being, past the thoughtless age of boyhood, will wantonly murder any creature

which holds its life by the same tenure that he does.

Gandhi as well advised us all, "The Greatness of a nation and its moral progress can be judged by the way its animals are treated" (cited by Kon, 2000). Even the great inventor Tomas Edison felt empathy on this issue. He said, "Non-violence leads to the highest ethics, which is the goal of all evolution. Until we stop harming all other living beings, we are still savages" (cited by Kon, 2000).

In the final analysis we must come to understand that our treatment of each other in our own species is but a reflection of the barbaric cruelty and narcissistic tyranny we exercise towards the sentient beings of other folds. Until we gain a better, higher treatment of our brethren of the feathers, and fur, and fins, and scales, we will never attain a level of true morality and peace amongst ourselves. In this light, vegetarianism could be justly understood as a necessary element of our own species' planetary survival. The student is strongly encouraged to emulate these great geniuses mentioned above and to explore the validity of my claims for themselves.

11). Know that the LPR is the basis of all Western Ritual Magick. It must be practiced habitually. In so doing, if rightly performed twice daily, recognizable positive results will be gained in a quarter year, and if thrice daily, within one month.

# On the Qabalistic Planes of Existence and the Divisions of the Human Soul Compared to the Buddhist System

Through the discipline of Magick, Socratically interpreted as coming to know God and the universe by "Knowing thyself," the student will eventually arrive at the acute, if even painful, realization of the component nature of his own being whether in this incarnation or another. Like the Taoist system,[34] in

---

[34] Taoism describes the unity of the human being as a trinity of components: Li (body), Yi (mind), and Qi (spirit).

Western terms the aspects of mind, body, and spirit, though separately defined, incorporate to form the unity that is a human. It is this same concept of Unity within Trinity that forms the Christian conception of God as Father, Son, and Holy Spirit, as well as the Hindu-Vedantic conception of Brahman (the All God) as composed of the three deities Brahma (creator), Vishnu (preserver), and Shiva (destroyer). The great Egyptian formula of IAO, discussed earlier, is similar to this scheme in its configuration as Isis (birth/creation), Apophis (death/destruction), and Osiris (rebirth). Saint Patrick also alluded to this spiritual truth in his analogy of the clover leaves. And as Crowley (1970) wrote, "This first triad is essentially unity, in a manner transcending reason. The comprehension of this unity is a matter of spiritual experience. All true gods are attributed to this Trinity" (p. 2).[35]

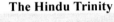

**The Hindu Trinity**

BRAHMA          VISHNU          SHIVA

Qabalistically, upon the Tree of Life, this Divine trinity is macrocosmically reflected in the Sephiroth of Kether, Chokmah, and Binah. Microcosmically reflected within humanity, this trinity is echoed in the social molecule of family – father, mother, and child – thus mirroring the basic building block of matter, the sub-atomic composition of the atom as proton, neutron, and electron. A mystical example of this structure would be the Yogic state of Pratyahara in which the Yogin, the

---

[35] See also *777 and Other Qabalistic Writings* for further Trinity formulas from Crowley (1993).

object perceived, and the act of that perception are understood as one. In the same way, what is termed the human soul, though acknowledged as a singular aspect of the human being's composite structure, is Qabalistically outlined in terms of the following triune formula:

1). **Neshamah**: The highest spiritual aspirations of the soul. The quest for the Holy Grail, the path of seeking salvation, the road of return, the pursuit of the Great Work, the striving for Gnosis. It is personified in the lessons provided by the stories of such solar figures as Osiris, Attis, Buddha, Mahavira, and Christ. On the Tree of Life Neshamah corresponds to the Three Supernals of Kether, Chokmah, and Binah. It is consciousness alone and unsullied, unalloyed by any taint of personality or environment. It is Buddha Nature, Zen's gateless gate, the Christos within each and all, the spark of Divinity, the ray from the One Spiritual Sun, and is physiologically situated in the reconstituted Pineal Gland of the awakened human; in the Ahben;[36] in the Philosopher's Stone.

2). **Ruach**: The intellect; composed of the logical, mental, and creative powers of the soul. It is both the scientist and the artist and corresponds to the six Sephiroth from Chesed to Yesod. It is the ego, the personality, individual affinities and personal preferences. It is physiologically situated in the higher neo-cortex or mammalian area of the brain.

3). **Nephesh**: The lowest animal emotions and intrinsic instincts. It is the id, the libido, the pleasure/pain principle, fear and desire, and the fight/flight/freeze reaction. It corresponds to the Sephira Malkuth and is physiologically situated in the limbic system or reptilian center of the brain.

To this traditional structure could also be added a fourth component, called **Guph** in Hebrew, denoting the material/corporeal/physical human body.

---

[36] Qabalistically speaking, and this is a great secret being imparted, the word stone in Hebrew is Ahben (sometimes transliterated as Ehben). This is a compound word of two parts; Ab meaning "father" and Ben meaning "son." "I and the Father are One," said Christ (John 10:30). "The stone the builders refused hath become the head of a corner" (Psalm 118:22). For the clever, these hints combined with the intimations stated above should be enough to connect the dots.

In some ways, and in some ways not, this Qabalistic structure holds parallels to the Buddhist conception of man's makeup. For purposes of comparison and contrast let us briefly examine this Eastern edifice as well. The primary difference in the Buddhist conception of Man's spiritual constitution versus the Qabalist's is the Buddhist denial of any permanent or individual soul (called Jiva in Sanskrit). This is perhaps the most telling difference between the Buddha's original teaching and that of his Brahminical predecessors, the latter reflected in such works as the *Upanishads* and the *Bhagavad Gita*, in which a human soul is presupposed, just as in the Qabalistic system. We must understand that in the final analysis, this seeming contradiction is ultimately irrelevant, as each system is but utilizing a different teaching device in attempt to explain or convey a transcendental truth that cannot be fully enunciated through mere reasonable and explicit verbiage.

In so doing, either scale of logical duality may be used in trying to awaken the student. One system says, there *is* a soul. One says there *is not*. While a seeming oppositional dichotomy, each system is using a different approach at opposite ends of the intellectual scale to but stir the student's banal consciousness beyond its normal confines. This is why when Mahavira, Tathagata of the Jains, achieved Awakening he exclaimed, "I am the All," while the Buddha Shakyamuni decried upon His enlightenment, "I am nothing" (Osho, 1974). Each is in actuality describing the same Truth, the same occurrence in different terms; a Truth that transcends normal human conditions and thus cannot be fully expressed or adequately explained in words. It can only be totally comprehended by those who have undergone that actual transformation. Thus, either technical articulation is accurate, but at the same time, limited and unsatisfactory for those who have not had the actual experience (and to the profane it seems utterly contradictory).

Thus, the Buddha, in contrast to Qabalah and Vedanta, declared there is no soul in Man; that Man is but a composite of ever-changing ingredients having no static or constant core. In modern times, Buddhist teachers have likened this teaching to the analogy of a flashlight beam. When its ray is spun around in a circle fast enough upon a wall such motion gives the appearance of an actual solid circle of light even though it is just the action of this process making it appear to be so.

However, like the Qabalah, Buddhism also reflects a composite schematic constituting the human being. Known as the Skandhas, this structure is divided into five categories. In Buddhist psychology the theory of the Skandhas is an outline in which the human individual, while acknowledged as a unity, however illusory (Maya), is still composed of multiple layers just as the many layers of an onion compose one onion. The individual, in complete agreement with Western developmental psychology, is seen as a compound interrelationship of various components. Sometimes in translating to English, Skandha is interpreted as "sheath" and sometimes as "aggregates," thus further lending to this stratified or nested idea in which each level is successive to the next like enveloping nests or cocoons. These five Skandhas, greatly simplified for the purposes of our discussion are (in the transliterated Sanskrit):

1). **Rupa**: form or matter – the physical body.

2). **Vedana**: sensations and emotions, the pleasure/pain principle.

3). **Samjna**: perception, recognition.

4). **Samskara**: mental formations and decisions triggered by an object.

5). **Vijnana**: conscious awareness, the slate or empty subjective space upon which all the other Skandhas arise.

These Buddhist conceptions are greatly similar to those used within the Brahmanical tradition as well, Buddhism being in many ways a development or evolution of the earlier Upanishadic teachings. The idea exists in such Vedic theory that a human being is composed of sheaths of existence called Kosas. These are Anna (body), Prana (life-force), Manas (mind), Vijnana (awareness), and at the core of these, the real Self - Jiva or Atman (the soul). Manas is further subdivided into four more levels: Sattvam Uttamam (the intellect or discriminating and perceptive faculty); Smriti (memory); Mahan Atma (the ego or principle of differentiation by which the individual personality incorrectly perceives itself as separate), also called Ahankara ("I-maker").

It should be noted, as with all religions and philosophies, Buddhism has undergone profound change and evolution throughout its many centuries of existence. Like all of the Abrahamic religions Buddhism too has fragmented into innumerable factions, denominations, and schools. In this light, we must acknowledge that the development of Buddhism under the great professor Nagarjuna (150 – 250 C.E.),[37] founder of the Mahayana (or "greater vehicle" system), turns this teaching of "no soul" (anatman in Sanskrit) upon its head, especially through his influence within the Tibetan variants of Buddhism through Padmasambhava, such as the Kargyutpa and Madyamihka schools (Evans-Wentz, 1968, p.173).

In the development of Nagarjuna's Mahayana doctrine we do see the development of a Buddhist conception of soul in the form of the Skandha Vijnana or consciousness. In the Mahayana doctrine it is consciousness that is seen as the root or core of the human composite upon which the other Skandhas are enveloped; that which is forever unsullied by existence; that which is the uncreated; that which is never born and never to die. It is the Vijnana that is seen as the one ray from the Divine, identical with it, that is the traveller, the knower, the witness, and the watcher of all successive existences throughout the Samsara. It is the Vijnana that is the subject of metempsychosis (reincarnation) that passes from life to life inheriting new Skandhas around it in each time and locale. While a comprehensive thesis on this topic is far beyond the scope of this work, in these brief explanatory comments we can easily see a closer connection, or parallel, between the Mahayana Buddhist and Qabalistic conceptions of Man's spiritual formation, and thus the perennial essence that underlies both of these religions in differing terms.

Regardless of whether the individual holds a Buddhist cosmology, or a Jewish one, or a Sufi, or Native American or any other spiritual perspective, it is irrelevant to the practice of the LPR (and most other forms of White Ritual Magick in general) as long as they be upon the Right-Hand Path in their quest. Through arduous practice, exacting analysis, and austere

---

[37] "Nagarjuna was the greatest of the Fathers of the Mahayana, having been... the thirteenth. . .in the direct succession of the Buddhist Patriarchs. He is believed to have been the reincarnation of Ananda, the Buddha's illustrious disciple. . .Nagarjuna was the transmitter of the Prajna-Paramita." (Evans-Wentz, 1968, p. 157).

contemplation of the LPR, the practitioner will come to realize the characteristics, powers, and deficits of their own soul's varying levels and differing qualities within whatever system they identify and by whatever school they choose their spiritual schematic and philosophical terminology. Like the uniqueness of a thumbprint or snowflake, such preferences will be based upon the individuality of the person and, as such, they matter not. As all the great sages have taught, there is more than one path leading to the summit of the mountain.

Qabalistically explained through the LPR, the divisive energies of the Nephesh and Ruach can be subordinated and coordinated to the higher aspirations and willful designs of the Neshamah. Or to put it poetically,

> Once harnessed, the demons
> Of our own hell
> Will carry the rider
> Higher and well!

Beyond the results on the levels of the subjective soul, the student must also realize the outcomes produced by the LPR upon objective levels of reality. The Magician must respect that the LPR manipulates potent elemental and spiritual energies and thus produces ripple-like effects throughout the planes of existence like a stone thrown in a pond. These results can be greatest upon the lower planes, but most assuredly affect causation upon the higher realms as well. As above, so below.

As Crowley (1970) explains, "The least gesture causes a change in man's own body and in the air around him; it disturbs the balance of the entire universe, and its effects continue eternally throughout all of space" (p. xx).

And Levi (1997), "There is. . .nothing indifferent in life, and our apparently most simple resolutions frequently determine an incalculable series of benefits or evils, above all in our diaphne with the great magical agent" (p. 49).

In light of these repercussive effects of any action, especially the complex and powerful ones associated with any spiritual practice, the student is reminded of the Wiccan wisdom contained within the Sistercraft's adage, *What you give out you will receive back seven-fold*. This is a significant warning to all occultists regardless of system and it must be adhered to! All Magicians must configure their ethics and practices accordingly or suffer the consequences.

Qabalistically, these planes of existence are classified into four strata. In this grimoire, however, I have altered this structure into five planes by the addition of the Astral as its own level. I have done this for two basic reasons. One, for the simple symbolism achieved of 4 = 5, or the Tetagrammaton reconciled with the Pentagrammaton (or put another way, the cross with the star, the universe with the self). This is, as we shall assess, one of the fundamental symbolisms and main goals of the LPR. Two, because while the Astral plane has been traditionally allocated to the lowest of these strata, I believe the data proves it unique enough to be classified as a level all its own. These divisions, reiterated from earlier, are as follows:

1). **Atziluth**: Pure Archetypal Deity, the source, the one, the Void, the Buddhist Shunyata, infinite and eternal, without quality or characteristic but with the potentiality for all.

2). **Briah**: The creative Archangelic plane.

3). **Yetzirah**: The formative Angelic plane.

4). **Assiah**: The active material universe of man and matter. This level is traditionally considered also as the realm of shells (ghosts), elementals, vampires, and demons. But as I argue, these creatures belong more properly to the level of the Astral (traditionally assigned to Assiah, but as stated above, is hereby changed in my schematic).

It should be understood that all levels of existence intermingle, blur as it were, into the others below and above it. In actuality they do not possess firm lines of demarcation like states in the union, nor do they have strict boundaries like geometrical figures. Instead they "bleed," so to speak, from one into another. For this reason, I consider the aforementioned beings as formal inhabitants of the Astral, though they may produce, in special instances, effects upon the material (as do poltergeists, for example). Human clairvoyants or psychics can similarly see or read the activity of these beings though they do not reside in the same time and place properly speaking.

5). **Astral**: Perhaps no other theory in the occult arts is as open to varied definition and debate as is the concept of the Astral plane. While the capacity of this treatise is not meant to cover such a voluminous topic, some fundamental points should be made. As stated prior, while usually assigned to Assiah, my experience has shown that the Astral does not so easily fit into such a neat and simple diagram. I believe, as do many occultists, that it overlaps in its influence upon and in its receptive effects from the other planes and upon the component levels of Man's constitution. Classical sources of instruction should be sought out for further elucidation on this notable topic so that one's Magickal repertoire is well versed in such discernment.[38]

In comparison to this Qabalistic arrangement, the Buddhist conception of the planes of existence, per the Mahayana, is remarkably similar, again lending itself to the argument that all Truth is One in the final analysis when stripped of all cultural or temporal dross. In the Mahayana system reality is reflected in what is called the Trikaya, or three Divine bodies. These are outlined as follows:

1). **The Dharmakaya (causal realm)**:    Pure, formless consciousness, the One Source, unlimited and unbounded, the Void (Shunyata), emptiness infinite and eternal, without quality or characteristic but with the potentiality for all, identical to the Qabalistic Atziluth, and corresponding within the Consciousness of Man as deep, dreamless sleep.

2). **The Sambhogakaya (subtle realm)**:  The creative level of existence, where the archetypal (Platonic) forms or ideas exist noumenally to yet be affected into material manifestation; corresponding to the Qabalistic levels of Briah and Yetzirah. In the consciousness of man, it is consistent with dreaming and certain meditative states.

3). **The Nirmanakaya (gross realm)**:  The sensory motor world of phenomena corresponding to the Qabalistic Assiah. It conforms with the waking state of consciousness in Man.

Like my addition of the Astral plane as its own separate level in the Qabalistic pattern above, to the Mahayana's I also add another stratum for clarification. This is known as the **Bardo** realm within the Tibetan schools. The Bardo is, to drastically over-simplify, the after-death state where the

[38] For examples see Crowley (1970, pp. 143-155, 245-264, 362-379); Crowley (1994, pp. 356-366, 380-390); King, (1997, pp. 63-95); and Regardie (1994, pp. xxi, xxiii, 9, 54-55, 67, 70-71, 108, 155, 159, 162, 340, 463-465, 47-474, 467-468).

individual consciousness abides before rebirth into another womb and corresponds to what we term the Astral Plane in Western occultism. The Bardo, taken together with the Nirmanakaya and the Sambhogakaya constitute the realm of the Samsara (Sanskrit for "round and round"), which correctly understood per Buddhism comprises only Maya (illusion). Unlike the Western attitude, all that we see, smell, hear, taste, feel, and think is not considered "real" by our Buddhist brethren for all in the Samsara is subject to Annica (or transience). Only the Dharmakaya is considered real as it is the only thing (if "thing" it can be called) that is not subject to change. Likewise, only the Dharmakaya belongs properly to Nirvana, both terms being synonymous with each other. The only difference is that Nirvana denotes the state of consciousness achieved in an individual when one has become realized to their oneness with the Dharmakaya and thus freed from their Avidya (spiritual ignorance). For a complete exposition of this concept of the Bardo the earnest student is directed to the *Bardo Thodol* or *Tibetan Book of the Dead* (Evans-Wentz, 1971), a book so spiritually significant that C.G. Jung admitted to always carrying it in his coat pocket wherever he went (Evans-Wentz, 1971, pp. xxxv-lii).

Before ending this section, it should be remarked that the philosophy of the after-death state shared in the *Bardo Thodol*, stripped of its cultural trappings and Tibetan terminology, is nearly identical to that espoused in the systems of Theosophy, Qabalah, and Magick. Those familiar with these Mahayana teachings may compare them to what Dr. Regardie (2004) explains in the *Tree of Life:*

> Theurgy conceives the removal of the enclosing sheaths from the soul after death of the physical body in very much the same way as does the Theosophy of Madam Blavatsky.[39] Following

---

[39] For a thorough exposition of the system expounded by Madam H.P. Blavatsky, one of the most influential occultists of all time, see her seminal works *Isis Unveiled* , *The Secret Doctrine,* and *The Stanzas of Dzyan.* As the primary founder of Theosophy, along with such other influential members as H.S. Olcott, C.W. Leadbetter, and Annie Besant, Theosophy would undergo, like most religious systems, many divisions, schisms, and developments in its

evolution over the past century and a half. Besant and Leadbetter would, as is historically infamous, break with Theosophy after championing it, to promote J.D. Krishnamurti as the New World Teacher or Matreiya. Krishnamurti's teachings would turn Theosophy's basics on their head, teaching that we are our own saviors (much as Buddha did), disavowing the Theosophic premise of a hierarchy of Ascended Masters as necessary for Humanity's awakening. Theosophy would see itself split and changed into various denominations and branches. Among these some of the most notable being the Lucis Trust and Arcane School of Alice Bailey (an organization highly influential in the spiritual direction of the United Nations, for good or bad, take it as you will), the I Am Movement, and the Summit Lighthouse of Mark and Elizabeth Clare Prophet. Like all religious systems, each of these branches has their proponents and detractors, some saying they are the "authentic" successors to Blavatsky's original, while condemning others as fallen from the fold. Some seem to possess a more anchored teaching to the ancient mystery traditions, while others seem to reflect rehashed principles easily found elsewhere combined with nothing more than dogmatic metaphysical assertions from the "authority" of channeled sources via mediumship. I leave it to the individual to decide which is which for themselves.

As in any magico-mystico endeavor, the student pursuing these, or any other system of supposed spiritual enlightenment (as well as my own presented here) is always sternly warned, **caveat emptor,** as well as – **judge it by the fruit it bears.** The six watchwords of the true occultist must always be, **doubt, doubt doubt** and **proof, proof, proof.** Without this the student will be drawn into ridiculous assertions of improvable nonsense. Personal experience only, and not avowals made by tradition or authority, must be the sole guide of the rightly directed aspirant.

Perhaps the most important barometer to ascertain whether a supposed religious guru or alleged spiritual master is full of bullshit or not is a simple commonsense judgment that can be easily made over their lives – that is, <u>do they walk the walk or just talk the talk?</u> Such an easy gauge would have, for instance, kept many sincere searchers from drinking the Kool-Aid at Jonestown. Such an easy gauge would have kept many eager and thirsty from falling into the insidious mind-control, profit-based snare of L. Ron Hubbard and his personal abortion that has come to be known as the Church of Scientology. Such an easy gauge may have also kept the Beatles, and many others of the affluent class (like director David Lynch), from wasting their time under the hypocrisy of Maharishi Mahesh Yogi. It is well documented in a plethora of sources that all of these "holy men" stole from and screwed their followers (literally and figuratively) all the while demanding their students' utter commitment to mental and financial subservience to them.

Remember o' reader, in regards to the Magickal and Mystical disciplines – anyone can preach it; damn few really do it. If saying it and doing it were the same thing, how easy the Path of Return would be for us all! Hypocrisy would be the Way, and then any politician or bureaucrat could be our role model, our guru, our Master. We would not need to go to the Ashram or Sangha or Order for guidance, we could simply attend our local city council meeting! Those Who Know, the Ones who actually live the lofty concepts they preach, are truly diamonds in the rough, souls as rare as sapphire and platinum. Only towards

the death of the body, which is the visible
vehicle of the higher principles, the Real Man,
perfectly intact though minus the physical
body, is thrust onto the Astral Plane. Gradually
he ascends to the several Palaces which have
been self-created by the mode of life just
passed. . .assimilating his earthly experience,
and building them into faculty for a further
incarnation. Magic, following the Qabalists,
embraces the philosophic idea of the
Reincarnation or *Gilgolem* of souls. (p. 351).

Furthermore, when we consider the statement made by Christ
that John the Baptist was Elijah returned, we can again see that
the basic spiritual premises espoused in the East versus the
West are not so far removed from each other as we may think.
Exoteric fundamentalism's insistence of only a single life
allotted per person before facing eternal judgment pales when
one realizes the words of its own Savior. Moreover, the concept
of reincarnation was advocated by many of the early Church
Fathers, like Origen, before they were wrongfully condemned
as heretics by those only interested in securing earthly power
for themselves. When we further consider the "bad hand" that
so many people are dealt, such as being born into poverty,
illness, abuse, and so on, can we really believe God to be truly
all-loving and just if this is but the single lifetime that such
individuals are forced to endure?

In agreement with this perspective, the astute scholarship
presented by G.R.S. Mead (1931) in his *Fragments of a Faith
Forgotten*:

Some of the outstanding elements or practices
associated with the teachings of the...
esotericism which distinguishes 'heretical'
Christianity from 'orthodox' Christianity, may
be briefly outlined as follows:
1). The view that the Christos, made manifest in
the flesh of Jesus, is the mystical archetype of

they must the sincere occult postulant always endeavor to gravitate.

the Primal Man, the A-dam; that the Christos is innately present in all men and capable of being realized by them. . .the Buddha, too, is said to be similarly innate and realizable.

2). The doctrines of unerring cause and sequence in regard to thought, word, and deed (karma), and rebirth based on these.

3). A doctrine concerning divine hierarchies that constitute an unbreakable chain of being, of which man is a link; and the corollary teaching that ultimately all living creatures, members of One Body, will attain Deliverance by virtue of knowing the Mysteries of the Gnosis.

4). A doctrine of emanations, or of the descent of the divine into generation, comparable to that of the Mahayana; and thus a doctrine of preexistence, such as the learned Origen of Alexandria held to be Christian and for belief in which he was anathematized.

5). A highly evolved mystical symbology.

6). The use of mantras, or words of power.

7). And particularly an eschatology. . .which, unlike that of exoteric Christianity, is supra-sangsaric; the exoteric Christianity eschatology being entirely sangsaric because of the exoteric teachings that the human principle of consciousness does not pre-exist before man's birth, that man lives but one life on earth, that after death man is destined to pass an endless eternity either of blissfulness in Heaven or of suffering in Hell. (as cited in Evans-Wentz, 1968, p. 34, footnote #1).

While this section reflects but a desultory inspection of the views contained within the Qabalistic Magickal viewpoint and that of the Mahayana Buddhist systems regarding the human soul and the planes of reality, this exposition should be sufficient in forming the necessary foundation of a coherent and working cosmology for the Magician. However, the student is earnestly warned not to accept any of this verbiage as gospel fact, for to do so would be to fall into the error of blind faith, into the morass of dogma; that is, to accept metaphysical speculation as truth based on authority or tradition. The student is adamantly encouraged to find out for themselves whether such theory be true for them or not. Nevertheless, with the resources cited herein, a map to the territory has been provided for the aspiring student to easily find their way through the useless and unproductive plethora of briar and wilderness that unfortunately and inherently exists within the subject of esoteric studies. I thus indubitably assert that such sources will be beneficial and productive to anyone's spiritual progress if they remain committed to such study and practice. In this endeavor the LPR will likewise prove a mighty tool in the carpenter's chest for building their new Temple of the Deity.

# Component Formulae of the LPR: Physical Mechanisms

While later chapters will investigate how the LPR can be metaphorically compared to other psycho-physical disciplines such as Yoga and Martial Arts, for the purpose of gaining a deeper comprehension, in this section we will break down and study the basic components of the ritual from a strictly Magickal perspective beginning with its sensory-motor elements. In this regard the LPR can be surmised to contain the following three ingredients of motion and posture: that of the legs (or feet), of the torso (or spine), and of the arms (or hands).

The motion of any of the bodily components in the LPR, like that in any Magickal ritual, must be efficient, graceful, balanced, and precise. The use of the legs in one's footwork, as Crowley (1970) writes, should be light and sure like that of a tiger or cat. The circumambulation within the LPR (if being performed in the temple), or rotation (if being performed in a more confined, solitary place), is instructed to be always deosil (clockwise) even during banishment.[40]

---

[40] Widdershins is traditionally used for banishment purposes in Magickal operations while Deosil is for invocation. However, this does not apply to the LPR, as banishment or invocation is affected by the directional tracing of the Pentagrams and not by the ritual's rotational (or more properly described,

As in seated meditation, or as in the practice of any breathing-based psycho-physical meditative practice performed standing (such as Tai Chi Ch'uan or Qigong), the spine should be held straight, erect, and tall during the LPR. This is not only for the obvious phallic, and thus creative symbolism, but also to foster suitable open breathing that facilitates strong tones and vibrations in all of the ritual's vocalizations, as is taught in any

**Dr. W.Y. Evans-Wentz (February 2, 1878 – July 17, 1965) in Sikkim with his Guru, the Lama Kazi Dawa-Samdup (circa 1920's).**

circumambulational) direction.

**Alexandra David-Neel (October 24, 1868 – September 8, 1969): Adventurer, scholar, and accomplished Tibetan Buddhist; the first Western woman to penetrate the sacred city of Lhasa and have an audience with the Dalai Lama. A true pioneer and a genius in Eastern Esoteric studies.**

singing art such as opera. Proper upright posture also promotes the correct flow of internal energy through the nervous system while performing the LPR. In Yoga this would be explained as allowing the proper flow of prana through the nadis. In Tantra this would be explained as allowing the proper flow of kundalini through the chakras. In Qigong this would be explained as the proper flow of qi through the dan tiens. And in Qabala it would be the flow of the Ruach Elohim through the Middle Pillar.

While the artistic etching or tracing of the Pentagrams and enclosing circle of light or flame in the empty space of the performance area is primarily a mental visualization during the LPR, the arm and hand movements utilized to do so must be laboriously practiced in order to achieve expert development. To be exact and balanced in these motions, to be able to form precise geometric shapes in midair, is really easier said than done and takes dedicated, repetitious drilling to eventually master. Furthermore, as Regardie (1994) instructs, "In all cases of tracing a Pentagram, the angle should be carefully closed at the starting point" (p. 282).

Once a practitioner has attained their own rhythm and feel for the proper execution of the LPR, it should be performed in exactly that same way every time. This exactitude and consistency creates a unique identity to the Magician's own particular expression of the ritual. It also provides a direct Karmic link between all of the successive rituals performed. This link will not only aid in intensifying the Magician's aura, it will work to build the chain of elemental current (or force) created by the LPR[41] empowered by the practitioner's focused Will and projected imagination.

This is not to say that creative variations or purposeful modifications of the base LPR form are not permissible or useful. On the contrary; adapting, altering, tailoring, customizing, or flavoring the ritual to specific uses, to other needs and/or ends are of course acceptable, just as Crowley did with his LPR variation – The Ritual of the Star Ruby. [42]

---

[41] Its "egregore," if you will.
[42] See Appendix F.

However, this should only be attempted once the practitioner has mastered the base form of the ritual. More advanced functions of the LPR must be developed upon the basic application. The temple cannot be built roof first. It must be erected from the ground up, starting with a firm foundation. In so doing, the practitioner creates a Central Sun around which their Magickal solar system will thus flow in its revolutions.

# Component Formulae of the LPR: Mental Visualizations

The primary ingredients of the LPR reside in the visualization of the pertinent images therein. In the basic, or foundational form of the ritual, this consists of the Pentagrams, the Hexagram, the Flaming Circle, the elements, and the Archangels. In more advanced or creatively complex forms of the ritual this could also consist of such appurtenances as the Hindu tattvas, [43] Hebrew God-names, elemental weapons, corresponding directional deities or devas from other systems, and so on. The student is pointed to the extensive correspondences provided in the appendices of this tome for further direction on this matter. The ability to visualize these forms in their proper shape and proportion is in no way easy, and as we shall later discuss, represents a form of Yogic Dharana. In fact, progress in the LPR can be partially gauged by the individual's self-assessment of the increasing ease and accuracy by which these forms and symbols are lucidly visualized.

As visualizations, however, it must be understood that these symbols and forms are not to occur internally, that is, within the "mind's eye." While acts of imagination, they must rather be made and thought of as projections onto EXTERNAL REALITY ITSELF. For maximum efficacy in the ritual the visualizations must be seen as literally floating in front of and around you. This, of course, is a very difficult achievement as well, and like all Magickal practices, requires much repetition to

---

[43] See Appendix A.

attain even a rudimentary level of skill. But, rest assured, through habitual reprise such ability is acquired.

Do not be discouraged that Magickal dexterity, like any talent worth procuring, happens slowly but steadily. The aspiring Magician, especially today in the West, must discard a "modern-American-industrial-fast-food-drive-up-microwave-mentality" where everything is given quickly, where everything wanted is gained right now, in this instant. True dedication to Magick, or any other occult endeavor, is a lifelong commitment, just as Karma is an eternal process. I would remind you that to become a Master of any single Martial Art, for example, takes more time in the dojo than it takes for a doctor to become a brain surgeon or for a pilot to become commercially certified in a jetliner. Likewise, for further illustration, realize that the Lakota Sioux Shaman must train, study, and vision-quest for at least 16 years to achieve their "first level of power," and there are three more levels after that! (Elk, 1991).

Do not doubt that benefits will be gained from the LPR even in early stages of practice, but long-term dedication will unveil immensely more. With sufficient experience the practitioner will come to understand that these projected symbols are more than mere visualizations. They are being formed **in the Astral Light itself** by the exercise of creative imagination coupled with focused Willpower through the medium of the ritual's component activities. This insight is the very secret behind enacting all Magickal current and affecting all Magickal change in any occult operation.

# Component Formulae of the LPR: Vocalizations

The primary vocalization techniques in the LPR consist of spoken declarations and vibration of the Divine Names which, as we shall later see, act similarly in function as the Yogic spiritual discipline of Mantrayoga. Some areas of the LPR are pronounced in proper Hebrew with the Magician bearing intimately in mind the definitions, etymology, symbolism, and correspondences of these words. The remaining areas of the ritual can be verbalized in the practitioner's own vernacular.

Understand, these words possess power in and of themselves and are not to be taken lightly (Cavendish, 1983, pp.

123-141). In ancient times, and not incorrectly, these words were interpreted in a more animistic way; that they were living, spiritual entities. This interpretation is not merely absurdity or superstition, but holds a deeper truth. Today, through the lens of our Holy Science, this living power intrinsic in word and thought may be surmised in the following way, by the following three Laws:

1). A thought can be expressed in spoken word and thus creates a SOUND. A sound is a form consisting of the vibration of waves and is acknowledged in our reality through the auditory system.

2). A thought can be expressed in written word and thus creates an IMAGE. An image is a form consisting in the reflection of light and is acknowledged in our reality through the ocular system.

3). A thought can be expressed in action and thus creates MOTION and CHANGE. Motion and change are the molecular basis of all wave, particle, and life-form's existence in our reality and are acknowledged through all our sensory means.[44]

To the advanced aspirant let it be known that it is in these three Laws that the Mystery of the LOGOS, or the Word Made Flesh, as recorded in the Gospel of Saint John, is revealed and explained.

# Vibration of the Divine Names

To the spiritual ascetics of Asia the vibratory chanting or recitation of mantras and sutras constitutes a fundamental form of religious devotion and spiritual practice. In contrast, instruction in the proper technique of Magickal vocal vibration in the West is an area sorely lacking in the annals, grimoires, tomes, and books of shadow within occult literature. There are two reasons to which this can be attributed. One, because most modern day, arm-chair variety of New Age occult dabblers – noses still wet, breath stinking of mother's milk, and bellies full

---

[44] Alchemically speaking, the motion of subatomic particles is the Quadrature of the Circle on a molecular and quantum level. The Newtonian theory of gravity as a force, or the Einsteinian-Relativity theory of gravity as the curvature and shape of space-time, is the Quadrature of the Circle on the galactic and universal levels.

in front of their smartphones – do not have the scholastic
fortitude or attention span to have adequately studied this skill,
nor do they have the raw experience of sufficient practice to
have gained any real ability. Two, because vibratory technique
is best conveyed through actual personal instruction by a
competent Master or Guru and is more difficult to acquire
through the medium of written text.

I know for a fact that such hands-on instruction,
fortunately, does still exist. In Paul Foster Case's order, Builders
of the Adytum (BOTA), formal classes in vibratory methods are
provided to high level initiates called "Pronaos Counselors."
Other formal Magickal orders pursue this discipline as well
such as the Aurum Solis, AMORC, certain Wiccan covens, and
so forth. Whether the Ordo Templi Orientis (OTO) has been
able to preserve this faculty in its instruction is left to question.

Most people, unless they live in a modern occult Mecca or
are born into an experienced intergenerational occult family, do
not have access to such prominent organizations or teaching
and must make do with literary sources and self-instruction.
This is not an illegitimate endeavor in any way when no other
resource is available (and to such a path it is this tome's purpose
to hopefully contribute some value). Let us thus survey some of
our primary sources for a sampling of spiritual insight into this
skill area.

The astute occultists Chic and Sandra Cicero share,

> Divine names are not simply spoken in ritual,
> they are intoned or vibrated. Scientists have
> only recently become aware of what magicians
> have known for centuries – that all matter is
> vibratory energy. A physical phenomenon
> known as harmonic resonance shows that if one
> object starts to vibrate strongly enough, another
> object nearby will begin to vibrate or resonate
> with the first, if both objects share the same
> vibratory rate.
>
> The magician vibrates the god-name in order to
> affect a harmonic resonance between the deity
> as it exists within his own psyche and as it

exists within the macrocosm. Therefore learning how to vibrate divine names is crucial to the working of effective ritual magic. The name should be intoned in such a way that the student is able to notice a strong vibration in the chest cavity and even the entire body. (Regardie, 2004, p. 176, endnote #8).

It should be noted that in regard to this concept of "harmonic resonance" cited by the Ciceros, aspirants are again directed to the teachings of Paul Foster Case and his Order BOTA. Specifics to these teachings are omitted here due to my own personal pledges of honor and oaths of secrecy to said Order, but I can obdurately declare that BOTA's lessons covering this area of occultism are of the highest benefit to the student and to the collective good of Mankind. What I can relate for the advanced (yet only in the form of my own poetic blind) is this:

> In Bethlehem, with Mary's milk,
> The right vibrations applied to sand
> Will arise to the pinecone,
> And give birth to the Alchemist's Ahben,
> The Chintamani – the Yogin's Sacred Gem.

Furthermore, as the Ciceros relate in their endnote,". . .the deity as it exists within his (the Magician's) own psyche. . ." This illustrates a vital teaching identical to a secret lesson contained within the Mahayana Buddhist system as well. As the Tibetan Kargupta school of the Mahayana teaches; in the final analysis, **in the ultimate sense**, all deities, all devas, all dakini, all heruskas, all demons, and all pretas, have no real objective, external existence, but only exist within the One Mind. It is only the unattained, the profane and the ignorant, who wrongly believe otherwise.

In this teaching we are met with a contradiction in comparison to other occultic views; whether we view the deities and other spiritual beings as objective or subjective personas. It could be said that in this teaching exists one of the great paradoxes of all occultism. The deities <u>are</u> objective to our own egos. They are seemingly separate to our own personal, individualized existences. But they <u>are</u> also subjective in regards to their relationship to the One Great Mind, out of which and of which we are also, part and parcel, an expression. Yet also are we this same totality though we experience this vast existence in single, distinct, apparently isolated forms. Thus, both views can be seen as true. Both hold validity depending on which perspective we afford reality, though neither alone, one without the other, really sums up the amazing Mystery of our manifestation. This teaching is perhaps incommunicable through words alone and must rest in some admitted confusion awaiting the individual's own awakening to such a level of obscure understanding.

Regardie (1994) also shares the following important instruction. "In the pronunciation of these Names, thou shalt take a deep breath and vibrate them as much as possible inwardly with the outgoing breath, not necessarily loudly, but with vibration. . ." (p. 284). He likewise advises, "The Names should be pronounced inwardly in the breath vibrating it as much as possible and feeling that the whole body throbs with the sound and sends out a wave of vibration directed to the ends of the quarter" (Regardie, 1994, p. 54).

Elsewhere he further states,

> In vibrating the Divine Names, the Operator should first of all rise as high as possible towards the idea of the Divine White Brilliance in KETHER keeping the mind raised to the plane of loftiest aspiration. Unless this is done, it is dangerous to vibrate only with the astral forces, because the vibration attracts a certain force to the operator, and the nature of the force attracted rests largely on the condition of mind in which the operator is.
>
> The ordinary mode of vibrating is as follows: Take a deep breath and full inspiration and concentrate your consciousness in your heart, which answers to Tiphareth. (Having first... ascended to your Kether, you should endeavor to bring down the White Brilliance into your

heart, prior to centering your consciousness there).

Then formulate the letters of the Name required in your heart, in white, and feel them written there. Be sure to formulate the letters in brilliant white light, not merely in dull whiteness as the colour of the Apas Tattwa. Then, emitting the breath, slowly pronounce the Letters so that the sound vibrates within you, and imagine that the breath, while quitting the body, swells you so as to fill up space. Pronounce the Name as if you were vibrating it through the whole Universe, and as if it did not stop until it reached the further limits.

All practical occult work which is of any use, tires the operator or withdraws some magnetism, and therefore, if you wish to do anything that is at all important, you must be in perfect magnetic and nervous condition, or else you will do evil instead of good.

When you are using a Name. . .you must remember that the Sephira to which the Rose and Cross are referred, is Tiphareth, whose position answers to the position of the heart, as if there are letters in it. (Regardie, 1994, p. 487).

The Alchemical Order, The Philosophers of Nature (1997) have stated the following regarding the vibration of Divine Names:

. . .remember that the sounds created should be deep, resonant, and cause a subtle, if not exhausting, vibration throughout your entire body. They should be imagined as being inhaled and then spoken or shouted to the ends of the universe and returning again to you. This can also be done slowly and progressively, adding color and quality to each letter over time. The Word is the vehicle of the will and of thought. That is why magicians can utter words that may seem devoid of meaning. However, we can say that these words are energized by them because they know what to expect from their vocalizations. In addition, these words, through repetition, acquire charge which still increases their power of action. . .In addition, the magical theory considers that the vibrations triggered by human voice have he power to fashion the. . .substance of the Astral Light into various forms according to frequency, amplitude, intensity, and the resonance of the emission of the sound, but also to attract to our world the attention of various metaphysical entities. . .With regular practice we can rather quickly feel at will an intense tremor in the entire body under the impact of the vocalization of a single word. Also, practice will allow the student to contain at will the vibratory effects to a specific part of his body. . .

The throat is directly connected to our power of speech and creation. Through it we communicate to others, be they human, animal, or Divine. It is the quickest way to turn something into a reality in the material world, for sound itself is both transient and permanent. Once a word is spoken it is gone, yet its meaning, and effects remain forever. A word spoken cannot be taken back.

Words crystallize or make tangible our innermost thoughts. The more complex the thought, the more complex the word to describe it. These complexities act as a verbal DNA, or programming, creating a sense of visible and invisible conditions that become our life.

How often have we said something in haste, jest, lust, or anger only wishing later that we could undo what was done? If mortal speech is so powerful, than how much more potent is our speech when magically directed?

Initiated man is a transformer of energy. A layman who pronounces a word disturbs the air of the physical world but his word has little resonance in the higher frequencies. On the other hand, the initiate has reestablished the links between the different levels of his consciousness. That is, he reestablished contact with the various vibratory levels of the universe, and the more he advances on the initiatory path, the better the contact between his various planes.

Therefore, contrary to the layman, when the initiate talks, he disturbs the higher vibratory levels and if his word conforms to the original language he will then create the very thing designated by the word, through harmony will radiate the vibrations which are the thing itself ...If voice can crystallize a condition, through judicious use of voice, we can realize conditions that are preferred by us. When combined with the use of Hebrew letters and the powers they manifest, we can begin to direct our inner energies in any manner we see fit. . .

The Bal Shem, or 'Master of the Name,' was one of the most remarkable aspects of Medieval and Renaissance Jewish Qabala. For these Rabbis, nothing was impossible, and miracles are said to have been performed by them simply through the spoken expression of one or more of the names of God. (p. 22).

Mike Benjamin

Thus, this internal emphasis on the vibration shows a parallel to the motives of Western Alchemy, the purpose being, according to the prodigious Frater Superior of the Paracelsus Research Society – Frater Albertus (1974), the "raising of the vibrations" (p. 14). In contrast to this internal emphasis, however, the student is also advised to imagine the vibration extending infinitely out into the universe. This works to equilibrate the vibration, internal to external.

The following should also be taken into careful consideration. With each vibration, the student should feel his aura radiate its brilliance in a color of high frequency, such as white, sapphire, silver, or gold. You should feel the energy flow out into the Dynamic Sphere in all directions and back again. While all of the Chakra (bodily Sephira) should be aglow, the Anahata Chakra (Tiphareth) is the central focus of the LPR corresponding to Art, Beauty, the Adeptus Minor grade, the 5 = 6 formula, and the Rose of the Cross.

As will be instructed later, the LPR manipulates energy by using the appropriate elemental weapon in alignment with the heart Chakra (Tiphareth Sephira). This energy is not only projected horizontally outward, but also received back horizontally inward. Thus an orbit is created extending to and fro like a circuit. As Regardie (1994) explains, "These then are the two processes: the Invoking Whirl related to the heart. The Expanding Whirl related to the aura" (p. 492). These processes relate respectively to the individual acts of intention and attention, as well as the Kosmic actions of involution and evolution.

In addition, the action of the ritual creates not only such a horizontal aspect of energy, like a tide ebbing and flowing, but is also balanced with a vertical line of energy as well. To Chinese Qigong and Tai Chi Ch'uan adepts[45] this vertical orbit is analogous to what is termed in their systems the "greater circulation" or "great orbit" of Qi (or life energy) which constitutes the basis of Taoist internal alchemy (Yang, 1989). In Qabalistic terms it represents the Ascending Path of the Serpent united with the Descending Path of the Lightning Bolt (or

[45] The author holds advanced black belts in three different martial arts systems, including a style of Kung Fu that incorporates a form of Tai Chi Ch'uan.

116

Flaming Sword) upon the Tree of Life. Tantrically it is the orgasmic ejaculation of Kundalini from the Muludhara Chakra in the perineum to the Ajna Chakra in the third eye (or Pineal gland) and its descent again in the flaccidity that follows. To the Wiccan it is the growth of the new Spring's corn and the killing scythe of Winter's first frost. This horizontal and vertical extension and reception of energy also represents within the LPR a formation of the Cross and is thus indicative of the FIAT LVX.

The vertical orbit's primary purpose is to sustain the Magician's power as a direct link through the ascending Spiritual Hierarchy back to the Prime Source; to Divinity or "God" (or in Buddhist correlation, to the Dharmakaya). In this sense the vertical orbit is both INTERNAL and ETERNAL. The horizontal orbit, in balancing contrast, is the medium of Magickal current that can be sent out to affect change in the environment in accordance with the Will. In this sense the horizontal orbit is EXTERNAL and TEMPORAL (or in Buddhist correlation, is of the Samsara). Both are needed in equilibrium to form the harmonized whole (which in Mahayanic understanding correlates to the realization that the Nirvana and the Samsara are not two, but one, both arising from Shunyata). Also know, for those able to mentally conceptualize it, hidden within this structure of energy-orbits intersecting within the heart (i.e. Anahata/Tiphareth) is a three-dimensional model of the Qabalistic Tree of Life.

Before finalizing some concepts about the actual vocalizations made in the LPR we must first clarify a few points made by Regardie relating the Stella Matutina's teachings. He writes that the letters of the word to be vibrated in the LPR should first be formulated in the heart. He says that in advanced stages the Hebrew letters of the God-Name should be visualized and projected from Tiphareth (the heart Chakra) to the center of the Pentagram traced in space as the corresponding syllable is being vocally vibrated. He then becomes somewhat unclear in his instruction saying to "vibrate the Name as many times as there are letters in it." This is somewhat confusing as it does not clarify whether he means to vibrate the entire Name repetitively for each number of letters in it or to vibrate each letter singularly as a syllable.

Whatever his actual meaning, I believe, through my own practice and the ensuing inspiration gained, that I have formulated a more apropos method of so doing, both sound in its symbolism and proper in pronunciation. As we have seen, each Divine Name vibrated in the LPR is a Tetragrammaton or four lettered word for God; namely YHVH, ADNI, EHIH, and AGLA (the meanings of which will be later defined). Though spelled in four letters, by some methods of phonetics they are correctly pronounced in three syllables. [46] Thus, the three syllables in each Tetragrammaton, vibrated to the four cardinal directions form a zodiacal correspondence to the zodiacal triplicities[47] and the order of the zodiacal spirits[48] as seen by the simple mathematical formula of multiplication thereby created: $3 \times 4 = 12$. Such a rendering of the Tetragrammatons' pronunciation into three syllables likewise correlates to the pronunciation of the Archangelic names invoked in the climax of the ritual which are also composed of three syllables. Such an act crafts the zodiac encircling the Magician by this act of Will, Imagination, and Vocalized Vibration. This is but one of the ways in which the LPR symbolically and visually creates the presence of the Universal Mandala or Wheel of Ezekiel (to be further elucidated in the section "Metaphors of the LPR").

Regarding the vocal vibratory technique actualized in the LPR, the student is urged to contemplate the following ideas:

1). In audible sound quality, the vocalized vibrations should be akin to the sonorous, musical quality heard in Gregorian and Tibetan chant.

2). There will be an individual "flavor" to each student's vibrations based on the uniqueness of every voice, its tone, tempo, and so on. A vocal pattern is, after all, as unique as an individual's fingerprint.

---

[46] I differ with Regardie's instruction for pronouncing the Divine Name YHVH as it is spelled, with four syllables, for the reasons conveyed in the text regarding the Astrological correspondences established with the alternate three syllable pronunciation used herein.

[47] See Appendix A.

[48] See Appendix A and Levi (1996).

3). A complete "Total Breath," as used in Tai Chi or Yoga[49], should be utilized through the vibrated release of each syllable.

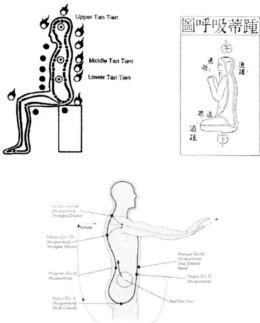

**MODERN AND ANCIENT RENDERINGS OF THE TAOIST GREAT ORBIT (OR GREAT CIRCULATION) UTILIZED IN QIGONG AND TAI CHI CH'UAN.**

---

[49] Proper training in Total Breathing is as important for the Magician as it is to the martial artist. Its basic instruction is as follows: Stand erect, posture straight, shoulders back but relaxed, tongue to the roof of the mouth (to connect the body's two main energy channels and thus establishing the Taoist "Great Circulation" of internal energy, or Qi). Inhale deeply through the nose, expanding the abdomen first, filling the lungs like a glass of water, from bottom to top, using the entire capacity of the lungs. Exhale through the mouth in reciprocation of the inhale; chest contracting first, lungs emptying top to bottom, abdomen contracting last. This style of breathing is known by many names. In the martial art of Juko-Ryu Kijutsu it is called the Total Breath (the name used in this text). In the martial art of Aikido it is called the Bell-Shaped Breath. In Tibetan Buddhism, it is the Pot-Shaped Breath. In Tai Chi Ch'uan it is called the Bellows Breath and the Pre-Natal Breath, as this is the breath we use upon birth and then as infants, only to forsake (into Post-Natal Breathing) as we grow older. This is the healthiest method for breathing for the positive benefit of the internal organs, digestion, the cardiopulmonary system, and internal energy.

Mike Benjamin

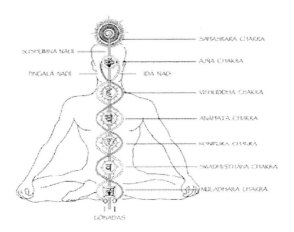

**THE CHAKRA (OR ENERGY "WHEELS") SYSTEM PER HINDUISM & KUNDALINI YOGI.**

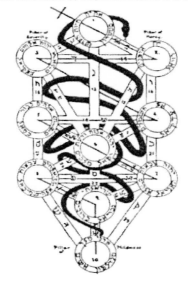

**THE QABALISTIC TREE OF LIFE DISPLAYING THE PATH OF THE ASCENDING SERPENT AND THE DESCENT OF THE FLAMING SWORD.**

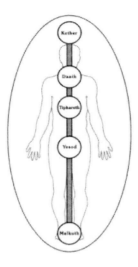

# TWO RENDERINGS OF THE
# QABALISTIC MIDDLE PILLAR

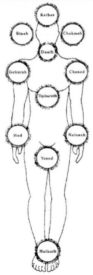

# THE INTERIOR STARS (CHAKRAS)
# OF ALCHEMY

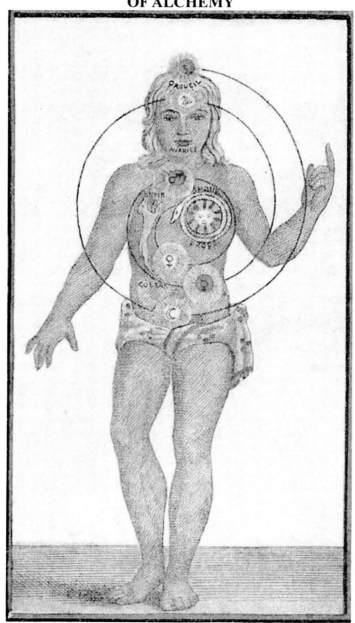

4). Generally, the pitch of the vibration should rise through the first half of the vibratory exhalation and descend through the last half.

5). Altering pitch and tone can also create a necessary or applicable emotional component suitable to the specific needs of the ritual. Crowley (1970) notes that banishment should possess a tone of "icy indifference," while consecration (implying invocation) should be in a tone of "love and fervor" (pp. 106-107). I would add that banishment should have an air of sovereign authority and learned confidence, while invocation should hold a tone of sincere and reverent humility.

6). This final point will only be fully understood with practice and experience. I will touch on it no more than to say that when performing the correct vibratory method an involuntary physical convex "bowing" backwards of the student's body, like a slight backbend, centered at the bodily Yesod (i.e. the Taoist Dan Tien, the Yogic Svadhisthana Chakra, the Japanese Hara, etc.) will occur.[50]

## Spoken Declarations

There are three spoken declarations within the LPR regarding the Divine Names, or Tetragrammatons, that are not executed with vibration as outlined above: 1). The Qabalistic Cross; 2). The Invocation of the Archangels; and 3). The climax of the ritual which I refer to as the Declaration of the Great Work. While these three areas are not formally vibrated per se, they still absolutely possess intrinsic power in their nature and processes. In this regard I have discovered through extensive

---

[50] This is the human body's physical center of gravity and energetic focal point located one to three inches below the navel and about one third of the way back from the navel to the spine. In Japan this point is called the Itten or the Hara, center of Ki. This is the insertion point of the wakizashi (short sword) in the Samurai suicide ceremony vulgarly called Hara Kiri (belly cutting), but formally known as Seppuku. In China this same point is called the Dan Tien (field of elixir) and is the center of Qi. Taoism teaches there are three Dan Tiens in the body; the navel point, at the heart, and in the center of the forehead. The martial art of Tai Chi Ch'uan is primarily interested in the lowest Dan Tien considered the main reservoir of Qi. In acupuncture this point is called the Qihai (Sea of Qi). Note also the correspondences to the Middle Pillar model of Qabalah and the bodily Sephira of Kether, Tiphareth, and Yesod.

performance of the ritual that the following instructions should be adhered to.

The Qabalistic Cross may be sincerely and reverentially whispered, or contrastingly, it may be boldly, loudly, but respectfully stated. The practitioner should experiment with pitch, tone, volume, tempo, emotional content, and so forth, in order to suit their own personal inclinations and character; to discover their own proper "frequency" and to meet the given needs at hand for performing the LPR. However, at the conclusion of this process, the "Amen" should be sung in one Total Breath; the first syllable ("Ah") in a rising pitch, and the second ("men") in a descending one.

The Invocation of the Archangels should be in a gradually ascending emotional pitch, beginning with a steady stoic declaration of Raphael, and growing in emotional fervor and volume through each successive Archangelic invocation until the ecstatic, fevered pitch of the climax;[51] the Declaration of the Great Work; the verbal avowal of the 5 = 6 formula.

# The Intellectual Composition of Magick

In order to fully outline the ingredients pertinent to the Magickal composition of our discussion, it is necessary to reiterate some points while examining some concepts to be left to the student's further inquiry. As previously touched upon, the Magician, to be a balanced whole and not a boat with one oar in the water, must be a duality of both priest and scientist. They must be both artistic-transcendentalist and rational-empiricist. They must possess a deeply understood and completely reconciled balance between the opposing faculties of logic and faith. The arms of their cross must be equilibrated, otherwise fanaticism and/or bigotry is created, as well as conflict or cognitive dissonance within their internal intellectual processes.

---

[51] In various writings, Crowley has repeatedly likened this ecstatic, fevered, trance-like burst of fervor required at a Magickal ritual's climax to a sexual orgasm. I would also add that this state, as closely as can be described, is likewise akin to a synthesis of the physiological euphoria associated with the orgasm coupled with the psychological energy of a panic attack, or perhaps more accurately, the adrenalin rush of the fight/flight reaction.

As Taoism teaches, it is the fundamental imbalance of these opposing forces, of Yin and Yang, that creates all forms of disease, madness, ignorance, poverty, and evil. It is this imbalance that is personified in the Bible as the war in heaven and the ensuing division drawn as such between heaven and hell. It is displayed in the Biblical Fall from grace, microcosmically manifested in the "trenches dug within our hearts." It is thus the internal harmony between both our physiological and psychological energies, emphasized by such diverse sources ranging from Lao Tzu to Eliphas Levi, that is essential to the healthy maintenance of the self and necessary for the proper pursuit of the Great Work.

In addition to this requirement of spiritual equilibrium, other varying intellectual factors prove of vital importance in the pursuit of all White Magick and are fundamental to the right use of the LPR, such as memory, focus, concentration, sincerity, and benevolence. Of all the varying intellectual factors, however, none are as primary to successful Magick as are the faculties of Will and Imagination.

Levi (1996) writes,

> To control the Willpower and make it subservient to the Law of Intelligence – this is the Great Work of our. . .art. Ceremonies which are performed without intelligence and without faith, in the absence of the higher aspirations of the soul, are but superstitious observances which tend to degrade those who take part in them. It is an error to attribute magical power to ceremonials, for magical power exists only in the trained Will of the operator. For this reason is the Magical Axiom true, that the Sanctum Regnum – the Divine Kingdom of God – is within us. INRI, Intra Nobis Regnum Dei. (p. 19).

He continues,

> Imagination is the eye of the soul, and it is therein that forms are delineated and

125

> preserved, by its means we behold the reflections of the invisible world. It is. . .the apparatus of magical life. . .because this faculty exalts the Will and gives it power over the Universal Agent. (Levi, 1996, p. 19).

Only surpassed by the quality of Love, it is these two faculties of Will and Imagination (represented in the Major Arcana by The Chariot and the Empress, respectively) which raise us closest to the Creator's essence and allow us to emulate Him in this lowly image every moment of our lives. Hence, the Magician's Will must be constantly strengthened and progressively purified. "Resist the devil and he will flee. . ." (James 4:7, King James Version). To this end, as exemplified by Jesus in the wilderness with Satan, or Buddha under the Bodhi tree with Mara, practices and behaviors which breed resistance to all forms of temptation are beneficial to this aim. Such methods as fasting, abstinence, chastity, all forms of self-sacrifice to others, and any self-imposed act of personal suffering through discipline work to foster improved Willpower in the practitioner.[52]

In this same vein, the student is prompted to contemplate the real meaning behind the priestly vows of poverty, chastity, and obedience. This is not only a triune ethical structure designed to remove all superfluous worldly concerns contraindicated to the monastic pursuit of the Great Work. These rules are also intended to positively fortify and spiritually purify the Will. All of the extensively drawn-out proscriptions, processes of purification, and moral protocols preliminary to the Abramelin Magick and the *The Key of Solomon* are precisely intended for this reason.

---

[52] This is a Levi-based opinion. However, to balance this theory, Crowley advised "But exceed! Exceed! Strive to ever more!" (*Liber Al Vel Legis*, II: 71-72). Rosicrucian poet William Blake likewise advised, "The roads of excess lead to the palace of wisdom" (Blake, 1995). I would advise that the student find a balance of the ascetic and the Bohemian, exercising what Buddha taught as the Middle Path; the Mahayana's concept of Madyamihka as also espoused by Nargajuna. Moderation in all things should be the guiding premise of the student, and not as I lived in my own youth, the life philosophy of "moderation in moderation!"

In considering this faculty, one's Imagination must be broad-ranging, unbiased, of a multiple perspectives, and artistically creative. It must be capable of both minute, specific detail, and contrastingly, of grandiose and elaborate expansion. It must be equally versed in analysis and synthesis, *solve et coagula*. Deep investigation and appreciation of all the fine arts, sciences, and social studies are essential to its development. However, besides Magick, some subjects are better suited to the facilitation of this faculty than are others. I have always personally found poetry, art, Kempo, music, literature, philosophy, painting, and history to be highly fruitful in this regards. The student may also find the controlled (and not habitual) use of organic psychedelics helpful, such as marijuana, psilocybin, D.M.T., and so on, if they not be of the personality or physiology susceptible to acquiring addiction (and thus detrimental to well being) or other ill health effects from such Eucharistic experimentation.[53] Again, on the opposite end of the scale, complete abstinence and sobriety may be, to the proper temperament, the more effective spiritual path. "To each

---

[53] Crowley would have advocated this experimentation, while Levi most assuredly would not. The student is directed to examinations covering both ends of the drug spectrum; advocacy as well as condemnation. Suggested sources include *Drugs and Magic* edited by George Andrews; *Plants of the Gods* by Richard Schulte and Albert Hoffman (inventor of LSD), *Junky* by William Burroughs; *The Cocaine Papers of Sigmund Freud* edited by Dr. Robert Byck, and the extensive research of psychedelics for shamanistic purposes and inter-dimensional alien contact as researched by Terrence McKenna. I would argue that the student needs to keep deeply in mind the stark difference between the utilization of psychoactives for religious ends (such as Ahyahausca when used by the Amazon basin's indigenous Shamans or the Medicine Men's use of Peyote in the Native American religion), versus the use of such substances simply for the leisure pursuit of "partying" so prevalent now in modern Western civilization. These differing usages are literally night and day, like the difference between H2O when used for watering a plant versus one's experience when drowning in the surf. And those who utilize Aldous Huxley's proponent views on psychedelic experimentation to justify the latter usage above incorrectly grasp his arguments which are, rather, solidly rooted in the former utilization of such. His warnings of the use of drugs for our own enslavement in his classic *Brave New World,* while written in the genre of science fiction, border more on prophecy. The reader is strongly encouraged to see his equally prophetic 1958 interview by Mike Wallace (available on Youtube) for further chilling accuracies over what the future (our present) would hold for the overly medicated.

their own" in discovering which fork in the road leads to Shambhala.

Although Crowley has provided perhaps the most comprehensive and understandable theorems in describing the workings of Magick in *M.I.T.A.P.*, he elaborates upon two significant concepts worthy of examination in this context. One is the quality he calls "Enflaming thyself in prayer." (Crowley, 1970, p. 129) This mental state is composed of an emotional exaltation akin to the artistic creative impulse, almost akin to a feeling of mania. This is combined with an actual overwhelming physical surge of energy, or what I term a Qi or Pranic cascade. The Sephirotic (or Chakra) path that this cascade bodily follows will be explained later.

Crowley has repeatedly likened this fevered, ecstatic, dervish state to the orgasm. My own experience has not proven it quite so euphoric and I compare it to an orgasm coupled with the feeling of a minor panic attack or adrenalin rush. It is both internal in the way it is relayed through the body's energy meridians (i.e. Yogic nadis or Taoist jingluos) and external in the way it is emanated through the Aura or Body of Light. One of Magick's primary purposes is the development of this Light Body and it is also one of the primary purposes behind the practice of the LPR. The progressive steps of the LPR, or those of any truly Magickal ceremonial ritual, are designed to foster a necessary disassociation with extraneous reality through the contrasting action of intense mental concentration and focus of Willpower. It is this tension between such fire and ice, between Yin and Yang, that creates the necessary strain to nurture the inflamed condition and is the rudimentary recipe for the manipulation of Magickal current.

The self-styled Great Beast, in agreement with Tibetan Buddhist teachings, likewise emphasized being "free from the lust of result" (Crowley, 1994) as a prerequisite quality for success in Magickal practices. The principle of this seemingly apathetic, unbiased, indifferent impartiality, its purpose and function, is similar to that of Silence. Like the discipline of Silence (which is designed to focus power by not wasting it in useless conversation, but in saving it for application to actions), this lesson is likewise designed to harness and focus the Magician's power purely, without wasting or dispersing energy on unnecessary concerns or superfluous worry over outcomes. While the Magician is to have faith in the hoped for effect of their ritual, they must also have the contrasting Buddhist separation to not care whether the results prove as they wish. In this way they pay careful mind to the workings of Karma, the Universal Law of Cause and Effect, that plays in all places and moments eternally, and which ultimately proves in every result and situation of life, whether successful or failing in man's eyes, as totally and utterly purposeful to the Divine Plan. Freedom from the lust of result is thus achieving a state of mind subordinate to God's Will; of accomplishing the true meaning of the word Islam ("surrender") by conquering our own limited scope of circumstances and our inherent human tendency towards selfish desire for success in all our worldly efforts.

Lastly, the mental state of Dhyana, achieved only through disciplined meditative or Yogic practice, is also essential to all Magickal ritual. While a more thorough exposition of this concept will follow later, for now it will suffice to discuss a few chief points. In this state of mind the individual considers themselves, the object perceived, and the act of that perception as a unity. Dyhana is thus very similar to what Dr. Scholem (1975) has explained, in regard to Qabalistic theory as, "The dialectical relationship of mutuality and magical rapport existing between the active Godhead and all created things." (p. 111).

Dyhana is essentially the comprehension of the Oneness that exists between All. It is the shattering of the illusion of separateness; the comprehension of the Unity of God, creation, all sentient beings, and all things together. (This is the primary difference between the Right and Left-hand Paths. The former strives to overcome this illusion in pursuit of truth and liberation. The latter works to antithetically reinforce it). This unity revealed in Dyhana is the nature and essence of the Magickal link.[54] To so acquire Dyhana, the Magician must be able to suspend their wrongful disbelief in their Unity with the All and circumvent the deceiving ego that is always striving for the illusory sense of separateness. To this end, the student is

---

[54] For thorough expositions on the nature of the Magickal link, see Crowley (1970, Ch. XV) and Frazer (1951).

emphatically encouraged to study, absorb, and thereby live the incomparable teachings of a true living Buddha, the Master Eckhart Tolle.

In summary then, this is the formula to our spiritual equation:

$$WILL$$
$$+$$
$$IMAGINATION$$
$$+$$
$$ENFLAMING\ THYSELF\ IN\ PRAYER$$
$$+$$
$$FREEDOM\ FROM\ THE\ LUST\ OF\ RESULT$$
$$X$$
$$\underline{DYHANA} =$$

$$MAGICK.$$

# Techinal Performance of the Ritual with Component Analysis

The ritual form hereby related is my own personal version which proves but a slight variation over the original. I offer it here for posterity as such differentiations have proven to me most valuable. The student is welcome to use this or the classic LPR as taught in the introduction to this work (or in other various Hermetic resources). Note that the lessons contained in this tome are applicable to both.

## Beginning Declaration

State firmly, *"I announce to all sentient beings within the range of my voice and the light of my aura that an act of Magick is about to commence. All benevolent are welcome. All malevolent will be hereby removed!"*

## Performance of the Opening Qabalistic Cross

1). Eyes may be opened or closed, posture upright and confident, facing East, take thy weapon (air dagger or fire

wand) in thy right hand and with it touch the third eye
(forehead) symbolizing Kether[55] and say "ATEH."
2). Lower thy weapon and touch the heart symbolizing
Tiphareth and say "MALKUTH."
3). Touch thy weapon to the right shoulder symbolizing
Joachin[56] and say "VE-GEBURAH."
4). Touch thy weapon to the left shoulder symbolizing Boaz[57]
and say "VE-GEDULAH."
5). Grasp thy weapon between both hands in front of thy heart
as if praying and say "LE-OLAHM."
6). Raise thy weapon in the same hold skyward and sing
"AMEN."[58]

# Analysis of the Opening Qabalistic Cross

The student should realize the obvious correspondence between
this act and the Lord's Prayer and contemplate the deeper
meaning of such within the context of *Matthew* 6:9-13. However,
this opening exercise is primarily meant as a method of
vertically aligning the energy currents of one's descending
bodily Sephira (Chakras) by calling down the Divine White
Brilliance from the Ain Sof Aur through the Divine Sephira
beginning in Kether, down Jacob's ladder, into our own Kether,
down Daath in the nape of the neck, to Tiphareth in the heart,
out to Joachin and Boaz in a balanced flow, to Yesod in the
abdomen (below the navel and between the hips), ending in
Malkuth at the soles of the feet. Thus, though brief, the

---

[55] Note the universal correspondence to this energy center in the forehead. In
Kundalini Yoga it is the Ajna Chakra; in Taoism the highest Dan Tien; in
Qabalah the bodily Sephiroth of Kether; in Alchemy the Adytum of the Temple.
**Descartes felt this point, which he identified with the Pineal Gland, to be the
location of Will in the brain.**

[56] The Pillar of Mercy upon the Tree of Life; the Pillar of Cloud in the Old
Testament; the White Pillar of Solomon's Temple in Freemasonry. See Clegg &
Mackey (1929, pp. 779-782).

[57] The Pillar of Severity upon the Tree of Life; The Pillar of Fire in the Old
Testament; the Black Pillar of Solomon's Temple in Freemasonry. (Clegg &
Mackey, 1929, pp. 779-782).

[58] Translation of the Hebrew Qabalistic Cross:  Ateh = "thou art." Malkuth =
"the kingdom." Ve-Geburah = "and the power." Ve-Gedulah = "and the glory."
Le-Olahm = "forever" (or "unto the ages").

Qabalistic Cross is similar in function to the Middle Pillar exercise.[59]

The Qabalistic Cross also acts as an invocative placation to God, an appeal to His power and majesty calling down the grace of the Holy Spirit and the intensity of the Sacred Fire into the Magician. In contrast, it is also the first step in the LPR at raising the Magician's state of consciousness beyond Nephesh and Ruach into Neshamah, out of Assiah through the ascending strata of Yetzirah, Briah, and into the ultimate goal of Atziluth.

The Qabalistic Cross possesses its own limited banishing properties as well for the cross symbolizes, amongst other meanings, the LVX formula – Light In Extension – the Light that at the moment of creation, at the Big Bang (the Beginning of the Whirlings), drove away the ocean of darkness and the chaos of the limitless void. Note also that "Malkuth" is stated while touching Tiphareth. This is because Malkuth, "the Kingdom," is the essence of Tiphareth, or the soul's "beauty." Again to reiterate, as Christ taught, "The Kingdom of God is within you." (*Luke* 17:21, King James Version).

For astute students of the Major Arcana, the following lines of numerical symbolism coupled with their Tarot significance are also hereby hinted at for meditation/contemplation as inherent in the movements of the Qabalistic Cross:

**\*In the initial movements**, the weapon touches the body on four points, forming the Cross, the Tau. By implication of the number 4 we have, through Tarot, The Empress (4th Key) and the Emperor (Key 4). By implication of the Tau, we have

[59] **The Middle Pillar Exercise**: A). Perform an opening Qabalistic Cross with an empty hand. B). Visualize thyself standing in Solomon's temple, facing West; the Black Pillar on the right, the White Pillar on the left. Imagine these Pillars reflected in turn, down the shoulders and legs. C). Take a Total Breath and raise thy consciousness to Kether. "Light the lamp" above thy head and vibrate EHIH. D). Imagine the Divine White Brilliance descending down from the Macrocosmic Kether into thine own Microcosmic Kether, through Daath in the nape of the neck, to Tiphareth in thy heart. E). Vibrate SHADDAI EL CHAI and imagine and feel the Light flowing down to Yesod in the point below thy navel. F). Establish Malkuth in thy feet in the same way but vibrating ADONAI HA-ARETZ. G). Imagine the Light extended through thy body as the glowing Middle Pillar of the Temple, balanced between Joachin and Boaz, from Kether to Malkuth, Tiphareth shining in glorious radiance, and thine aura splendidly illuminated. H). Conclude with the Qabalistic Cross.

through Tarot both the Hanged Man (Key 12) and the Universe (or World), Key 21. As 4 is achieved through 1 + 3 or 0 + 4, so are the following combinations possible: The Fool (1st Key) and then High Priestess (3rd Key); the Magician (Key 1) and the Empress (Key 3); the Fool (Key 0) and the Emperor (Key 4).[60]

*The fifth movement brings the weapon centered to Tiphareth, symbolizing the Magician as the Pentagram, the Microcosm, Yeheshua or Yehovasha, the Adam Kadmon. By implication of the number 5 we have, through Tarot, the Emperor (5th key) and the Hierophant (Key 5). As 5 can be achieved by 1 + 4 and 2 + 3 and 0 + 5, so are the following combinations possible: The Fool (1st key) joined with the Empress (4th Key); the Magician (Key 1) joined with the Emperor (Key 5); the Magician (2nd Key) joined with the High Priestess (2nd Key); the High Priestess (Key 2) joined with the Empress (Key 3); and the Fool (Key 0) with the Hierophant (Key 5).

*The sixth movement raises the weapon from Tiphareth above their head symbolizing appeal to the Godhead, to Kether, to the Macrocosm – thus, the Hexagram. By implication of the number 6, through the Tarot we have The Hierophant (6th Key) and The Lovers (Key 6). As 6 can be achieved by 1 + 5, 2 + 4, and 0 + 6, we are thus given: The Fool (1st Key) and the Emperor (4th Key); The Magician (Key 1) and The Hierophant (Key 5); The Magician (2nd Key) and The High Priestess (3rd Key); The High Priestess (Key 2) and The Emperor (Key 4); and The Fool (Key 0) and The Lovers (Key 6).

# Tracing of the Pentagrams and Vibration of the Divine Names

1). Eyes wide open, posture straight and upright, face East and trace the Earth Pentagram from forehead to hips to banish with thy weapon. See the Flaming Star. Upon completion, align thy

---

[60] Upon the Tree of Life, the paths leading from Tiphareth through Yesod to Malkuth are, respectively, The World (Key 21) and Temperance (Key 14), or in the Thoth deck, The Universe and Art. For an exhaustive analysis of Tiphareth and its correspondence to the 5 = 6 formula and Adeptus Minor grade see Case (1985).

weapon with thy Tiphareth (thus pointing at the Star's center) and using a Total Breath per syllable, vibrate: YHVH ("Ya – Ho – Vah"). Envisage the Star blazing and behind it see a piedmont blue sky filled with wispy stratus clouds of white and light gray floating in a steady wind. Feel the wind and smell the scent of fresh ionized air. Once the vision is solidly formulated, see this elemental scene dissipate into nothingness leaving but the Void. Simultaneously formulate within the mind only, as naught but an audible whisper, the thought, *"In the Ineffable Name of God, I banish air."*

2). Rotate a quarter circle deosil tracing the horizontal arc of flame from the first star with thy weapon, arm outstretched fully, as if cutting through space. Face South and trace the Earth Pentagram from forehead to hips to banish with thy weapon. See the Flaming Star. Upon completion, align thy weapon with thy Tiphareth (thus pointing at the Star's center) and using a Total Breath per syllable, vibrate: ADNI ("Ah – Do – Ni"). Behind the Star envisage a raging fire like the surface of the sun. Feel great heat and smell the scent of sulphur. Once the vision is solidly formulated, see this elemental scene dissipate into nothingness leaving but the Void. Simultaneously formulate within the mind only, as naught but an audible whisper, the thought, *"In the name of the Lord, I banish fire."*

3). Rotate a quarter circle deosil tracing the horizontal arc of flame from the prior star with thy weapon, arm outstretched fully, as if cutting through space. Face West and trace the Earth Pentagram from forehead to hips to banish with thy weapon. See the Flaming Star. Upon completion, align thy weapon with thy Tiphareth (thus pointing at the Star's center) and using a Total Breath per syllable, vibrate: EHIH ("Eh – Heh – Yay"). Behind the Star envisage crashing tsunami waves, torrential rivers in flood, and monsoon rains. Taste the salt and smell the brine. Once the vision is solidly formulated, see this elemental scene dissipate into nothingness leaving but the Void. Simultaneously formulate within the mind only, as naught but an audible whisper, the thought, *"In the name of the I Am, I banish water."*

4). Rotate a quarter circle deosil tracing the horizontal arc of flame from the prior star with thy weapon, arm outstretched fully, as if cutting through space. Face North and trace the Earth

Pentagram from forehead to hips to banish with thy weapon. See the Flaming Star. Upon completion, align thy weapon with thy Tiphareth (thus pointing at the Star's center) and using a Total Breath per syllable, vibrate: AGLA ("Ah – Guh – Lah"). Behind the Star envisage a towering mountain; Olympus, Meru, Everest, Ararat, Albigensia; the great umbilical cord connecting Heaven and Earth. Smell the soil and taste of the dirt. Once the vision is solidly formulated, see this elemental scene dissipate into nothingness leaving but the Void. Simultaneously formulate within the mind only, as naught but an audible whisper, the thought, *"In the name of the Eternal Almighty, I banish earth."*

5). Rotate a quarter circle deosil tracing the horizontal arc of flame from the prior star with thy weapon, arm outstretched fully, as if cutting through space returning to the East, thus completing the Flaming Circle around thee. Realign thy weapon back with thy Tiphareth and the first Star's center.

# Analysis of the Tracing and Vibrations

While the ritual proper detailed here is utilized to banish, whether the Magician is executing the LPR for this purpose or utilizing its invocative variant, both operations will work to invoke the Divine energies and Archangelic forces that follow. However, the LPR, unlike other Magickal rituals, does not alter its circumambulation (or more aptly described, rotation) to vary its effect; that is, to alter its action of banishing versus invoking. Classically, invocation calls for deosil motion, banishing is usually widdershins. In contradiction to this general rule, in the LPR the operation is altered by the direction utilized in the tracing of the Pentagram with the dagger (or wand) in the space

in front of the Magician. [61] For banishment, as we have shown, the Earth Pentagram is utilized. For invocation, reciprocate. Furthermore, as shown above, in banishment the elemental visualizations are seen to dissipate or disintegrate. In invocation these visions are formulated and then left to be.

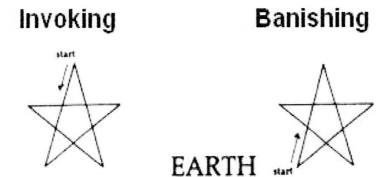

**Invoking**

**Banishing**

EARTH

**Earth Pentagrams for Specific Usage in the LPR**

---

[61] As a general rule of Magickally using the Pentagram, trace towards the elemental point to invoke the element and away to banish. The LPR uses only the Earth Pentagram, however, as according to classical instruction. Also note that in other Magickal evocations, the Pentagram should be point up on the altar for lighted spirits and point down for infernal. When considering the action of the elements in regards to the Tetragrammaton; air is for banishing, fire for consecration, water for purification, and earth for materialization.

# The 4 Elemental Pentagrams for Banishing and Invocation

For advanced aspirants, these may be used per direction in artistically compounded exercises of the LPR, with the corresponding Pentagram being utilized per each direction. In the basic form of the ritual, only the Earth version is used towards each direction (per classical instruction).

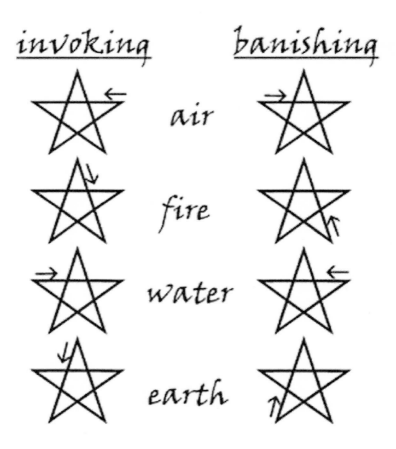

In regard to the shape, size, and color of the Pentagrams traced in the LPR, the following details are of importance. These figures must be drawn geometrically exact, for all intents and purposes, and the practitioner must be sure that the end line connects with the first point so as to close the angle created. Beginners may find this precise drawing difficult at first, but will gain improvement in each performance and refined skill with repeated practice. As we shall later examine, this aspect of the ritual composes a form of Yogic Dharana.

In size, the Stars should extend from Kether to Yesod; that is, from the forehead to the center of the body's gravity just below the navel (Yogically speaking, from the Ajna Chakra to the Svadisthana Chakra). In this way the center of the Star is aligned with the Magician's heart center, Tiphareth (or in the Yogic system, the Anahata Chakra). Thus, the heart of the Magician is centered to the heart of the Pentagram; the individual to Yeheshua, the practitioner to the principle of Salavation, Atonement (at-one-ment), Resurrection.

By use of the LPR or any Magickal act, the Astral light becomes, as occultist Chris Monnastre explains, "malleable by focused and concentrated thought." (Regardie, 1994, p. xxiii). However, I vary with her suggested color schematics to be used. She instructs in the forward to Regardie's (1994) *The Golden Dawn* to visualize the Star as etched in "blue flame flecked with gold not unlike a gas flame." (p. xxiii). Thus by her scheme this would seem to be a blend of the two color polarities naturally occurring within the Astral Light. In my opinion, for banishment, the color of the Star should be in piercing blue-green, and for invocation, in glowing yellow-red.

As Levi ellucidates,

> All these wonders (of Magick) occur by means of a single agent which the Hebrews. . .called OD. . .we shall refer to it as the Astral Light, following. . .the school of Martinez Pasqualis... Mirville called it the devil and the ancient alchemists called it AZOTH. . .it is the vital element, manifesting itself in the phenomena of warmth, light, electricity, magnetism, and flowing through all terrestrial globes and all

living beings. Within this very agent are manifested the proofs of Qabalistic doctrine regarding equilibrium and the movement of double polarity, one pole attracting while the other repels, one producing heat and the other cold, one giving a yellow-reddish glow and the other a blue-greenish light. (1973, p. 158).[62]

Also, as you rotate deosil through the ritual's steps, you must visualize your weapon etching a curving trail of flame from Star to Star. In Solar or Magickal performances this flame is usually golden, like the Aurora of Sol or Apollo. If the LPR is being used for Lunar or Wiccan purposes this flame may be in silver, like the moon's glowing aura or the halo of Diana. In advanced practices this circle may be seen as a flaming snake whose mouth comes back to swallow its own tail (like the Magician's belt in Tarot Key 1 of the Major Arcana). In this way the circle symbolizes the Ouraboras serpent, the symbol of the Astral light, of eternity and the cycle of rebirth.

While the vibratory method of vocalization has been covered earlier, the meanings behind these particular Tetragrammatons should be understood by the Magician, for they are not (as the "barbarous names" in some Magickal rituals) without real definition. The Eastern name, YHVH, the name of the Semetic conception of the All Spirit (originally a tribal volcano god) has been long debated as to its proper pronunciation with such variations as "Yah," "Jah," "Ya-hoo," "Ya-way," and "Je-ho-vah," being the most encountered in religious and mystical teaching. The pronunciation of three syllables as "Yah-ho-vah" is most applicable for usage in the LPR in regard to the frequency that this sound, as a mantra, achieves for the Magician's mental state.

Most importantly, however, beyond the name and its spoken sound, is the formula contained within the name itself. As was stated prior, the four Hebrew letters of this name represent the four Platonic elements of fire, water, air, and earth – or in modern understanding, the four states of matter being radiant energy, liquids, gases, and solids. In this way the

---

[62] See also Levi (1996, Book 3, Ch. 3) and Crowley (1970, Ch. XVIII).

ancient Qabalists rightly understood the composition of the material Universe, stating that the Name of God is contained within all. These letters also represent the formula of the family unit as father, mother, son, and daughter. In Christianized Qabalah they also stand for the four Gospels of the New Testament and their four Saints: Matthew, Mark, Luke, and John – as well as the four holy animals symbolic of these Saints: the man, bull, eagle, and lion (seen in the corners of Keys 10 and 21 of the Major Arcana).

The Southern name, ADNI, is a representation of the Tetragrammaton which can simply be translated as "Lord." It is this word that we find in Sanskrit origin as "Ahdi." Being pre-Semitic in origin, in Sanskrit it is utilized in such Yogic terms as the meditative state of Samahdi, meaning union with the Lord; that is, being united with God or Brahman by moksha (liberation) through Yoga.

The Western name, EHIH, is representative of the name God gives Himself in His encounter with Moses upon Mt. Sinai in the story of the burning bush. There God said unto the Hebrew's greatest wizard, "*I AM*." In agreement with the central tenets of Eckhart Tolle's (1999; 2005) teachings, it is this self-awareness, this self-consciousness, this awareness aware of itself within us (the faculty we all possess that can say and know and feel "I AM") which is the source of Being itself. It is the dimensional intersection in which we are one with God. It is the Divine Spark in the core of our hearts, the Buddha Nature, and the Christos. It is the place where Jesus could declare from within Himself that "I and the Father are one," and that the Great Yogis of India could identically announce, "The Atman is one with the Brahman." It is towards discovering this truth that the great Guru Ramana Maharshi taught only a single spiritual practice – that of *Nan Yar* – the self-inquiry of asking "Who am I?" It is this same result that Socrates aimed at when he left his most profound of all injunctions to each of us. "Know thyself" he preached, the result being the most important lesson we could ever learn as human beings.

The final Northern Tetragrammaton, AGLA, is unlike the previous Hebrew words in that it is actually a *Notariqon* (or Qabalistic acronym) for *Atah Gibor Le-olam Adonai* –"You, O Lord, are mighty forever." This is sometimes presented as the variation, *Athah Gabor Leolah, Adonai* – "Thou art powerful and eternal, Lord."

Returning to the exercise of the LPR, as you vibrate these four Divine Names, you should see the Pentagrams growing brighter, illuminated by your vibration. In addition to visualizing and feeling the presence of the respective elements per direction, the practitioner may experiment with what I term "rolling correspondences." This is the application of a much more vast set of correspondences in your directional visualizations in which a panorama of images is rolled through, beginning with the element, then switching to further symbols, images, Magickal words, or other Divine names corresponding to that element. Examples to this effect can be found in Appendix A of this volume or can be gained by consultation with Crowley's (1993) *777* and Godwin's (1994) *Cabalistic Encyclopedia*. In advanced stages of perfecting this additional exercise, the Magician will no longer need to willfully perform such rolling correspondences, but will find that, with ample practice, this stream of connected images associated with the

**The Great Indian Sage, Sri Ramana Maharshi (1879 – 1950) and his close friend, the realized cow, Lakshmi.**

direction and element will occur automatically and without effort, if the Magician wants it so. This is but an example of Yogic Dhyana inherent to the LPR that shall be extrapolated in a following chapter.

Lastly, but of no small substance, upon the completion of each direction's vibration and visualization the practitioner should feel a brief moment of complete inner stillness, peace, and calm before proceeding to the next direction. This momentary mental quiescence can be likened to what is called "Zanshin" in Japanese martial arts. As Budo Master Fredrick J. Loverett (1987) explains:

After you have executed a perfect technique, you are left with a good feeling, a sort of aftertaste. This is called Zanshin, 'remaining spirit.' During this period. . .all of the proper things you did. . .are still present in a heightened state. . .such as perfect balance, intense external awareness, and spiritual focus. During this. . .you are as close as you can come to operating at peak performance without actually doing anything. It is a moment of great stillness – you do not move and it seems as if the universe were holding its breath. Zanshin is an instant of silent exaltation when you are savoring the memory of perfection. (pp. 74-77).

# Invocation of the Archangels and the Declaration of the Great Work

1). Facing back to the East after fully rotating around the four cardinal points, extend thy arms out to the sides in the form of a Cross and remain. Whisper, "Light in Extension."

2). Then, declare with authority, not of command or domination, but in an attitude of alliance:

"BEFORE ME STANDS RAPHAEL!"
Visualize his towering manifestation behind the Eastern Star, wings outstretched o'er the quarter.
"BEHIND ME GABRIEL!"
Visualize him towering behind the Western Star, wings outstretched o'er the quarter.
"TO MY RIGHT HAND MICHAEL!"
Peripherally visualize him towering behind the Southern Star, wings outstretched o'er the quarter.
"TO MY LEFT HAND AURIEL!"
Peripherally visualize him towering behind the Northern Star, wings outstretched o'er the quarter.

3). Still remaining in the posture of the Cross, cry out in the fevered trance of climax:

## "FOR AROUND ME FLAMES THE PENTAGRAM
## AS IN THE COLUMN SHINES THE SIX-RAYED STAR!"

4). Visualize the interlaced Hexagram, parallel to the ground, at the height of thy Tiphareth, thyself as its center.[63]

5). With this climax achieved, then visualize the scene as a whole: Pentagrams ablaze; the circle of fire surrounding thee; the radiant Archangels towering around; the Hexagram aglow; and the Brilliant Clear Light of God shining down upon thee through thy Middle Pillar and out into thy aura shining golden like the sun in every direction of the Dynamic Sphere infinitely into the Universe. Feel the incoming surge of energy, the Pranic/Qi cascade throughout thy body. Experience a final state of Zanshin while still in the form of the Cross.

6). Conclude with the Qabalistic Cross, as in the beginning, thus completing the cycle (or circle) of the ritual.

7). As a form of denouement, or epilogue to the ritual proper, rotate back around the circle one more time, stopping at each cardinal direction, and reabsorb the images thou hath projected back into thyself. As all of these have been birthed by thee, they must be taken back into the operator to prevent any serious depletion of magnetism. In this way the LPR is a Microcosmic metaphor reflecting the entire Macrocosmic manifestation of Big Bang to Big Crunch, as it were. Just as God has given the Universe out of Himself; just as Brahman went forth into Leela, "to play," so does all return ultimately to its Original Source.

---

[63] The Hexagram point will thus be aligned to the centers of the East and West Pentagrams; the North and South Pentagrams being aligned to the Hexagram's angles.

## Eliphas Levi's Sigil of AZOTH

# Analysis of the Invocation and Declaration

Analysis of the climax of the LPR, which contains within its growing intensity the invocation of the Archangels and the declaration of the Great Work, is somewhat complex. We will attempt a cursory detail of such explanations below to better illumine for the student the various correspondences and symbolisms inherent in the ritual's performance. Each of these factors shall be covered individually in the sequence in which they are performed.

In assuming the shape of the Cross, the Magician is forming their body into a living hieroglyph of potent power symbolic of significant esoteric principles. Its most obvious correspondence is to that of the Christos and His crucifixion. Along with this historical occurrence, however, there is also a deeper esoteric principle espoused beyond that misinterpretation held by fundamentalism. This is the concept of the Sacrificial God; of Christ, Attis, and Osiris, gleaned from the Solar principle (witnessed by our prehistoric ancestors and imprinted upon our collective unconscious) of the source of life (Sol) being born every morn, dying every dusk, and being reborn again, day after day. In truth, this principle was witnessed by the Moon worshipers as well in the observation of the waxing and waning of their lunar goddess. What is philosophically derived from these Macrocosmic occurrences is the Universal principle of the eternally progressing process of birth, life, death, and rebirth in all things.

It is analogous to the self-sacrifice of all cultural heroes as documented by the great Mythologist Joseph Campbell (1949) and his thesis of the "Hero's Journey." In such a quest, as reflected in stories as diverse as Buddha to Christ to King Arthur, the protagonist begins the journey in one state of being or consciousness (i.e. Prince Siddhartha Guatama under his father's care and luxury; Christ the Carpenter). He then experiences challenges and adversity that are threatening of his life and/or soul (i.e. Prince Siddhartha seeing poverty, old age, sickness, and death and seeking release from the Samsara in meditation under the Bodhi Tree, only to be assailed by the great demon tempter Mara as he draws nigh to such achievement; Christ in the wilderness with Satan). He then overcomes or defeats this enemy and in so doing gains the boons, the treasure of such victory; the ascended, the awakened, the newly illumined condition (i.e. Prince Siddhartha enlightened to Nirvana and thus reborn as the Buddha; Christ upon the cross). The hero then returns from whence he came to share such boons with the multitude and thus redeem their unregenerate condition (i.e. Buddha preaching to the multitude and starting the Sangha; Christ resurrected).

In the Western esoteric traditions this process is symbolized in Tarot's Greater Arcana by the series of Keys 11,

12, and 13 (or Justice, the Hanged Man, and Death) taken together as a whole, as one teaching. These keys hold the same teaching as that of Joseph Campbell's (1972) Hero's Journey and as that of the Bodhi Tree and the Cross. Briefly speaking, Justice (Key 11), symbolized in the Key by the sword and scales held by the Justice figure, stands for the process of Karma in our lives; (Karma meaning "work," denoting the actions we choose) and the ensuing cause and effect that results from such actions. As the Western Mysteries teach, as well as in Buddhism, all beings are destined to eventually come to a point in their incarnations, and through the process of their personal Karma, where they become enlightened, awakened, taking the next step in the evolutionary process and achieving Divine at-one-ment.

In so doing they undergo a death, symbolized by Key 13. This death is not an end, but a new beginning, a new birth (as the seed in the top left corner of the key symbolizes). Likewise, to the profane and unlearned, death is an end seen in what is erroneously viewed by them as the Key's seemingly setting sun. But the sun in this key is not an end. It is not dusk, but rather, it is the dawn; the new and golden morn that gives birth to what Christ called "the New Creature" – the state of being achieved when one has truly been born again into that which is **more than human**.

This New Creature, the Homo Novus birthed from the seed of Homo Sapiens, is the Hanged Man (Key 12). The Hanged Man is hung upon a Tau, upon a Cross, symbolizing the Universe to which he is intimately intertwined without separation (as the rope that holds him illustrates). As Buddha taught, everything contains everything else. The One is in the Many, and the Many are in the One. He is not separate, but One with That. He is the realizer of the Vedantic truth "Tat twam asi." He hangs upside down because his perspective on all of life, his view of reality, is completely opposite to that held so dear by the rest of unenlightened humanity; the rest of the unregenerate who fear themselves as single, isolated beings separate from everything else; the lie that, as Eckhart Tolle (1999) and many other spiritual Masters so rightly teach, is the basis of our false sense of self, of the ego; of *that* which we **are not**. The Hanged Man reflects what is identically taught in the Kargutpa school of Tibetan Buddhism. In their *Precepts of the*

*Gurus* it is taught, "The Great Man differs in every thought and action from the multitude" (cited in Evans-Wentz, 1968, p. 99).

This same process of transformation is also hidden within the name of the Gnostic God IAO (Regardie, 1994, p. 12). Magickally interpreted, this name represents an acronym, or formula, consisting of the Egyptian mythos of Isis, Apophis, and Osiris (Crowley, 1970, Ch. V). Isis, goddess of nature, represents the generative or creative process of the Universe. Apophis, murderer of Osiris, represents the destructive processes thereof. And Osiris, the god born again from the pieces Apophis has cut him into, decries the rebirth that arises, like a phoenix from the ashes, from the entropy intrinsic to the manifested Kosmos. It is in the individual the same process outlined above as birth, death, and rebirth; and as well within human consciousness it is both the artistic process and the spiritual Hero's Journey.

The Cross created by the practitioner's posture in this stage of the LPR is four sided and thus representative of the square; symbolic of order and of the material Universe. And as the Fifth Knowledge Lecture of the Golden Dawn relates,

> In each of the four (Qabalistic) worlds. . .are the
> ten Sephiroth of that world, and each Sephira
> has its own ten Sephiroth, making four
> hundred Sephiroth in all – the (Qabalistic)

> number of the letter Tau, the Cross, the
> Universe, the completion of all things.
> (Regardie, 1994, p. 77).

It is the four directions, the 4 elements, the 4 Archangels, and the four letters of the Tetragrammaton. It is this square which is enclosed by the ring of fire connecting the Pentagrams formed by the ritual, and thus also symbolizes Alchemy's Squaring (or the Quadrature) of the Circle.

### Leonardo DA Vinci's Vitruvian Man (the Squaring of the Circle) Superimposed upon the Pentagram

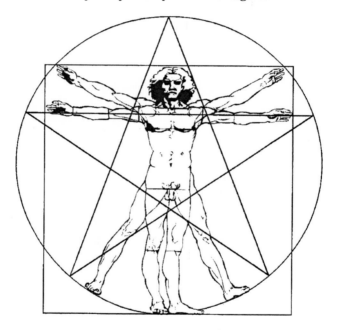

As representative of the number 4 and the four elements, the Cross likewise represents the Magickal formula of FIAT LVX or *flatus (air), ignis (fire), aqua (water), terra (earth) – Light in Extension*. While another form reflective of the Tetragrammaton, this formula also displays the act of God's creation as FIAT LVX (which is a Latin derivative for "Let there be light") and thus reflects the act of visual creativity and Imaginative Will that the

Magician is exercising in the act of the LPR. FIAT shows the elements used to create the Universe and LVX (pictorially hidden within the Cross-posture physically held by the Magician) is the prime substance of such elements; the basis of all matter and energy. It is God's light and the medium of Magickal current. In the West it is OD, AZOTH, and the Astral Light. In the East it is Prana, Qi, and Ki. It is, in short, the inherent principle of life and motion in all manifested things.

Let us now turn to the Invocation of the Archangels for numerous ideas in need of elucidation. Their names should be pronounced in three syllables for the reasons previously explained (i.e. in order to form a vibratory correspondence to the three syllables pronounced in the Tetragrammaton, to the Zodiacal triplicities, and to the Zodiacal Spirits of the Elements). The following is the proper pronunciation of these names with their Hebrew meaning:

> **RAPHAEL** (God who heals): *"Rah – Fy – El."*
> **GABRIEL** (God is my strength): *"Gah – Bree – El."*
> **MICHAEL** (He who is like God): *"Mih – Ky – El."*
> **AURIEL** (Limitless light of God): *"Or – Ee – El."*

Dr. Regardie teaches that the Archangels should be visualized as towering figures, but remains reticent in their further appearance (1994, p. 55). Classical interpretations of them as beautiful, androgynous beings of luminosity are most typical and perhaps somewhat objectively accurate, but are not exclusive interpretations. The student is left to their own creative abilities as to how to envision them, but is encouraged to experiment with proper color correspondences for their robes and radiances (as revealed in Appendix A). It is, however, strongly suggested to utilize the following weapon correspondences that correlate to the elemental weapons inherent to the respective direction and which relate to the nature and agency of the Archangel wielding them:

> Raphael – stave and/or wand.
> Gabriel – golden trumpet and/or goblet.
> Michael – flaming sword and/or dagger.
> Auriel – scroll and/or pantacle.

151

Know also that the personified images of the Archangels act as receptacles for the energies invoked and act to spiritually shield, protect, and fortify the Magician. They should face you when invoking and look outward from the circle when banishing. Some sources say they should appear halfway between you and the traced Pentagrams. I utilize an alternative positioning in which they appear behind, or outside the Stars, wings outstretched and touching each other, thus creating a secondary shield of protection in addition to and enveloping the Flaming Circle created.

As four that make this additional ring around you, they again represent the Square in the Circle. As four they again represent the Tetrad, and by the Pythagorean formula thereof, are also symbolic of the Hexagram.[64] They are also indicative of the Four Pillars of Heaven in Egyptian mythology which hold aloft the endless canopy of space, the Mother of Heaven, Nuit. The Magician thus becomes the fifth and central pillar of this scene; the Tetragrammaton transformed into the Pentagrammaton; the elements crowned by Spirit; God incarnating as Man; Jehovah as Yeheshua.

# A Final Meaning Behind the Archangels

An aerial view of the directional sequence followed in their invocation matches the directional series of the hand's motion in the Qabalistic Cross. That is, East, West, North, South as compared to up, down, right, left. This progression also matches the intended steps of all Magickal ritual: air to banish; water to purify; fire to consecrate; and earth to manifest. Or to state it in Biblical symbolism: it is God's breath into Adam; followed by Noah's flood; then the fires of Armageddon;

---

[64] See Appendix E for the Formula of the Tectractys and the Tetrad's relationship to the Hexagram. Note also that the Tetrad is the numerical sequence upon which, as the Pythagoreans assert, the Universe is built: 1+2+3+4=10; ten being the Decad and the Sephiroth upon the Tree of Life. This echoes the metaphysical premise of Taoism as well which teaches from the One (the Tai Chi or Grand Ultimate) came the Two (the Yin and Yang). From this two came the four (the four elements) and from the four came the myriad changing things that compose the Kosmos.

ending with the establishment of the New Jerusalem. ". . .on earth as it is in heaven." As above, so below.

Following the Archangelic invocation is the absolute climax of the ritual which I referred to in my terminology as the Declaration of the Great Work. The student must come to feel that with each proceeding stage of the LPR their consciousness, their state of mind, and their emotional content are being exalted higher and higher, escalating step by step until they reach the fevered, trance-like, orgasmic, dervish state of "enflaming thyself in prayer" thus declaring the verbal equation of the Great Work: "For around me flames the Pentagram as in the column shines the six-rayed Star." This phrase is, of course, a statement equal to the $5 = 6$ formula of the Adeptus Minor grade in the Golden Dawn hierarchy. It is the reconciliation of the Microcosm with the Macrocosm, of the Pentagram and the Hexagram, of Man with the Universe. In Western terms it is Gnosis, Salvation, Redemption, Atonement – the expiation of sin and entrance to heaven. In Eastern terms it is Samadhi, Satori/Kensho, Moksha, Nirvana – the release from Samsara's cycle of Karma.

My particular phrasing of the LPR's climax, slightly altered from Crowley's and Regardie's,[65] creates a symbolic visualization of vital meaning. The "column" in which the Hexagram shines is the fifth column mentioned before, created by the Magician. Thus, the practitioner of the ritual, who is the Microcosm (the Pentagram), has now become the Hexagram (the Macrocosm); and conversely, the four quarters of space surrounding the individual, normally considered the Universe, has now been imprinted with the four flaming Pentagrams of the Man. Thus, that which is above has become that which is below, and vice versa.[66] The two great manifestations of spirit, Man and the Universe, the subjective and the objective, have become equated.

This is not to say, fool-heartedly, that the Great Work will be accomplished with one or even one million performances of

---

[65] Crowley's (1970) LPR typically states ". . .and in the column. . ." while Regardie's (1994) Stella Matutina wording omits any mention of column, instead stating, "Before me flames the Pentagram and behind me shines the six-rayed star."

[66] See Crowley *Book Four* (1996, Part II, Ch. XI).

the LPR. For the occultist, the LPR is but one means to this end, and in such a one's repertoire it needs to be supplemented with other Magickal and Mystical practices fitting of the student's personality and needs. There is, as we have said in agreement with the sages of all times and locales, more than one path that leads to the summit of the mountain, more than one raft that floats to the other shore. Perfection, after all, is a continuous journey and not a final destination. Evolution is never completed, but is an unending expression of Spirit-in-action, as All is Spirit, or as the Tibetans say, "all is Ati." It is our obligation, however, as students of the Magi's art, to always strive for such a goal, to always earnestly seek the all-embracing wisdom and unending compassion characteristic of all the true Gurus, Tathagatas, Bodhisattvas, and God-men of history. As that carpenter from Nazareth who became a Buddha advised to us all, "Be ye perfect just as your Father in heaven is" (*Matthew* 5:48, King James Version).

The Hexagram visualized in the ritual's climax can be of two differing color schemes. The student is instructed to experiment with both and choose that which offers the greatest clarity in their mental projection. The first color scheme is of white and black interlaced triangles. The white will point to the East in correlation to the Solar correspondence of the dawn and ascending light. The black will point to the West in correlation to dusk and the descending night. As previously discussed, the interlaced and equal triangles represent the Macrocosmic duality of manifestation: the Taoist Yin and Yang; the Yogic Lingam and Yoni of Shiva and Shakti in conjugal union; the two Vedic aspects of the Almighty Mother, Tara and Kali; the Zorarastrian war between Ahriman and Ormuzd; the Greek mythos' Zeus and Hades, Apollo and Diana; and the Judeo-Christian Jehovah and Lucifer in their respective heaven and hell.

In Christian eschatology the two triangles represent the Holy Trinity (Father, Son, and Holy Spirit) and the diabolical trinity (Satan, Beast, and False Prophet). In this duality resides the essence of freewill, of choice, as the polarity of temptation, of the dichotomy of sin versus righteousness. These dual principles reflected in the emblem of the Hexagram also relate the intrinsic qualities of the Astral Light (also called the Prime

Substance in Magick and Alchemy) observable in all of the manifest Universe. These properties are attraction and repulsion, coagulation and dissolution, involution and evolution, growth and entropy.

For the Wise, however, for Those Who Know, this duality reconciles itself in Advaita, in the non-dual One, in the Unity prior to the Kosmic manifestation of such Yin and Yang. Thus, beyond the Macrocosm or Universe, as a symbol of Deity the Hexagram expresses God's transcendence of this same duality by the singularity of the shape's two interlaced triangles. It likewise expresses Deity as the Unified source for this manifested duality. In such an Advaitic and Qabalistic sense, God is both creator and destroyer; God of love and God of wrath. He is both the Pillar of Mercy and the Pillar of Severity on the Tree of Life. God is, as Isaiah 45 expresses in the Old Testament, "The Lord of Light and of the Darkness," or in Nietzsche's teaching, that which is beyond good and evil. It is the Deity unified in both His manifest guises seen in His Creation; as the Limitless Light of the Ain Sof Aur and as the Chthonic, Saturnian essence that Crowley emulated so well. The Great Source is the It, the Grand Androgyne, that One which breaks into the He and She, god and goddess; not only the LVX, but the NOX – the Dark God of Rabbi Ben Simeon immortalized hieroglyphically in the art of Eliphas Levi as Baphomet, the Witches' and the Templars' god, or the Goat of Mendes.[67]

---

[67] The Dark God of Rabbi Ben Simeon is, in truth, an Advaitic teaching within Qabalah that shows the Unity of God in the relative duality we see in His creation; of God being both sides of the coin, so to speak, originator of Good and of Evil (Scholem, 1977). This is obviously related in the Biblical allegory of God being the creative source of Satan. The Rabbi's Dark God is symbolically analogous to the lower black triangle in the Hexagram (Crowley, 1995). It is hieroglyphically represented throughout the occult by various forms, such as the Goat of Mendes, the Templar's alleged "ass-headed" god, and the devil of the medieval witches' black sabbath (Levi, 1996). Baphomet is perhaps the most famous form of this teaching. Crowley (1995) (and Fr. Montague Summers as well) argue that Baphomet is etymologically derived from the Latin "bapho" and "metis," meaning "fountain of wisdom." Levi (1996) argues that this figure has the identical meaning to that hidden within the form of the Egyptian sphinx; the sphinx being a composite creature made up of the Four Sacred Animals and thus is a representation of the Tetragrammaton formula. He relates that its origin comes from the Hebrews, being based upon the figures found legendarily upon the Ark of the Covenant that were sphinx-like creatures; part bull, part cherubim. This form as a Holy symbol was later profaned by the vulgar and

**The Interlaced Hexagram**
**The Qabalistic symbol equating to the Taoist Yin and Yang,**
**expressing God's Advaitic Unity (the Taoist's Tai Chi or "Grand**
**Ultimate") which breaks into duality in order to manifest the**
**Universe of polarities.**

---

Satanized by the False Church under the corrupt medieval papacy in their attempt to establish religious monopoly upon the earth. Adepts have preserved this form's real meaning for centuries despite fundamentalism's (and Satanism's) attempt to proliferate its evil connotations in their ridiculous literalism (Gardner, 1991). This subject would need its own treatise to cover adequately.

## Eliphas Levi's Baphomet:

**(From the Latin, *bapho-metis,* "fountain of wisdom," according to both Crowley and Montague Summers) – it is the Goat of Mendes; Pan, god of Nature; Janicot, the Witches' Horned God; and the Templar's idol for which they were burned at the stake for heresy by the false church.**

**Levi's hand-sign (or mudra) of Baphomet.**

**Crowley's version of this mudra.**

The second color-scheme for the Hexagram consists of blue and red. While this is obviously representative of the elements water and fire, or purification and consecration in the ritual sense, it can be applied in two ways. The first is to be followed and the second discarded. With the red triangle pointing East towards the sunrise and the blue pointing West to the sunset, it shows the Magician aspiring towards the Divine Source (symbolized by the Sun), and the grace of God descending upon him like the baptismal waters of the Holy Dove.

In contrast, the inversion of this color scheme holds an altogether different meaning that should be avoided by the practitioner of White Magick. The blue, when switched to the East, stands for the "water of life," the blood sacrifice being offered to God as Sol. The red then becomes God's tongue of flame descending to lap up the burnt offering upon the altar. This is Black Magick and thou must commit it not! We strongly part ways with Crowley on this issue and remind the student that Frederick Loveday, the notorious pencil-necked Thelemic "saint," got what he deserved for what they both did to that poor innocent cat in Cefalau!

To Crowley's (1976) question in the *Book of the Law*: "Is... God to live in a dog?" (II:19) I answer, YES! God lives in every creature, in every plant, in every rock, in every element. As the Mahayana teaches, all beings possess Buddha Nature; or identically, from the Gnostic viewpoint, all things contain the Christos. This truth is echoed by innumerous great Sages from all times and many locales. Our own American Transcendental genius, Henry David Thoreau said, "I saw a muskrat come out of a hole in the ice ... While I am looking at him, I am thinking what he is thinking of me. He is a different sort of man, that's all" (cited by the International Vegetarian Union, 2012). Or the Great Indian Saint Sri Aurobindo, "Life is life - whether in a cat, or dog or man. There is no difference there between a cat or a man. The idea of difference is a human conception for man's own advantage" (cited by Brennan 2013). Or from the Prophet Mohammed, "And there is not a creature on the Planet Earth nor a bird that flies with its two wings, except they are nations equal to you" (Quran 6:38). And from the Old Testament, "For that which befalleth the sons of men, befalleth beasts, ... As one dieth so dieth the other. Yet they have all one breath. So that a man hath no pre-eminence over a beast" (Ecclesiastes 3:19, King James Version). And as the Christos taught in the Gnostic scriptures regarding this Universal God-essence in the Each and in the All, "Split a piece of wood: I am there. Lift a stone, and you will find me there" (Gospel of Thomas, saying 30).

As Evans-Wentz correctly asserts in a way unifying of Eastern and Western esotericism, and thus completely akin to our own arguments,

> . . .all living things, sub-human as well as
> human, are potentially Buddhas, or, in the
> Gnostic Christian sense, Christs. Accordingly...
> what men call differences are merely
> differences of illusory external appearances.
> Inately, all things are the One, and thus, in
> essence, indistinguishable. . .as Bodhi-dharma,
> the first of the Zen teachers, taught, all things
> contain the Buddha nature from beginningless
> time.

Furthermore, to commit blood sacrifice for power, or any other purpose (such as experimentation, hunting, profit, or the like), is pure evil – period – regardless of what the left-hand path, or their scientific counterparts, the vivisectionists, teach. The Tibetan Mahayanists say that to sacrifice an animal to the Deity is like killing an infant for its mother (Evans-Wentz, 1968). Praise be to the vanguard that is PETA and the heroes who compose the ALF![68]   Avoid all those who claim otherwise. **Pashu Ahimsa,** [69]  non-harm to animals, as exemplified by the

---

[68] For classic works on the modern  philosophies behind the birth of the environmental rights and ensuing animal rights movements the author recommends such groundbreaking personal favorites as Rachel Carson's *Silent Spring,* Marston Bates' *The Forest and the* Sea, Tom Regan's *The Case for Animal Rights,* Birch and Cobb's *The Liberation of Life,* and ANYTHING by the great ecologian Thomas Berry. In addition to PETA and ALF, the seeker is also encouraged to support the vital work of the Humane Society, the ASPCA, and the AAVS.

[69] Regarding Ahimsa and Pashu Ahimsa, the student is reminded of the well-known Eastern precept **Ahimsa Paramo Dharma** (*"Non-violence is everyone's religious duty"*). Make no mistake about this concept. Ahimsa (non-violence as a

## Buddha's pacifist and vegan lifestyle is the Path of the Wise. The

spiritual principle and life practice) IN NO WAY IMPLIES PACIFISM. Ahimsa as such, in our modern times, has been distorted by misinterpretations of such important social figures as Gandhi and MLK Jr. In such a misreading of history (what the eminent eco-poet Derrick Jensen has called "putting on the Gandhi mask") **any** use of violence in **any** circumstance is declared morally wrong. Such a rendering seems to forget Gandhi's own charge of "Where there is only the choice between cowardice and violence, I would advise violence." Or as Orwell warned as common-sense, "Pacifism is objectively pro-fascist."

The "Gandhi Mask" is further contradicted by the founders and perpetuators of the Ahimsa philosophy itself, namely the Vedanta, Jain, and Buddhist religious schools. The Jain and Hindu scriptures and law books explicitly support the use of counter-violence against attackers and criminals, and such persons are not intended to be protected by the philosophy/obligation of Ahimsa. Likewise, we need not forget the Buddhist Shaolin who believed that Nature Herself reflected every creature's right to self-defense. Thus Kung-Fu was considered an integral component to the monk's personal development and existential survival in a most-often dangerous world. After all, how could the Dharma be proselytized if its emissaries were not capable of surviving in the inimical Samsara in which the Sangha was to be built and preserved? What Ahimsa really presupposes is a way of life in which violence is shunned at all practical costs; in which the use of force is an absolute last resort when no other options for safety or peace otherwise exist. In this way Ahimsa perfectly reflects the philosophy supported throughout the great martial arts traditions as well – that violence, the use of fighting skill, is a last resort to conflict resolution, is an utterly solemn and grave responsibility, and is only utilized when forcibly evoked by another's evil actions against ourselves, loved ones, the Earth, or other innocents. Ahimsa can be codified into three basic rules:

A). **Panatipata – the first rule is to abstain from taking the life of a sentient being.** This rule likewise implies the principle of reciprocal force legally expected in situations of modern self-defense. However, this rule does not surpass the potentiality for a legitimate lethal force situation.

B). **Pashu Ahimsa** – non-violence to animals. Intimately related to the above concept of Panatipata, the first reference to the moral teaching of Pashu Ahimsa comes from the *Kapisthala Katha Samhita* of the *Yajurveda* (8th Century B.C.E.). Around this same time the *Chandogya Upanishad* taught the concept of Sarva Bhuta which barred the use of violence against all creatures.

C). **Manu Smriti – Prohibition against the wanton destruction of plant life.** This concept, of course, does not imply that people cannot eat plants. Rather, it is as if the ancient Asian seers peered ahead through the veils of time to see our current eco-crisis. This concept, so crucial for us today, dictates that such ridiculously selfish human actions like deforestation, clear cutting, open-pit mining of mountains, butchery of old growth trees, and other destructive practices against the biosphere must stop!

To this effect, let us not forget the prophetic words of the Cree Indian Nation; an adage reflective of our species' history and our modern culture's character that we must strive to ultimately prove wrong: "Only when the last tree has been cut down; only when the last river has been poisoned; only when the last fish has been caught; only then will the white man realize that money cannot be eaten."

Mike Benjamin

only sacrifice to be made by any Magician is as exemplified by Christ – the sacrifice of oneself for the good of others. Such is the Way of all true Bodhisattvas!

**Seal of the noble and heroic Animal Liberation Front.**

*"Animals are not ours to eat, wear, experiment on, use for entertainment, or abuse in any way."*
**-The PETA philosophy.**

**From Mahavira to Shakyamuni, such is the Truth related by all real Tathagatas and Buddhas.**

# Chapter 3: Metaphoric Reflections on the Ritual

"There are metaphors more real than the people who walk in the street. There are images tucked away in books that live more vividly than many men and women. There are phrases from literary works that have a positively human personality... sentences whose sound, read out loud or silently (impossible to hide their sound), can only be of something that acquired absolute exteriority and a full-fledged soul."

-**Fernando Pessoa**, *The Book of Disquiet* (2002).

# The LPR as Art and the Creation of the Universal Mandala

To reiterate the thesis of this grimoire, or "grammer," of Magick: The LPR is the fundamental practice of all Occidental occultism and Western Magick. It is the egg from which all Golden Dawn ceremonial ritual is hatched and the void to which they all return. Properly understood it is the Medicine of Metals and the Stone of the Wise. In its perfected form, it is the fulfillment of the Great Work; it is Gnosis, the 5 = 6, the reconciliation of the Microcosm and the Macrocosm, of the Samsara with Shunyata, of Maya with Nirvana.

On a deeper level of introspection, an analogy could also be drawn with the LPR between such seemingly diverse practices as Yoga, the Japanese Tea Ceremony, and Tai Chi Ch'uan. All are designed as methods of moving meditation to harmonize the triune aspects of Man (mind, body, and spirit) through the application of physical movements coupled with mental exercises. In this way the LPR can be understood as what Deepak Chopra (1995) calls a Thought Experiment. This is simply ". . .a way of leading your mind into new places, making it see things differently" (Chopra, 1995, p. 8). This, teaches Chopra, is one of the basic spiritual methods which must be acquired to live the "Way of the Wizard." As he relates, "The wizards knew something deep and important – if you want to change the world, change your attitude towards it." (Chopra, 1995, p. 8).

To become a Wizard – a Magus – a Magician, you must alter your attitudes; you must sublimate your consciousness and raise your vibrations; you must change your conventional ways of thinking and the mundane perceptions and conceptions shadowed and sheltered in our modern concrete and steel reality; you must expand the knowledge base from which you draw and relate your experiences; you must be enhanced and intensified; you must, in short, become a "human 2.0!" The LPR proves to be the fundamental method of all Occidental esotericism towards these ends. As we now proceed to investigate the metaphorical interpretations of this ritual we shall discover how it fulfills these lofty goals for the dedicated aspirant.

In the Magician's hands the LPR is a living form of Magickal art. Art can be defined in its broadest sense as the external expression of one's internal creativity. This creativity is formulated in part by the synthesis of the individual's emotional sensitivity and spiritual awareness harnessed through mind and manifested through body. All true art is Magick, to echo Crowley (1970). The natural artist exists because of an inherent aptitude in spiritual acuity that expresses itself in creative action. The reciprocity of this idea is also true; that all real Magick is of an artistic nature, the key ingredients to both disciplines being the Imagination initiated and guided by focused Will.

In art, as in Magickal ritual, the raw mental, emotional, and spiritual qualities of the practitioner are concentrated by Will and implemented by Imagination into an alloy of creative action. Such is the impetus of this grimoire, and so likewise is the essence of the LPR. In its performance the LPR becomes the Magician's painting. The sphere of the Astral Plane, and all the Qabalistic worlds, are the canvas. The Astral Light (or the Od or Azoth) become his paints. And his Imagination, enacted by a focused Will, expressed through his body's faculties of sight, speech, and motion, become the brush.

Unlike most art, however, that which is created by the LPR is not arbitrary or left up to the Magician's fancy or inspiration. Like a Karate Kata, the ritual's movement is specific and is meant to be precisely performed in in the same exactitude in every execution. The vision or scene created by it, both mentally and Astrally, is intended to be identical each time. This maintains a Karmic link between all of the practitioner's exercises of the LPR, thus building the Magician's storehouse or egregore of Divine, Archangelic, and elemental force generated. It also creates a profound three-dimensional picture both surrounding the Magician and incorporating him or her into it.

This scene has been described with many names, and as we have already examined, holds deep esoteric symbolism. To Qabalists, it is the Wheel of Ezekiel. In Shamanism it is called the Wheel of Life. To exponents of the Tarot it is representative of Key 10 of the Major Arcana (the Wheel of Fortune). To the Native American it is the Dream Catcher. To Buddhists it is the Wheel of the Dharma and the Samsara. To Taoists it is the Yin-Yang and the I-Ching. To Freemasons it is the Square and the Compass. And to the Magus it is the Magick Circle or Pantacle. As Carl Jung (1970) extensively examined, other than perhaps the Tree of Life, no other motif in symbolism is as fundamentally and universally intrinsic to the structure of the human unconscious as is this Magick Circle, which he termed by its Eastern name – the Mandala (pp. 41-44). This picture, this Astral painting formed by the Magician's visualizations in exercise of the LPR, is precisely the creation of this symbol, which we shall term the Universal Mandala, and now enter into a thorough interpretation.

From the Sufis, to the Lamas, to the Navajos, Mandalas in some form have been represented in the art and/or religion of all cultures in all times. Psychologist Leonard George (1995) relates an important etymological, as well as spiritual insight worthy of quote for our studies, into the Mandala regarding its Buddhist and Tantric forms. Dr. George writes:

> In Sanskrit, mandala literally means 'circle.' Some scholars have argued that the term derives from the roots 'mans,' mind, and 'dala,' to dilate – hence, 'mind expander.' The circular images called mandalas have been used as potent means of altering consciousness, especially by practitioners of Buddhist Tantra. Generally, a deity is depicted at the center of the Tantric Buddhist mandala. . .In concentric rings surrounding this central figure, other spiritual beings and objects are portrayed. Frequently the mandala is divided into four quadrants, each a different color and populated by different kinds of beings. The entire image represents the palace of the central deity. At the same time, it symbolizes the universe. In Tantra and other forms of Mahayana Buddhism, the world of enlightenment and the phenomenal world are thought to be the same place, viewed

in different ways. The world, viewed
spiritually, is a mandala. . .In the main Tantric
meditation practice. . .the meditator identifies
with a deity in order to awaken the
corresponding aspect of enlightened awareness.
The mandala is often incorporated into
(spiritual) practice. The meditator studies the
mandala until every detail can be reproduced
in the imagination. Then the practitioner
merges with the central deity, acquiring its
powers and characteristics. The universe is
visualized as the mandala, one's own divine
palace, filled with deities and surrounding one
in every direction. Such practice is not
considered a mere escapist fantasy; rather, the
mandala portrays the truly divine state of the
world and oneself, which is hidden by our
ignorance. . .Carl Jung believed that the circular
form of the mandala represented the human
personality's instinctive drive toward
wholeness. (pp. 163-164).[70]

Though relating the tantric Buddhist teaching with regard to the
use of Mandalas, in this marvelous exposition by Dr. George we
see explained the very purpose and efficacy of the LPR as a
spiritual exercise as well. By use of the LPR the Magician is
creating such a Mandala with himself. When understood in this
light it is easy to comprehend the assertion that the LPR is a
major pathway, or catalyst, in the pursuit of Wisdom, in
fulfilling the Great Work, in accomplishing Gnosis.

---

[70] In the Tibetan Buddhist systems, this use of mandalas as meditative
devices, as well as the use of the mandalic deities for the same
purposes, is extensively detailed by Evans-Wentz (1969). In Western
occultism, an identical practice is likewise employed known as
assuming the god-forms. Both Crowley (1970) and Regardie (2004)
provide exhaustive explorations of this Magickal practice. While this
type of Magick is beyond our present examination, another version of
this discipline will be will be detailed later in this treatise in regards to
its application through the use of the Major Arcana of the Tarot and in
keeping with Dr. Paul Foster Case's teaching of this technique.

Mike Benjamin

In similar tone regarding the primacy of this circular symbol as a potent medium of philosophical insight, but in a much more poetic form, the great American Transcendentalist Ralph Waldo Emerson opens his essay *Circles* with the following powerful insights:

> Nature centers into balls,
> And her proud ephemerals,
> Fast to surface and outside,
> Scan the profile as the sphere;
> Knew they what that signified,
> A new genesis was here.

> The eye is the first circle; the horizon which it forms is the second, and throughout nature this primary figure is repeated without end. It is the highest emblem in the cipher of the world. St. Augustine described the nature of God as a circle whose center was everywhere and its circumference nowhere. We are all our lifetime reading the copious sense of the first of forms... Our life is an apprenticeship to the truth that around every circle another can be drawn; that there is no end in nature, but every end is a beginning; that there is always another dawn risen on mid-noon, and on every deep a lower deep opens. (cited in Richardson, 1990, p. 189).

The Buddhist Wheel of Dharma (or Dharmachakra), representative of the 8-Fold Path, and the Samsara (the "round and round" of manifest reality). At its center is the symbol of the Trikaya.

**The Taoist Yin-Yang surrounded by the I-Ching.**

**A Tantric Mandala.**

**A Native American Dream Catcher.**

**The Magickal Pantacle.**

**The Masonic Square and Compass.**

We will now look further into the actual shape of the Mandala created by the LPR to elucidate its further significance as a Magicko-Spiritual practice. It is not necessary to reiterate the meanings behind the projected images of the LPR, but to examine the scene as a whole; the living artistic image created by the Magician which we have termed the Universal Mandala. There are two primary shapes created by this ritual, of the practitioner centered within the circle of symbols. The first is the shape of the upright Magician centered within the circle. The second is when the Magician assumes the shape of the Cross within it. These two forms alone convey such advanced occult doctrine that it cannot be a coincidence that the inventor(s) of the LPR, whoever he or she was, was not devising a ritual which simply bore arbitrarily or culturally narrow connotations. What was constructed in this method is a practice that strikes at the heart of the Collective Unconscious, at the homo sapiens race-consciousness, through the activation of Universal archetypes. Whoever the LPR's inventor was, he or she understood that this ritual's efficacy would be applicable and significant to adepts of any place, in any century.

When we consider the shape of the Magician as an upright being centered within the circle, the most obvious meaning to be allocated to this figure is the apparent phallic and reproductive symbolism. The Magician is the erect phallus, the active principle in Nature, and the circle in space is the feminine womb, Nature's passive principle. Here is shown the God and Goddess, all of the other dual paradigms heretofore examined, and the formula of IAO described elsewhere. This symbolism is likewise representative of the artistic energy being used to formulate the ritual which is akin to the reproductive faculty or sexual drive; the libido of the Freudians and the Kundalini of Tantric Yoga.

This shape of the phallus and womb, or lingam and yoni, also suggest that this figure is indicative of the Gnostic Demiurgos, the force which created the Universe. It is the Heavenly Father uttering the FIAT LVX, causing a single point in the feminine Void to become the unending expanse of manifestation.[71] Just as one sperm enters the ovum to create human life, so does the Word of God enter the emptiness of nothing to bring forth the galaxies! And what is the Logos made Flesh that can create the Universe? This is another deep occult secret holding perfect harmony with modern science. As we have said, a word can be written and thus seen, being composed

---

[71] For any astrophysicists reading this work perchance, note the significance of the Mandelbrot set: $Z = Z^2 + C$.

of light and particles. A word can also be spoken and thus heard, being composed of waves and vibrations. In complete agreement with modern physics, it is these two properties, particle and wave, that compose the entire Kosmos.

In pondering the linear posture of the Magician we may also ascribe to him/her the shape of the number 1. The circle of the Universal Mandala created can be ascribed the number 0. In this contemplation an entirely different, yet equally valid symbolism is inferred. As 1 and 0, the Pythagorean decad (the sequence of 1 to 10) is represented in this figure as well. Unlike the Qabalists who theorized that the Universe is built upon the letters of the Hebrew alphabet (represented upon the Tree of Life as its 22 connecting paths assigned to the 22 Keys of the Major Arcana), Pythagoras theorized that the Universe is built upon numbers. Pythagoras believed that the decad (corresponding to the Qabalists' ten Sephiroth upon the Tree of Life), being the basis of all mathematics and geometry, was thus the structure of all Creation. The Universe, he argued, is founded on numbers.

Also, the four quadrants of the circle, corresponding to the four elements, Archangels, and letters in the Tetragrammaton of the LPR, also correspond to the Pythagorean tetrad, or the sequence of numbers 1 through 4. These added together $(1 + 2 + 3 + 4)$ equals the decad (10). They thus show the totality and completion of Creation as hidden within the Tetragrammaton. It is also interesting to note that in our current internet-driven Aquarian age, all computers operate upon the binary code which is based upon nothing but the combinations of the numbers 0 and 1!

Let us now interpret the Universal Mandala in the light of Freemasonry. This unveils other levels of meaning as a result of applying the Craft. If we utilize the Great Masonic Emblem as a key to the Universal Mandala we unlock two interpretations, both valid in application to the figure created by the LPR. If we translate the Emblem's center "G" as meaning God, the Mandala reveals a triple spiritual meaning between the relationship of God to the Universe and to humankind. First, God is the center of the Universe, as earlier reflected by Emerson (quoting St. Augustine); the center that is everywhere and the circumference that is nowhere. Second, humankind, as created in God's image, is the center of their own Universe as well, since the experience of existence, for each of us, comes only from our seeming individuality which perpetuates the illusion of our separateness from all other things. (And it is this fundamental error suffered by our minds that spiritual awakening is meant to abolish). Third, the center of humankind, once awakening or Gnosis has been achieved, is discovered to be God, the Divine Spark; and in so knowing this Mystery, our illusion of separateness comes to an end.

When implementing the Great Emblem's "G" to the LPR as meaning Geometry, a more mathematical and architectural understanding of the Universal Mandala is gained. In accord with the ancient Greek aphorism, the Masons agree that "God geometrizes." As such, God then becomes the Grand Architect of the Universe. From this view, in the LPR we can see the Magician become the point, as the center of the ritual; the body's erect posture, the line; the field of vision, the plane; the ring of fire, the circle; and the figures traced, angles. Thus, within the Universal Mandala created by the ritual, all of the geometrical forms required by Hiram Abiff for drafting, engineering, and constructing King Solomon's Temple are readily present.[72]

The circular structure of the LPR's Universal Mandala is also reflective of theories within the Masonic sciences of physics, astronomy, and chemistry. In regard to physics and astronomy, in one way the circle represents Newtonian theory[73] where the celestial movements of moons around planets, planets around suns, and galaxies awhirl, are attributed to gravity as being a force. In another way, the circle can also represent the Einsteinian theory of relativity[74] where gravity is attributed, not to a force, but to the actual curvature of the space-time continuum itself.

In either case, we know that a line extended far enough upon a globe comes back to its own starting point, thus being, paradoxically, a circle. Arguably, this would be the same result

---

[72] The author achieved the 32nd degree (Sublime Prince of the Royal Secret) in Scottish Rite Freemasonry in the Valley of Freeport, IL. 1995.

[73] $F = G \times \dfrac{m_1 \times m_2}{r^2}$

[74] $E = MC^2$.

if a line were extended far enough through space. The idea of astronomical infinity is still possible, however, in a similarly paradoxical way. Though the boundary of the Universe (the "ring-pass-not") is finite, it is still in constant expansion at the speed of light (186,000 miles a second) away from its starting point, the Qabalistic Rashith Ha-Galgalim (or "beginning of the whirlings;" another name for Kether). This starting point is the Big Bang in astronomy and is expressed by the FIAT LVX formula in Magick. This concept is also symbolically expressed in the occult by the Equilibrated Cross, the Cross within the Circle, and the Svastika,[75] all of which the LPR creates through the image of the Universal Mandala.

Chemically speaking, this constant expansion moving the Universe away from its starting center[76] is also the same motion inherent in all forms of energy and within the atomic structure of matter. Like the Magician at the center of the Mandala with the images in orbit all around, so also is the molecule with its nucleus and sub-atomic satellites in orbit around it; or to be more precise, electrons in orbit around the proton-neutron

---

[75] Levi (1997) states, "The cross, which produces 4 triangles, is also the sacred sign of the duodenary and on this account it was called the Key of Heaven by the Egyptians" ( p. 12). Astronomical interpretations of the basic forms of the Cross are as follows:

Equilibrated Cross – The center intersection of the Cross shows the infinitesimal point of no dimension from which the Universe is born and its expansion outward in four dimensions (the three physical dimensions of length, height, and width, plus time), called by science the Big Bang and by Magick the FIAT LVX.

Svastika – Usually associated as a solar symbol and emblem of the seasons' flow, the Svastika also shows the birth of spiral galaxies, the solidification of star systems from the whirling of primordial gasses, and the establishment of gravity and orbits. The arms of the bent Cross also point in the correct direction of most celestial motion; that is, in an eastward or clockwise rotation when viewing the Earth from above the North Pole.

Solar Cross – The cross within the Circle shows the establishment of the material Universe in its seeming mechanical form of cyclical rhythm and timing; the clock all wound up and set to tick on its own. "And on the seventh day God… rested" (Genesis 2:2).

[76] Not, at least, until the reversal of the Universe's expansion as seen in the Doppler Effect, and the ultimate implosion of it back into itself in the same infinitesimal point from which it sprang. Science calls this the Big Crunch, but Western Adepts know this entire process of Universal creation and dissolution as but the opening and closing of the Rose; while in the East this is the slumber and awakening of Brahman.

cluster. Alas, it cannot be stated too many times – As above, so below!

In addition to the Freemasonic interpretations offered above, Crowley's Thelemic system, expressed in terms of the Egyptian mythos, is also applicable as a key to unlocking further understanding of the LPR's meaning as the Universal Mandala. Let us examine the mathematical and emblematic principles of 0 and 1, expressed by the flaming ring and the standing Magician, seen through this perspective. As previously stated, 0 is a symbol of the Void, the Prime Nothingness from which all Creation sprang. In its circular shape, without beginning or end, are also implied the concepts of eternity, infinity, the sphere, and the horizon. In the Egyptian pantheon this is personified as the goddess Nuit, Mother of space. In the Thelema's primary holy book, Crowley's (1976) *Liber Al vel Legis* (The Book of the Law), its channeled author, the Spirit Aiwass, explains Nuit: "I am known to thee by the name Nuit. . .I am Infinite Space and the Infinite Stars thereof. . .O Nuit, continuous One of Heaven, let it be ever thus; that Men speak not of thee as One, but as None" (I:21-23).

In addition to the shape of the Magician seen as the number 1, interpreted as a line, 1 can also mathematically stand for the geometric point. In addition, the Magician's position within the universal Mandala created by the LPR, is its center. In regard to this view, the 1 is personified as the point and the center (in the Egyptian pantheon) as Nuit's groom, the god Hadit. *Liber Al vel Legis* continues,

> I, Hadit, am the complement of Nu, my bride. I am not extended. . .In the sphere I am everywhere the centre, as she, the circumference, is nowhere to be found. . .I am the flame that burns in every heart of Man, and in the core of every star. I am Life, and the giver of Life, yet therefore is the knowledge of me the knowledge of death. I am the Magician. . .I am the axle of the wheel, and the cube in the circle...for it is I that go. . . (II:1-7).

Mike Benjamin

Also of interest in this vein, in Egyptian mythology Chaos and Wind begot Maat, goddess of the Air, who was born in the form of an egg, the shape of which became our number 0. In all ancient cultures the concept of air is directly related to the principle of the life-force and of breath, as in the Hindu Prana and the Chinese Qi. In Egyptian, Maat is a word also meaning both "mother" and "matter." And in early French Tarot decks, the Fool (Key 0), assigned to the element of air, was originally called "Le Mat."

As is evident from even these slight hints, the Egyptian mythos provides deep lessons in the occult concepts of humanity and the Kosmos, of the Microcosm and the Macrocosm. It is no wonder then why such historically important figures in both ancient science and esotericism, such as Hermes Trismegistus and Pythagoras, were so heavily influenced by Egyptian teachings. This is also true of modern occult masters like MacGregor Mathers and Crowley. To the ancient adepts of Egypt who held the keys to the Mysteries of their mythos, science and religion were indeed one system that unlocked the secrets to both the individual and Nature. Their genius is obvious and easily exemplified by cultural examples of their elaborate theology manifested in such literature as *The Book of the Dead*, the library lost at Alexandria, their vast system of language expressed in hieroglyphics, and their architectural masterpieces of engineering like the Sphinx and the Pyramids.[77] While much of the world was barely beyond the hunter-gatherer stage of our cave-dwelling ancestors, Egypt, the Oz of the Nile Valley, was in a state of advanced civilization that in many ways outshone our own modern society.

---

[77] Current evidence as reported in the Orion Correlation Theory of such researchers as Robert Bauval, Adrian Gilbert, and Graham Hancock suggests that the three Pyramids of Giza are set out in direct, exact proportion to the three stars composing the belt in the constellation of Orion (known as Osiris to the ancient Egyptian Priest/Astrologers and as Michael in Qabalistic astrology). Air shafts leading to the burial chamber of the Pharaoh in the Great Pyramid have been calculated to have pointed at Orion's belt on the Summer Solstice during their era. It is believed that this architecture was purposed as a "launching pad" for the Pharaoh's soul (ka) to merge with Osiris in the heavens. The masonry and engineering of the ancient Egyptians expressed a technology and mathematics unsurpassed even today!

Our final consideration regarding the Universal mandala created by the LPR is the ritual's climax and the Magician's assumption of the form of the Cross within the Circle. This symbol has been called by various names in occultism and is represented by many emblems. It has been signified by the Rosy Cross, the Solar Cross, the Phallic Cross, the Rose and Sword, the Ankh, the Svastika, and so on. Its meaning is nearly as extensive as that of the Pentagram and Hexagram and needs to be fully investigated by the student. For instance, the Golden Dawn's lamen, the "Formula of the Rosy Cross," is a comprehensive hieroglyphic representation of this symbol's varying levels of occult significance.

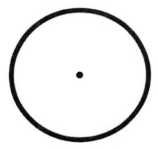

**The Point within the Circle** – sign of Hadit within Nuit (and astrological symbol of the Sun).

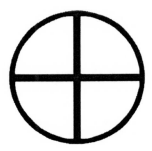

**The Cross within the Circle** – also called the Solar Cross (and astrological symbol of the Earth).

A Rosicrucian interpretation of the Cross within the Circle holds important relevance to this examination. As the author Magus Incognito[78] (1949) writes in *Secret Doctrine of the Rosicrucians:*

> . . .the World Soul (animus mundi) – the first manifestation of the Eternal Parent. . .(is) a Bi-sexual Universal Being. This Bi-sexual Universal being, combining within itself the elements and principles of both Masculinity and Femininity, is known in the Rosicrucian teachings as the "Universal Hermaphrodite" and the 'Universal Androgyne.' The term 'Hermaphrodite' is defined as: 'an individual which has the attributes of both male and female.' The term came into use through the legend of Hermaphroditus, son of Hermes and Aphrodite, who, while bathing, became joined in one body with the nymph Salmacis. The term "Androgyne". . .is derived from the combination of the Greek words, "Andros," meaning "a man," and "Gyne," meaning "a woman." The conception of the Bi-sexuality in the Universal Manifestation, or Universal Being, is one met with on all sides in the ancient esoteric and occult philosophies in all lands. In ancient Greece, in ancient India, and in ancient...Persia, and Chaldea the doctrine formed an important part of the Inner Teachings. In its highest forms, this teaching lay at the very heart of the Ancient Mysteries, and resulted in the very highest and noblest conception of dignity and worthiness of Sex...In order to understand the symbology of the Universal Androgyne, it is necessary to first become familiar with the two ancient symbols of Sex. In all ancient philosophies and religion, we find that the cross + is the symbol of the

---

[78] A pseudonym taken by its alleged authors: William Atkinson of the New Thought movement, BOTA founder Paul Foster Case, and the possibly apocryphal Yogi Ramcharaka.

male; and the circle O the symbol of the female. In representing the Bisexual, the Hermaphrodite, the Androgyne, the two symbols, the Cross and the Circle, are combined in several ways. The original way was that of placing the Cross within the circumference of the Circle; but later usage preferred the various forms of the so-called "Phallic Cross," which consists of the Circle, or oval, sustaining the Cross which depends downward from it. Sometimes the Cross is represented by the letter "T," and the Circle as the letter "O." The well-known esoteric symbol, the Swastica, consists of a modified Cross, conceived as a "whirling wheel". . .The whirling Cross of the Swastica, when seen in rapid motion, presents the appearance of a Circle enclosing a Cross. This symbol. . .is one particularly sacred to the Rosicrucians, since. . .it represents the Universal Activity and universal Creation, symbolizing the Great Mystery of Occult Generation on all planes of life.[79] In the fanciful symbology of the ancient Rosicrucian Brotherhoods, the Circle was transformed into the Rose, and the Cross...into the Sword. . .The sign...symbolized the Mystic Union of the Rose and the Cross, from whence arose the name of the order, Rosicrucian. (pp. 55-57).

The "Anonymous Magician" also writes,

. . .the Cross surmounted by the Rose indicates that the "Rose" (the mystic symbol of the Divine) can be attained only by the suffering of the mortal life (symbolized by the Cross). . .The Sword attached to the Rose indicates that the Sword of Spirit must be actively employed in

---

[79] In the Rosicrucian cosmology, these ascending planes of existence and evolution are: elemental, mineral, plant, animal, human, angelic, and Divine.

> the Battle of Life, in order to win the reward of the Rose. . .The Cross surmounted by the Crown, indicates that the suffering of mortal existence, borne by the faithful disciple of Truth, will inevitably be rewarded by the attainment of the Crown of Mastery. . .The modified Phallic Cross indicates the Sexual Duality of the Manifested Universe – the Presence and Activity of the Universal male...and the Universal Female Principle. . . (Incognito, 1949, pp. 21-22).

Though this be a Rosicrucian teaching, in it is represented diverse principles reflected in other forms of esotericism. Such principles can be seen in Eastern sources such as the Taoist Yin-Yang symbol. Similarly, these concepts are also relayed in Eliphas Levi's (1996) "Unalterable Principles" and Western Magickal Theorems espoused in his seminal work *Paradoxes of the Highest Science* (pp. 135-158).

These last cruxes must be made in concluding our review of the Cross within the Circle. In so doing further insights should be imparted to the student regarding the significance of assuming the form of the Cross during the LPR's Invocation of the Archangels and Declaration of the Great Work:

1). The Rose of the Rosy Cross, symbolizing the Circle, is in the East represented by the Lotus and holds identical meaning as the Rose (i.e. infinity, eternity, awakening, gnosis, jnana, etc.).

2). Crowley's symbol of the Great Work (a cross atop a circle) is but a variation of the Solar Cross and holds the same meaning as those explained above.

3). Like Crowley's sigil for the Great Work, the Astrological symbols for Mars and Venus are but variations of the Solar Cross. They are representative of the Universal male and female principles, whose microcosmic energy-centers are respectively located in Yesod (the genitals) and Tiphareth (the heart).

4). The Egyptian Ankh, the sandal strap of the gods, is another variation on this symbolic theme of the Solar Cross and displays the Universal principle of motion inherent in all of

Creation; from the largest galaxy to the smallest sub-atomic particle; to the actions of the body to the processes of the mind. This Law of Motion is the intrinsic property of the Astral Light, of Prana, of Qi. "Come unto me is a foolish word, for it is I that go." (*Liber Al vel Legis*, II:7).

5). The Svastika, it must be noted, was a holy symbol for centuries upon centuries, in cultures ranging from the Jain to the Hindu to the Tibetan to the Native American. Only when usurped by the psychopathic motivations of the Nazis prior to World War II did its meaning change to one associated with evil. While still wrongly used today by such racist terrorist groups as the Neo-Nazis and Ku Klux Klan, and other nefarious so-called religious sects void of Truth or merit like modern Satanism, it is time this once sacred symbol be brought back to its accurate meaning and abdicated from such unjust thievery.

**The Egyptian Ankh.**

**Symbols of Venus and Mars.**

**The Svastika.**

**The Golden Dawn's Rose Cross Lamen.**

**The Rosy Cross – Symbol of Rosicrucianism.**

# The LPR Analzyed with the First Half of the Major Arcana of the Tarot

"My number is 11, as all their numbers who are of us.
The Five Pointed Star, with a Circle in the Middle,
and the circle is Red. My colour is black to the blind,
but the blue and the gold are seen of the seeing.
Also I have a secret glory for them that love me."
-*Liber Al vel Legis* (I:60).

As outlined previously, the scene created through the use of the Imagination guided by Will in the performance of the LPR is nothing less than the formation of what we have termed the Universal Mandala, along with all of the vast meanings associated with this form. We will now look at another interpretation of the ritual that will prove as extensively and philosophically profound. When we view the LPR through the revelations provided by the first 11 Keys of the Tarot's Major Arcana, a whole new vista of occult construal is thereby unlocked.

A comprehensive exposition of these Trumps, Key 0 through Key 10, (let alone the entire Major Arcana,) would require its own far-reaching volume and is beyond the scope of this focused work. It is the intent of this section to cover some of the Key's major precepts and how they pertain to a deeper understanding of the LPR. We will show how Trumps 0 through 5 relate the components of the LPR's execution, while Trumps 6 through 10, in contrast, express the functions of the ritual's composition.

Furthermore, while an exposition on the Tarot's other deck, the Minor Arcana (encompassing all of the varieties of human personality type) is not pertinent to this analysis, the four suits of the Minor Arcana hold obvious correspondence to the four directions/elements of the LPR's Universal Mandala. These are: Swords to East and the air; Wands to South and fire; Cups to West and water; and Pantacles to North and the earth. As we will see below in Key 1 (the Magician), these four suits correspond to the four Magical weapons of Magick and are contained on his altar.

These first 11 Keys of the Major Arcana will be surveyed not only due to their symbolic pertinence to our topic, but also due to the fact that the number 11, as Crowley correctly espouses in numerous writings, is the number of Magick; it is the sum of 5 + 6, of the Pentagram with the Hexagram, the Microcosm with the Macrocosm, and relates to the Magician in his or her utilization of the Powers of God, which are but the forces of Nature. The Tarot deck style to be examined will focus largely on that of BOTA's, designed by its founder Dr. Paul Foster Case. Interpretation of these Keys will be based on both Case's deck and those assigned to Crowley's Thoth version. Case's deck is a very slight alteration on the Rider-Waite deck designed by Pamela Coleman Smith, both of which are based on the more antiquated designs of Levi, Papus, Court de Gebbelin, Esseilles, Oswald Wirth, and others.

Legend, part historic, part apocryphal, explains that the first Tarot originated in the Middle Ages from the artistic efforts of a congregation of adepts from various esoteric spiritual systems who wished to preserve the Secret Teachings in a universal and comprehensive way. This would be achieved through hieroglyphic form using a combination of pictorial art, symbolic letters, and mathematical signs; their theory being that "a picture is worth a thousand words." The Tarot, in this author's opinion, remains the quintessential medium of conveying spiritual Truth and philosophical Wisdom. It should be studied deeply by all occultists and would-be Magicians. With cross-referencing of various systems it will be found that the Tarot is genuinely insightful for any seeker regardless of the particular path in which they are rooted. As a conveyer of the Truth that underlies all religions, it is as priceless a tool for the Sufi as the Buddhist as the Taoist as the Witch. Let not its usage of the Hebrew alphabet bias one into wrongly believing that it is only a resource for Qabalists.

0 – The Fool – Aleph:  The Fool, as the beginning of the Major Arcana's Tarot, is the Genesis of the Tarot Keys. Represented by the number 0 it corresponds to the Circle of the Universal Mandala. It likewise represents the Void, the Prime Nothingness, or "God," from which all things (all of Creation, Nature, and the Universe) emerged, and into which the images of the LPR are projected and the Divine Names vibrated. The number 0 is also correspondent to the Greek letter Omega ($\Omega$), "the last," just as the Hebrew letter assigned to this Trump, Aleph, is correspondent to the Greek letter Alpha ($\alpha$), "the first."   Thus, this Key shows in its symbolic circularity, expressed as the Alpha and the Omega,[80] "the first and the last," the concepts of unity, totality, eternity and infinity.

Etymologically, "fool" is derived from the Latin root "follis" meaning "bag of wind."  This is what the Fool carries in his sack upon his Wand of Will. This wind is the Ruach Elohim, the breath and Spirit of God, the breath that spoke the FIAT LVX, the breath breathed into Adam to give him life. This breath is the source or "material" of the Astral Light, the Prime Substance, the Universal Life Energy of which all matter and energy is composed, and which the Fool also hieroglyphically personifies.

---

[80] A name assigned to Christ in *Revelations* 1:8.

This Life Energy is known in the wisdom of all ancient cultures. The student is reminded that in Sanskrit it is Prana; in Mandarin Chinese it is Qi; in Japanese it is Ki; in Finnish it is Sisu; in Greek it is Pneuma; in Hebrew it is Ruach; in Latin it is Spiritus; in Alchemy it is Azoth; in Egyptian it is Ka; and in Theosophy it is Fohat. All of these words equally express the idea that human spirit, or energy, is intricately bound with the human breath. This is because the ancients, prior to modern medical discoveries, knew that the breath was the fuel of the body, though they may not have understood the modern explanation of oxygenation of the blood. They did, however, understand a deeper teaching still not grasped by our modern science; that beyond oxygen, the breath brings Macrocosmic energy into the Microcosm through the process of respiration. This is one of the primary teachings contained within such breath-focused disciplines as Yoga, Qigong, and Tai Chi. Breath *is* life, beyond metaphor, for we are all born with a cry and die with a sigh.

In the LPR, the Astral Light is not only used to form the projected visualizations, it is the prime ingredient through the Magickal use of the breath in the vibration of the Divine Names. As is taught in Mantra Yoga, the Names in and of themselves possess intrinsic energy or power when so used, due to both the conversion of breath into sound waves and vibrations, and the ancient meanings and philosophical associations assigned to the Names. Thus, the proper use of the Total Breath is vital in the LPR, as it is in all Magick, Yoga, Qigong, or Tai Chi. The energy processes it entails work to generate, intensify, and transform human spiritual energy into a useable physio-biochemical fuel.

In addition to the symbolic interpretation assigned above to Aleph, its literal translation in Hebrew means ox.[81] Even the

---

[81] The Fool also represents the descent of Spirit into matter or involution. As he walks looking upward, at the Divine Source he is destined to eventually return to after his grand journey (symbolized in this Key as the Sun), he is also about to fall off a precipice, symbolizing Spirit's manifestation into the corporeal (the allegorical Fall from Eden). This is another representation of the Hindu concept of Brahman entering into Leela – the great game where God (the One) becomes everything (the Many) and forgets Himself in order to just remember; or the Taoist teaching that the Tai Chi (Grand Ultimate) breaks into the Yin and Yang, which then form the innumerable changing things of the Universe. In Qabalah, this is represented by Kether becoming Binah and Chokmah, then the rest of the

very appearance of this word in English holds significance, for geometrically we can see the circle of the O next to the X, a cross. In Hebrew, the letter Aleph appears as such – א. This letter's form is written in such a way as to represent an arrow piercing a serpent. This exemplifies the Magickal teaching of the focused or aimed Will, represented by the arrow, in domination or control over the Great Magickal Agent, the Astral Light, universally represented in ancient symbology by the serpent or snake. This is due to the fact that the ancient Masters understood the properties of the Astral Light and its various Kosmic manifestations including the Sun's electro-magnetic radiation, lightning's electricity, the Earth's magnetism, fire's heat, and the stars' light. Being the root of such forms of energy, the Wise Ones seem to have chosen the Astral Light's electrical properties – consisting of peaks and troughs, ebbs and flows - and thus symbolized it in the form of the snake whose motion is similarly undulating. (More will be discussed about this phenomenon under Key 8 – Strength). As we have said, it is this substance, the Astral Light, or by whatever name one chooses, that the Magician works their art through ceremony and ritual. And it is in the LPR that the Magician works with it as a medium upon empty space, just as a painter applies their colors to a canvas.

**Ancient rendering of the Hebrew letter Aleph depicted as an arrow piercing a serpent.**

Tree of Life. This grand journey of the Fool, the process of Leela, the Hindu Divine Game where God has forgotten Himself and then quests on through evolution to remember who He is, is also echoed in Zen's **ox-herding pictures** that reflect Man's path from ignorance to enlightenment. In this context, note, that the Fool Key is assigned the Hebrew letter Aleph, meaning an ox!

Finally, the Fool also possesses meaning identical to that explained earlier about the Hanged Man (Key 12). That is, the one who has attained Magickal insight, they who have attained Gnosis, Moksha, Nirvana, see the world in complete antithesis, in total opposition, from that of the profane vulgar multitude still under the sway of illusion (Maya in Sanskrit) and ignorance (Avidya in Sanskrit). To such a multitude of unregenerate people, the Magus seems a madman, or a fool, for they are not taken in by the false phantasamagoria of life, or the desires and fears of the general populace, but rather, see clearly into the very nature of Reality.

This could easily be compared to, or illustrated by, the way the Native American Shamans were widely viewed by the first "civilized" contemporary Europeans who came into contact with them following the arrival of Columbus, the conquistadors, and the later pilgrims on Plymouth Rock. For most of those contemporaries, then, as it is in modern times, only the material world was "real." To the Shamans, however (as with the Buddhas, Tathagatas, Bodhisattvas, Arhats, Yogins, and Sages of all places and all ages), it was understood that waking life and materiality was no more than another layer of Brahman's unreal dream. How odd and ironic it was, and what an oxymoron, that this period of European history was termed the "Enlightenment" when it represented a turn from religion (however vastly erred its spiritual understanding was under the False Church) to the strict materialism of science.[82]

---

[82] And how tragic this "Enlightenment" would prove when, while still under the pangs of Western science's birth, these men would attempt genocide against the tribal peoples they contacted, all the while the False Church, in backlash to such growing materialism and science, would commit the psychopathic atrocities against female herbalists and midwives (as well as those noble and beautiful creatures, black cats) that became the holocaust we now call the **Burning Times**. (Note that because of the False Church's sociopathic slaughter committed against black cats, to this very day it is difficult to find a feline wholly black without some slight white in its coat! How odd in the West such gorgeous Beings are superstitiously considerd bad luck, while in the East, such as Japan, they are rightly considered good omen). In the Renaissance and Enlightenment era more innocent people were murdered in the name of the Prince of Peace by His self-imposed Catholic and Protestant elect over the ridiculous and irrelevant charges of witchcraft, heresy, and deviltry than were butchered in the 20th century by Hitler and Stalin combined! In regards to this utterly shameful period of Western history, all we practitioners of the arts of the

1 – The Magician – Beth: The Magician is represented in Tarot by the number 1 and thus geometrically corresponds to the point formed in the LPR by the practitioner in the center of the Universal Mandala. As the point, the Magician Key expresses one of the most vital mental faculties needed by the occultist, that of concentration, of unwavering attention upon a single purpose. As Crowley (1994) explained, Magick is the art of reducing all thought processes to one single purpose or goal (while Yoga is the art of then reducing this one thought to none – The Fool). The idea of the point shows the ability to mentally "zone-in" on a particular target, thus zoning out all other superfluous thoughts and mental distractions by the exercise of Will. The point expresses, just like aiming the sight of a gun, the concept of pure focus. In martial arts this term is expressed in Okinawan Karate systems as Kimei, the idea of striking to a pin-point target upon a body with perfectly aimed force. This is the same goal the Magician strives for, metaphorically speaking, in the act of Magick – to achieve the effect desired by an act of focused Willpower. In the LPR this one goal is idealized as the fulfillment of the Great Work, the 5 = 6.

---

Magi – we Qabalists, Alchemists, Hermeticists, Rosicrucians, Shamans, and Thelemites – must stand with our Wiccan and Neo-Pagan sisters and brothers and loudly declare, **NEVER AGAIN!** To such a situation, should it ever arise again, shall we gladly and ferociously take up arms against any oppressors and exponentially exceed our blood with theirs!

Beyond the point, the Magician's posture in this key, like that used in the LPR, is upright and again suggests obvious Phallic symbolism; the Phallus being in Magick a symbol of the creative impulse. In this Key we see the four elemental weapons correspondent to the four directions faced in the LPR, the four Tetragrammatons and their letters, the Archangels, the arms of the cross and so on. Upon his table, representing the Magician's field of operation, are the cup (water), the disk (earth), and the dagger (air). In his hand he holds the wand, another Phallic symbol, representing the Will and corresponding to the element of fire. The Magician is thus utilizing the Will as his tool and the Kosmic fire (the Astral Light or Great Magickal Agent) as the medium with which he is working. This, of course, holds obvious parallel to the action being exercised in the LPR.

In addition, the wand of will is held high while the Magician's other hand is held low, pointing at his altar table. This shows the action of the Magus drawing down the Divine White Brilliance (the positive flux of the Astral Light) from Kether, through himself as the medium of its channeling, and onto the altar table. This table is representative of the Magus' life and environment, the field of operation upon which he enacts his Magick. To this Key is also assigned the Hebrew letter Beth (ב), meaning house, representing the idea of civilization as embodied by home and family. It is upon these areas – life, environment, family, home, and civilization – that the Magician works royal his art for beneficent ends.

**THE OUROBORAS** – The Magician's belt in Key 1; symbol of creation and eternity; of the unity of evolution and entropy. Christ said, *"Be wise as serpents."*

Around his waist is entwined the Ouroboras serpent, symbolizing Eternity and also analogous to the Ring of Fire traced from cardinal point to cardinal point in the LPR. The sideways '8' above his head is the mathematical sign for infinity, embodied in the LPR's Universal Mandala by the circle, symbolizing the potential within energy, the Universe, and mankind as being inexhaustible. This entire scene shows the Magician as not only a transformer and channel of Divine energy, but as a catalyst of effect and change upon the world by their usage of Universal forces (symbolized by the elemental weapons) as directed by his Will and Imagination. In this regard, the LPR represents the fundamental Western esoteric practice so far devised to prime the occultist for the generation of Magickal energy (as embodied in the Fool – Key 0) and to introduce the student to the Willful control of such forces (as embodied in the Magician – Key 1).

2 – The High Priestess – Gimel: The High Priestess, assigned the number 2, geometrically represents the line, as the line requires two points thereby joined in order to create it. In the LPR it is the line, artistically speaking, that is the sole component needed for tracing the Pentagrams. Two is also, as we have examined, the number of Universal duality symbolized in the East as the Yin-Yang and in the West by the equilibrated

Cross and the Hexagram. The cross, as we have seen, is the form taken by the Magician's posture in the climax of the LPR and is also the symbol worn upon the High Priestess' heart, or Tipahreth, while the Hexagram is likewise being envisioned (a double duality thus invoking the Tetrad). Tiphareth, again, corresponds to the Adeptus Minor grade and is represented by the formula of the Great Work, 5 = 6, showing the reconciliation of the Microcosm with the Macrocosm. And it is the practitioner's Tipahreth, we remind the reader, that is the point with which the center of the LPR's traced Pentagrams align.

The High Priestess is astrologically attributed to the Moon, shown by the crescent horns holding a sphere upon her head. These are reflective of the horns seen in the iconography of the Egyptian Goddess Isis (who corresponds to the Greek Artemis and Roman Diana; all lunar goddesses of Nature and Magick). Just as the Moon receives and reflects the light of the Sun, so does the mind in its act of memory show the intellectual processes of receptivity and reflection. With the LPR, it is memory which proves the first mental faculty necessary for its execution, for the ritual must be memorized by heart in order to be properly performed by the Magician.

Memory is also symbolized in the High Priestess by the rolled Torah scroll she holds, upon which she inscribes all events. Torah (Hebrew for law) is correlative to the Buddhist Dharma and the Taoist Tao. This scroll is also representative of our individual memories and also of the complete recollection of the subconscious storehouse (known by the Jungians as the Collective Unconscious and to the Theosophists as the Akashic Record). It is into this record that the Buddha mined when he became enlightened, giving him an account of all his previous lifetimes, even those stretching back into his pre-human animal and plant incarnations. Through this amazing Kosmic insight he was shown the Oneness of all life and gained his total compassion towards all creatures, seeing that we all mutually suffer in this Samsara. It is because of this fact that Tibetans view all creatures as Mothers, and respect them as such, because at some point in our cycle of metempsychosis we have all been a Mother. This Akashic record can be accessed through advanced Magickal practices, some Eastern meditative techniques (like the Buddhist Sammasati meditation,[83] when highly developed), by those with real psychic or clairvoyant ability, in accurate remote-viewing (like the C.I.A. method taught by the Farsight Institute of Colorado), and sometimes in past-life regression therapies such as that pioneered by psychologist Stan Groff.

The student should also notice that the High Priestess sits as the Middle Pillar between the black and white pillars of the Temple, between those marked as Jod and Beth (or in Masonic terminology, Joachin and Boaz). These are also indicative of the Pillars of Mercy and Severity upon the Tree of Life. Her position of being balanced between the two shows her as having transcended them in harmony, of having reconciled them in balance. In the Western esoteric tradition this achievement is the initiate's quest for spiritual equilibrium, and in the East it is the treading of the Madhyamika, or Middle Path. This striving for liberation has been likened to traversing a razor's edge[84] or a straight and narrow path,[85] for it is one of extreme challenge and difficulty requiring great spiritual balance.

The High Priestess' position as the Middle Pillar also relates her representative mental function of memory, for it is in the present, the Now balanced between then and later, that past experiences are utilized for future contexts. This concept of the Now, this truth that the present is all there ever really is to reality (and of this concept being a great spiritual secret hidden in all mystic paths and that this secret is a primary gateway to human awakening), is the central tenet to the modern Master

---

[83] Sammasati is a Buddhist method of meditation in which the practitioner attempts to gain insight into his or her's life's karmic purpose by tracing back, moment by moment, the events of one's life, eventually into the infant era, and then even into the pre-birth *in utero* stages, and then potentially farther back into the Bardo realms, and then beyond this into one's previous incarnations. This is what happened to the Buddha upon his awakening under the Bodhi tree, with His Sammasati extending back into His previous human existences and then into His pre-human lives as animals and as plants and as minerals.

[84] "The sharp edge of a razor is difficult to pass over; thus the wise say the path to Salvation is hard" (*Katha Upanishad*, 1:3). It is from this verse that W. Somerset Maugham gained his title for the classic novel *The Razor's Edge* about a WWI pilot who finds enlightenment through the practices of Hinduism.

[85] "Enter ye in at the straight gate: for wide *is* the gate, and broad *is* the way, that leadeth to destruction, and many there be which go in. . ." (*Matthew* 7:13, King James Version).

Eckhart Tolle's (1999) entire system. To comprehend this principle fully is to shed the temporal state and enter eternity.

Such a teaching is likewise shared by some of the greatest philosophers in history. Thoreau (1980), too, wrote ". . .stand on the edge of two eternities, the past and the future, which is precisely the present moment." The Buddha also promoted this understanding when he preached, "Do not dwell in the past. Do not dream of the future. Concentrate the mind on the present moment" (cited in Carus, 2008). The great stoic Roman emperor Marcus Aurelius wrote in a similar vein when he stated, "...thou hast forgotten that every man lives the present time only" (cited in Elliot, 1937, p. 299). And, ". . .thou shalt strive to live only what is really thy life, that is, the present. . ." (cited in Elliot, 1937, p. 295).

Why this insistence upon focusing on the present? Because since the present moment, the Now, is all that truly is, to dwell in the past or in the future is to dwell in illusion (Maya) or unreality. Even when we remember the past, we do it in the Now. When that past occurred, it was the Now, *then*. When we anticipate the future with either hope or worry, again, it is done right Now. And when that future occurs, whatever the outcome, it too happens only in the Now.

**Now is the only time that ever is**. The assimilation of this fact helps us to shed our ignorance by perceiving reality as it really is and not as our egoic minds erroneously make it. This is why so many esoteric teachings stress this lesson as a path to awakening from our slumber of ignorance, and thus as a road to realizing God. To this effect, the great Sufi poet Rumi said in his poem *Masnavi*, "Past and future veil our sight from God." Likewise, his fellow Sufis have a saying, "The Sufi is the son of time present."

Meister Eckhart, the Medieval Christian mystic wrote,

> Time is what keeps the light from reaching us. There is no greater obstacle to God than time: and not only time but temporalities, not only temporal things but temporal affections, not only temporal affections but the very taint and smell of time. (cited in Blakney, 1941).

Christ taught his disciples to not look back if they wanted to be fit for the Kingdom of Heaven (*Luke* 9:62) and also to, "Take no thought of the morrow. . ." (*Matthew* 6:34). Russian mathematician and philosopher P.D. Ouspensky (1970)[86] taught that the present is the moment always poised between the streams of past and future that forever crash into each other. The seeming fluidity of time is really only a manifestation of the constant change, of the motion, that continually occurs in the space of the ever-present. This continuous transience of all things, manifest through movement (from the largest celestial bodies to the smallest sub-atomic particles), and known in Buddhism as Annica, is symbolized in the High Priestess by her blue robe which turns into the flowing water at her feet.

The Hebrew letter assigned to this Key is Gimel (ג) meaning camel. This word was anciently associated with the caravan, of coming and going on a quest or expedition. Hidden in this word is the idea of Campbell's Hero's Journey and the Magickal formula of IAO, both discussed earlier - the Great Pilgrimage every adept makes in both the strivings of this life, as well as in living life after life after life. In the symbolism of Gimel as the great quest, we also see suggested God's Kosmic process of involution and evolution; of the Great Spirit's implantation of Itself into the Each and the All, and its eternal process of arising from those states and conditions in continual change, growing back towards Itself as the One Source. Like a seed in the soil sprouting forth and climbing towards the Sun, it is what Jesuit evolutionist Teilhard de Chardin (1950) described as the Ground of Being reaching towards the Omega Point. In Hinduism this is likened to a grand game, called Lela, played by God, where Brahman becomes all things in forgetfulness of Himself only to eventually remember and return. It is also the Mahayana Buddhist conception of the Samsara where all follow the Path of life, death, the Bardo, and rebirth; at least, that is, until the attainment of Nirvana. Scientifically, it is the expansion of the Universe from the infinitesimal point of the Big Bang until its ultimate return in the Big Crunch.

This idea of going and coming, of leaving and returning, is mirrored in the LPR by the energy circuits created by the

---

[86] Considered the greatest student of G.I. Gurdjieff's Fourth Way School.

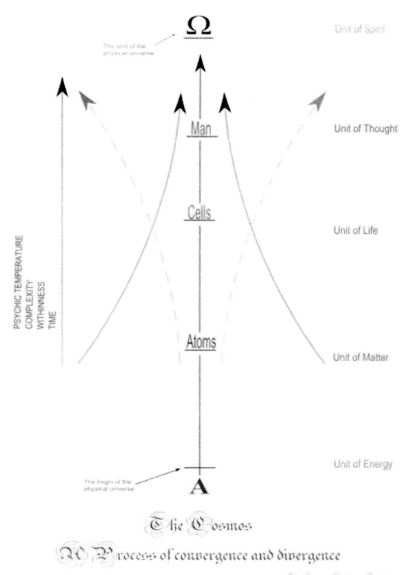

**A Diagram of the Kosmic Evolutionary Process per Teilhard de Chardin.**

**Isis – Egyptian goddess of Nature and Magick.**

**Diana – the Roman Isis and Greek Artemis.**

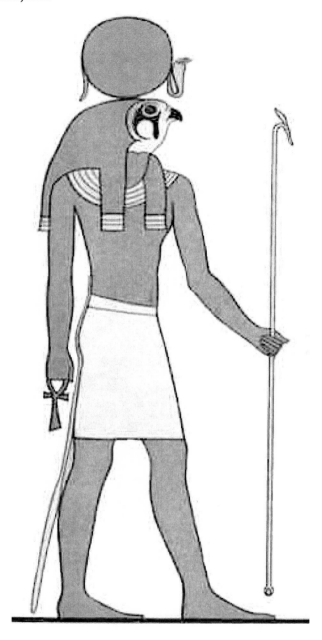

**Osiris – Egyptian god of regeneration and rebirth.**

vocalizations and visualizations performed by the Magician. The Magician's declarations and vibrations begin in silence, reverberate to the farthest reaches of space, and end in silence again, forming a complete revolution. The shapes and images in the ritual, the Stars and Archangels, begin as empty space, are thereby traced or projected, and are thereafter reabsorbed.

These currents of audible force and visual form created in the LPR are therefore in ebb and flow like the tides. They revolve like the phases of the Moon or the rising and setting of the Sun. They extend and retract like the phallus growing erect in stimulation to ejaculate its creative power, then returning to flaccidity again. They open and close like the blossoming and ensuing slumber of a lotus or a rose. They are the *ursa* entering the cave for a Winter's hibernation and exiting it in the awakening of Spring. They are Christ and Osiris, three days in the womb of death, arisen again to everlasting life.

Such manipulation of energy in the LPR is thus analogous to orbits and not lines. Whether in sound or image, the energies utilized expand out into the Universe and return again to their source, the Magician; just as the Ring of Fire that the Magician traces from Star to Star begins in the East, and ultimately, after a complete circumambulation, returns to end where it once began. Therefore, in this ritual's process is illustrated one of the central tenets of all Magick and spirituality: All things come from One Source and unto this One Source they are destined to return. Thus is participation in all forms of esoteric discipline often referred to as The Path of Return.

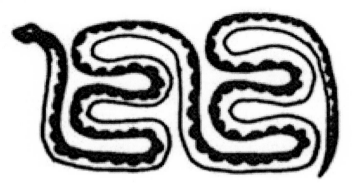

**Apophis (or Set) – Egyptian god of death; brother and slayer of Osiris.**

<u>3 – The Empress – Daleth</u>:  The Empress is assigned the faculty of Imagination, the mental creative process, as symbolized by the blossoming natural scene in which she sits. Tradition states that she is pregnant, thus again, personified by the fecundity of the plant life around her and expressive of Imagination as a force for creativity. In this way she astrologically corresponds to Venus, goddess of beauty, art, and the reproductive principle of Nature. This reproductive principle is not only expressed in sexual procreation, but also in the generative use of Imagination expressed by humans in such forms as arts, crafts, inventions, and all other forms of self-expression.

The number 3 assigned to the Empress is the addition of 1 + 2, or the union of the Magician (attention, focus, concentration) with the High Priestess (memory). Tradition states that the High Priestess is a virgin, and her union with the Magician transforms her into the pregnant Empress. Thus, the use of attention in gaining data about our lives and environments is stored in the faculty of memory for our recall. In this coupling is born our ability to expand upon such information and build new formulations or innovations upon the old data, the function of Imagination. The use of this process allows us to alter our existences, to cause change subjectively within ourselves or within objective reality in conformity to our applied Will. This is the very definition of Magick.

The number 3 is also indicative of the various Universal Trinities: the Christian father, Son, and Holy Spirit; the Hindu Brahman (creator), Vishnu (preserver), and Shiva (destroyer); Alchemy's salt, sulphur, and mercury; Taoism's yi (mind), li (body), and qi (spirit); the Qabalistic Neshamah, Ruach, and Nephesh; the formation of the Universal sound AUM; the Gnostic formula of IAO, and so on.

The Hebrew letter assigned to this Trump is Daleth (ד) meaning door. This shows the Empress as the door of life, through her womb, as a mother-to-be. It is also correspondent to the Imagination as this faculty proves the door to our own minds and creative powers. In the LPR the Magician must first use their Imagination to form and project the visualizations utilized (i.e. the Stars, elements, Archangels, etc.) until he or she has sufficiently developed their clairvoyant ability to actually see these shapes, these thought forms, literally created with the Astral Light by their act of focused Will.

**Venus – Roman goddess of love and femininity.**

4 – The Emperor – Heh:    The Emperor results from the transformation of the Magician who, when wedded to the High Priestess, becomes the Empress. It is thus 1 + 3 equaling 4; the first two prime numbers coupled together forming the first perfect square; the number assigned to this Key. The Emperor is a leader who rules his kingdom by use of attention, memory, and imagination applied by Will; the same mental formula necessary for the application of Magick. As previously examined, the number 4 also expresses all of the vast symbolism inherent in the LPR such as the directions, elements, names of God, the Cross, Archangels, and so on.

The Emperor's dominion over Nature through his power and sovereignty is also implied by his seat upon the cube. The cube consists of 6 sides and therefore expresses the idea of the Hexagram, symbol of the Macrocosm. His dominion and self-sovereignty is also implied by his armored war-attire, as well as the Ram symbol upon his throne-cube (the Ram being the symbol of Aries and astrologically attributed to Mars, the Roman battle god). In his hands he holds a scepter and a sphere, symbolic of the Solar or Rosy Cross, formed by the Magician's posture in the climax of the LPR.

All of these symbolisms are directly relevant to exercise of the LPR or as a prerequisite to any Magickal practice. The true Magician must be their own Emperor, self-sovereign, ruling over their animal instincts and lower appetites. They must be king of themselves by rightful exercise of attention, concentration, focus, memory, imagination, and willpower. The Emperor establishes the boundaries of his territory by battling and defeating his enemies. The Magician too must establish order in the chaos of the kingdom of the mind through the self-sacrifice of unwavering discipline. Likewise, by the formula of the LPR the Magician can establish organizational order over vast amounts of data relevant to nearly any facet of existence (as illustrated in Appendix A). This, the student will come to understand, is one of the fundamental practical applications of not only the LPR, but of the use of Tarot and the Qabalistic Tree of Life.

Perhaps the most important implication contained in the Emperor relevant to the LPR is in the Hebrew letter assigned to this Key, that of Heh ( ה) meaning window. These are the openings of the castle through which the Emperor surveys his kingdom. A window is also an aperture in a house (Beth - The Magician) that allows the flow of light and air (follis - The Fool). This relates the sense of sight (assigned to the Emperor and ruled by Aries) and the action of breath; the former used in the visualizations of the LPR and the latter being the source of Macrocosmic energy gained through respiration for the practitioner's Magickal usage.

Furthermore, in relation to this correspondence of sight, through the exercise of the LPR (and many other Magickal rituals and meditative practices as well), the student will eventually sharpen their innate psychic or clairvoyant abilities, known in antiquity as "second sight" or in Yoga per Pantanjali as one of the siddhis (or Magick powers). This is the ability to perceive the more subtle forms and inhabitants of Nature upon other planes of existence, such as the Qabalistic qlipphoth (ghosts or "shells"); the Alchemists' elementals (sylphs, nymphs, salamanders, and gnomes); the Celtic fairies, leprechauns, and elves; the Islamic djinn or genii of the desert; the Tibetan devas, dakinis, and pretas; and so forth.

As explained in BOTA's (1997) former literary organ, *The Portico*:

To discover the laws of the superphysical planes, one must have the eyes to see the facts of those planes; hence one of the principle aims of occult training is to develop a higher faculty of sight, now latent in most people, that enables its possessor to see things invisible to the untrained man. (p. 12).

And as the Rosicrucian poet William Blake (1995) stated, "As a man sees, so is he. As the eye is formed, so are its powers." In this same vein, but from the East, we also remind the reader of the advice provided by the Kensei (sword saint) Miyamoto Musashi in his strategic masterpiece, *Gorin No Sho (The Book of Five Rings)* (1974), written in the cave Regindo after prayer and meditation to the Buddhist goddess of mercy Kwannon: "Develop the two-fold gaze; perception and sight. Perception is strong. Sight is weak" (cited in Harris, p. 54).

**Mars – Roman god of war and masculinity.**

5 – The Hierophant – Vau:  At the number 5 we are met with the Pentagram and all of its glorious symbolism and meaning as already explained. As 5, the Hierophant sits halfway as the midpoint between the Fool and the Wheel of Fortune, Keys 1 through 10, the Trumps of our present examination. Also embodied are the five prominent figures of this card: the Hierophant; his two attendees; and the two pillars of the Temple. Like the High Priestess, the Hierophant's balanced position between these two makes him the Middle Pillar.

His headdress is a stylized egg, or yoke, derived from the Sanskrit root for Yoga, meaning union, again denoting the goal of the 5 = 6 formula; one's merging with God or the attainment of Yogic Samadhi. The LPR, as a Magickal exercise, also strives to achieve union, to accomplish harmony, between what the Hierophant and his two attendees personify. They are the sacred Alchemical triangle of Mercury, Salt, and Sulphur; the Taoist yi, li, and qi; mind, body, and spirit; the three aspects of our Being exercised in all art and ritual.

Traditionally, the Hierophant's shape is meant to be suggestive of a bell. Similarly, the crossed keys in the Trump are attributed to musical notes. Both these figures represent sound and vibration, which is why this card, in contrast to the preceding Emperor signifying sight, is attributed to the sense of hearing. Taken together these two cards directly apply to the LPR, for proper visualization and vibratory methods are essential to this exercise's highest results. HEREIN HIDES A GREAT SECRET FOR WHICH WE PROVIDE THIS VITAL HINT. **The very visualizations and vibrations of the LPR are specifically intended to cause direct auspicious effects upon the brain, via the ocular and auditory systems, necessary for fostering certain internal chemical and cellular developments, as well as organic evolutionary alterations in the central nervous system, required for further spiritual progress, psychic amplification, and Magickal buttressing of the human being. It is a way by which the human can consciously participate in the acceleration of their own evolution. It is a way by which the human can willfully co-create, in conjunction with the creative spirit of God, the birth of a new species faster than Nature would do so by Her own processes.** As the Golden Dawn pledge avows, through the sacerdotal art of Magick, we are to strive to become *more than human*. Personal oaths prevent further elucidation of this lesson, but sufficient information has hereby been relayed for the talented student to gain deeper insight into this Mystery through the use of meditative contemplation.

It can be said that what the Emperor is to clairvoyance, the Hierophant is to clairaudience. The student must, however, exercise keen spiritual discernment for it is a dangerous possibility that visions can be wrongly interpreted as clairvoyance while being nothing more than visual hallucinations akin to the symptoms of psychosis. This is similar to the phenomenon of clairaudience where voices heard could be nothing more than the auditory hallucinations symptomatic of schizophrenia. The true Inner Voice which the Hierophant symbolizes, however, is said to be unmistakable, clear, and never in contradiction to logic, conscience, or Divine love.

This power is catalogued in such diverse sources as the Abramelin system of Magick (once one has attained the knowledge and conversation of the Holy Guardian Angel) and in Pantanjali's Yoga Sutras as one of the Siddhis. It is what the Saints and Prophets have declared as the voice of God. It is, basically speaking, the reception of accurate intuition registered in the ears as spoken words.

The Hebrew letter assigned to the Hierophant is Vau ( ו ) meaning nail or hook. Used like the English conjunction "and" it grammatically shows a joining of words or nouns together, just as a nail can join two boards, or a hook can join a picture to a wall. In regard to the LPR, this again refers to the joining of the triune facets of the Magician's being (mind, body, and spirit) into a single, focused ritual act of Willpower. In this sense of joining, or union, Vau can also be considered akin to the Alchemical principle of Coagula.

Regarding the Hierophant's accoutrements, in his hand he holds a tri-barred Cross, a device likewise wielded by Shiva in Hindu iconography, standing for the three eras of time (past, present, and future), as well as the three aspects of God as Creator, Preserver, and Destroyer – which are but the reverse of the three aspects of time (i.e. the past always passes and is thus always destroyed in time's flow; the present is all there ever really is, and thus represents preservation; and the future is to come, and is therefore in a state of creation). Upon his other hand is tattooed a Cross. This exhibits his power and dominion over the elemental forces of nature, likewise utilized in the LPR. The lunar crescent at his throat, position of the Visuddha Chakra (attributed to self-expression and communication), shows the power of the voice for the conveyance of thought, memory, and imagination through the medium of sound, created and directed by the Will, and the reception of such knowledge through the reciprocal sense of hearing. As previously expounded upon, such use of language for the purposes of gaining and sharing Wisdom is personified in the Egyptian pantheon by the god of Magick, the ibis-headed Thoth.

6 – The Lovers – Zain:  At 6 we are met with the number of the cube, the Hexagram, and all the symbolism inherent in these as previously explained. Though traditionally ascribed to the faculty of discernment, this card is also a hieroglyphic analogy to the Tree of Life:  The Sun being the Ain Sof Aur; the Archangel's crown Kether and his heart Tiphareth; Adam and Eve the pillars of Mercy and Severity; the clouds Yesod; the mountain and ground Malkuth. The angel looks down, conveying the descent of God into matter (the Avatar), while the people gaze upwards representing the ascent of Man through the Path of Return back to God (the Buddha and Bodhisattva). Illustrated again in this scene is the Macrocosmic orbit of involution and evolution; Brahman's game of Leela. On a Microcosmic scale it relates the grand circulation of Qi through the body as taught in the Qigong exercises of Taoism. In Qabalah this is shown by the rising path of the serpent and the descent of the flaming sword on the Tree of Life. In the LPR these energy flows have been previously likened to circuits.

In the background is seen the Holy Mountain upon which the Hermit of Key 9 stands. It is Olympus, Meru, Albigensia, Ararat, Zion, Sinai, Calvary – the Axis Mundi. It is the umbilical cord connecting heaven and earth. This is what the Magician becomes in the LPR's Universal Mandala. He or she becomes the Axis Mundi, connecting that which is above with that which is below; a channel or bridge between the spiritual and the physical, just like their counterpart in Key 1 – The Magician.

The Hebrew letter Zain (ז) assigned to this Key means sword; a weapon used to cut or render things apart. This suggests the duality springing forth from unity in God's act of creation. In Qabalah it is Kether dividing into Binah and Chokmah. In Taoist terms it is the Tai Chi splitting into Yin and Yang. In this sense of cutting apart, the sword is also representative of the Alchemical principle of Solve.

Prior to the invention of the firearm, the sword was the ancient instrument with which nations literally rose and fell. In its straight double-edged form it represented the Cross to the Christian Crusaders. In its single-edged curved form of the scimitar it represented the Crescent Moon to their Muslim counterparts. It was the flaming weapon with which the Archangel Michael expelled Adam and Eve from the gates of Eden in the myth of Genesis. It was the tool legendarily used by St. George to slay the dragon. It is what exudes from Christ's mouth in John of Patmos' Revelation. And to the Japanese Samurai, its form as the katana was literally considered their soul.

In Magick, the sword also plays a prominent role as a tool utilized in formal ritual and other acts of banishment. Tradition teaches that in addition to light, open flame, wind, and the Pentagram, the point of the ceremonial sword is an effective weapon in casting out malevolent spiritual entities such as vampires, qliphoth, astral shells, specters, demons, and mischievous elementals. Though not the traditional weapon utilized for the LPR, it can be adapted to that purpose as well. Thus, just as in hand-to-hand combat, in Magick the sword can also be considered a formidable weapon. Its usage for either attack or defense, for protection or for slaughter of the innocents, mirrors the application of Magick in general, as white or black, hurting or healing.[87]

---

[87] The distinctions between White and Black Magick are not always easily drawn as Magick can be argued to be simply of the Gray or neutral variety. That is, just like a firearm or any other technology, tool, or weapon, Magick is only as good or evil, as White or Black, as the person who uses it (or as are their motivations for using it). Crowley (1970) states that any operation that is not intended to raise the Magician in a vertically straight line towards one's Holy

Mike Benjamin

**"Advaita" depicted in Hindu calligraphy.**

---

Guardian Angel is technically Black Magick (and, frankly, he would know). In other words, to use Eastern terms, any practice in which the aspirant is not striving for Nirvana, not following the Bodhisattvic path, is not holy. I would add this personal distinction as well: White Magick uses breath, light, sound, color, and so on, only for altruistic purposes, such as to heal, and never to harm. (By such a definition, however, Moses' plagues upon Egypt to free the Hebrew slaves would be one of the largest acts of Black Magick in history). On the other hand, Black Magickal practices often hold a perverted emphasis upon the use of bodily secretions such as blood, feces, sperm, vaginal fluids, urine, and so on. It is undoubted that any Magickal practice specifying such material ingredients is not of the Right-Hand Path of White Light! (The only exception I would add to this example is found in some forms of Taoist, Qabalistic, Kundalini, and Tantric Alchemy where the sexual fluids are used internally between husband and wife to foster health and longevity. In Norse heathenry, runes are often 'blooded' by their owner, that is to say, he or she will cut themselves and spread their blood on the runes, making them solely their own. But these are in no way the sacrificial, vampiristic, or coprophagic practices to which I allude above). To this effect, note that Crowley, despite all of his truly lofty erudition, wrote in the margin of his personal diary that the great Magickal secret of the entire Ordo Templi Orientis' system was to "eat your own sperm." Seems a far cry, an utmost inaccurate deviation, from the message of Jesus and the path of the Buddhas to which we of the Right-Hand aspire! But of course, as Crowley himself also admitted, in the City of the Pyramids his seat of council was on the left-hand side of the congregational chamber! However, I do not wish to deviate into too much dualism when Advaita is our goal. For a thorough and accurate deposition on the virtue espoused in the non-dual philosophy, in the transcendence of good and evil, see Evans-Wentz (1968, pp. 52 – 57) where he masterfully lays out the ideal of this view in ten precepts. Nietzsche too philosophizes on going "beyond good and evil." Note also that Crowley (1994) defines Magick as being White, Black, or Yellow, each being a different type, cosmology, and purpose. All of these theories are offered as important food for occultic thought.

7 – The Chariot – Cheth: The number 7 assigned to this Key correlates to the seven original planets of traditional Astrology, the seven Chakras of Kundalini Yoga, the seven Interior Stars of Alchemy, and the seven Sephira under the Supernal Triad of Kether, Chokmah, and Binah which constitute the human personality on the Tree of Life. It is also representative of the formula and geometric form of the Septenary and the principle of Phylactics, to which the Pythagoreans assigned the number 7 and gave it protective powers.

This last meaning is closely related to the pictorial form of this Trump, as the scene is one of a walled city surrounded by a moat being protected by an armed and armored warrior riding out to meet an approaching enemy. The city can be interpreted as the manifestation of geometry through architecture and operative masonry just as the soldier shows the manifestation of polity and law through force; this entire recipe being those ingredients necessary for the establishment of human civilization. The aspect of this scene is thus one of defense and protection, and when applied as an interpretation of the LPR, refers to the ritual's use as a means to build and fortify the Magician's aura, or Body of Light, as well as the ritual's practical use as an occult means of protection by its efficacy in banishing negative or malignant spiritual forces. The Hebrew letter assigned to this Key, Cheth (ח), relates to this concept of protection and defense, as it means a fence or enclosure, such as

213

Mike Benjamin

the wall that encircles and protects the city in the background. In relation to the LPR this is akin to the Magician's circle of protection made by the projected Stars, the vibration of the Divine Names, the Flaming Circle, and the Archangelic presences that compose what we have defined earlier as the Universal Mandala.

The Chariot symbolizes the physical body. The driver, crowned by the Pentagram, symbolizes the mind or consciousness. The two sphinxes drawing the contraption represent, like Plato's white mare and black stallion pulling the flaming chariot of the soul, the dichotomy of human logic and emotion, just as their color scheme of black and white is representative of the Universal duality of Yin and Yang. The sphinxes are also symbolic of the Tetragrammaton and the four elements, as these legendary beasts are an amalgam of the four Holy Animals (i.e. lion, man, eagle, and bull). This is precisely the hidden meaning behind the form of the Baphomet as well (as seen in Levi's famous illustration), and not the foolish and profane interpretation that it somehow represents the physical appearance of the nonexistent Christian devil.

The sphinxes, in their contrasting colors, also represent the pillars of the Temple and thus show humanity's body and mind as the Temple of Spirit. The driver is therefore also traditionally considered a warrior-priest. He is one who fights for the attainment of God. This is not meant, however, in the warfare way of the old Aeon, committing proselytizing atrocities through use of the inquisitor's fire and rack, nor the slaughter of the crusader's sword and ax upon others deemed infidels or heretics. It illustrates, rather, the combat of self-imposed discipline upon one's own unredeemed moral character against the enemies of desire and fear, and the valor of self-sacrifice altruistically directed indiscriminately towards all others.[88]

---

[88] Such also is the appropriate mystical translation of the Islamic concept of Jihad as espoused by its esoteric branch, Sufism, and often erroneously interpreted by its fundamentalist factions as war on others for the purpose of forcibly converting the "infidel." True Jihad is the war on oneself against the enemies of ignorance, avarice, lust, and covetousness. As echoed in the West in one line of the prayer by the Lakota Sioux Chief Yellow Lark (1887) to the Geat Spirit Wantanka, "Make me strong, not be superior to my brothers, but to fight my greatest enemy – myself."

In his hand the driver holds the Wand of Will. He sits beneath a canopy of stars and upon his apron are inscribed stylized Astrological symbols, thus displaying that every individual's unique character and personality makeup is, in large part, determined by the mixture of such Macrocosmic forces.[89] This vehicle directed by the warrior is thus an analogy for humanity's mind and body guided by Spirit. It is this Triune formula that constitutes the Unity that is humanity. And it is this formula that is exercised and strengthened by the practice of the LPR and all Magicko-Mystico ritual in general.

As a means of conveyance carried by its wheels, The Chariot also holds identical meaning to that examined under Gimel, the camel, in Key 2. Both of these concepts in relation to the life of mankind possess identical meaning as earlier related to the Pilgrimage of the Soul, the Path of Return, the Samsara, the Law of Motion, Karmic cause and effect, the Hero's Journey, Involution and Evolution, Leela, and so forth. In regards to the LPR, the wheels are obviously representative of the form of the Universal Mandala.

Perhaps this Key is best surmised by words found in the *Upanishads*:

> "Know the Self as the Lord of the chariot. Know the intellect as the charioteer, and the mind as the reins. . .He who has understanding for the driver of the chariot and controls the reins of his mind, he reaches the end of the journey, the supreme abode of the All-Pervading." *(Katha Upanishad, 3:3)*

---

[89] In the modern West, Astrology has fallen into ill-repute due to its generalized newspaper variety, and rightfully so with such lacking "info-tainment" as its main form of representation to the public. In the past this science proved the sister of Astronomy and was developed to an amazingly accurate degree by such ancient cultures from East and West as the Chaldeans, Mayans, Persians, Egyptians, and Chinese. We mustn't forget that both Christ's and Buddha's births were accurately predicted by Astrologers.

8 | STRENGTH | ט

8 – Strength – Teth: The entire meaning of this Trump – its number, name, letter, and picture – refers to the Great Magickal Agent, the Astral Light, and to its subjugation by will. THIS IS A GREAT SECRET. . .that by the conscious processes of humankind's mentality all the powers of Nature are subject to human usage and control. Likewise, on a psychological level, all of the forces of humankind's subconsciousness are equally subordinate to the suggestions and direction of consciousness.

The Hebrew letter assigned to this key, Teth (ט), means snake or serpent, as expressed through the very shape of the letter, which is meant to convey a snake curling up to swallow its own tail, as seen with the Magician's belt in Key 1. Here again is the symbol of the Astral Light as the Ouroboras: of eternity, of evolution and entropy, of the Universal process of building up and breaking apart, of Alchemical *Coagula et Solve,* of life and death as being intertwined, each proceeding from the other in endless cycles. As earlier stated, the snake was the Ancient Master's symbol for the Astral Light due to its wavy, undulating motion representing the electromagnetic properties of positive and negative, peaks and troughs, inherent to the electrically-natured Great Magickal Agent. The snake was also understood as a sign of the Astral Light's dual properties as both a healing or harmful agent; as the medium of both White and Black Magick. The snake cyclically sheds its skin and was thus a symbol of rebirth and renewal. It was also capable of a poisonous bite and the devouring of its prey whole, and in this way, was also emblematic of destruction.

The Astral Light, while a Magickal term and theory, can be fundamentally understood from a scientific perspective. It is the basic material (*prima materia*) from which all environmental forms are built. It can be seen fundamentally as electromagnetic radiant energy whose source is the sun. As both science and the esoteric teachings espouse, the sun provides the physical energy of our world and our entire solar system. It is from this fundamental energy that all things, simple and complex, are built. As science now understands, and as was known in the ancient Mysteries, energy is nothing but tiny fundamental particles or waves moving at incredible speeds. It is but the arrangement of these patterns of energetic movement or vibration that establishes what we think of as physical or corporeal matter. This comprehension is identical to the correct definition of the Astral or Sidereal Light.

In regards to humankind's dominion or control over the Astral Light, as this card hieroglyphically displays, the student is strongly urged to review the chapter entitled "The Devil" in Eliphas Levi's (1996) monumental *History of Magic*. It will suffice here to quote one brief statement that the Magus makes therein: "The will of intelligent beings acts directly upon this light, and by means thereof, upon all nature, which is made subject to the modifications of intelligence." (p. 169). It is by development of the Will, by the positive progression of intellectual faculties as facilitated by the discipline of Magick, and the dedicated practice of such rituals as the LPR in particular, that the aspirant will gain power from and control over this Universal Energy, named in this Trump as Strength, denoting the spiritual result gained by the Magician in so doing.[90]

---

[90] Crowley's Thoth deck wrongly minimizes this Key's meaning by making a Freudian error and reducing it to mere libido, hence Thoth's title of it as "Lust." He likewise makes a great error in assigning it as Key 11, juxtaposing it with his "Justice" Trump, called in Thoth "Adjustment," assigned as Key 8 (a naming that is actually quite relevant and an improvement upon the old wording, as far as meaning goes). Whether this juxtaposition of the traditional assignment of Keys 8 and 11 in the Thoth deck is an intentional blind on his part may be possible. But this is more likely due to his emphasis upon the Scarlet Whore of Babalon (sic) seen on this card, and his emphasis upon sex Magick as related through his naming "Strength" as "Lust," both so central to Crowley's system,

The card's picture depicts a youthful woman akin to the High Priestess. Like the Magician, she wears the sideways 8, symbol of infinity, above her head. She pets and plays with a yawning or laughing lion, thus showing her subjugation of the forces of Nature and her control over the animal passions. This Lion is the Lion of Judah, the Savior, and is also the Red Lion of Alchemy, another symbol of the Astral Light, Astrologically correspondent to the sign of Leo, the serpent-lion.

Advanced Adepts are here advised to note the deep and sacred mystery conveyed by this Astrological symbol, as well as this Tarot Key. We here provide a Qabalistic hint for those unaware. In Gematria, 358 is the numerical equivalent for the word Messiach, (Messiah or Savior). This is the same as that for Nachash – another name for serpent, but also meaning bright or "shiny one." This correspondence does not reveal some ridiculous Luciferian conspiracy, as erroneously touted by the fundamentalists (i.e. that occultists revere Satan as the Savior), but rather **an Occidental revelation of Kundalini Yoga**. Contemplate this hint very deeply students.

**Astrological Sign of Leo.**

---

that he reassigns 8 to 11 – the number he rightfully ascribes to Magick. However, such changing of numbers, in my opinion, establishes more error than clarity regarding these Keys' numerical significances and their meanings when taken as a whole as parts of the Pattern upon the Trestleboard.

G.D. member Arthur Edward Waite
(10/2/1857 – 5/19/1942),
co-creator of the Rider-Waite Tarot Deck.
*"Quod Tibi id Aliis."*

The number 8 assigned to this Tarot Trump is also Saint Martin's number for Christ, the symbol of the Aurum Solis system of Magick, and representative of the Ogdoad (Denning & Phillips, 1991). As Golden Dawn charter member and high-level Mason, Arthur Edward Waite (1995) stated, "Christian Gnosticism speaks of rebirth in Christ as a change unto the Ogdoad" (p. 75).

Beyond the Dharmachakra and eight-fold Path, the eight-pointed form also holds particular significance in Buddhism in regard to the life of the Great Guru Padmasambhava, the bringer of the Mahayana and Vajrayana systems to Tibet. In the account of his life as recorded by his chief adept, the great Buddhist nun Lady Yeshey Tshoygal (incarnation of the goddess of learning, Sarasvati), it is said that one of his great missions of life was to bring the Dharma to eight countries of his time: Jambu-mala to the east of his homeland; Par-pa-ta to

Mike Benjamin

**Sign of the Lords of Chaos in the Moorcock Mythos.**

**The 8-Pointed Star – Sign of the Ogdoad.**

**Seal of Aurum Solis.**

the south; Nagapota to the west; Kashakamala to the north; Trang-srong to the southeast; Lanka to the southwest; Lung-lha to the northwest; and Kekki-ling to the northeast. At the geographic center of this area rested the Dhanakosha Lake (of his homeland Urgyan), where it is said Padmasambhava was born in a water lotus. This lotus was created by a five-pointed dorje (dagger) that emanated from the Amitabha-Buddha in the Sukhavati Heaven. Thus, in this great circumambulation of missionizing, Padmasambhava, the Great Guru and Lotus-Born One, created a giant geometrical mandala throughout the geography! (cited in Evans-Wentz, 1968, pp. 101-106, 160-161).

9 – The Hermit – Jod: The number 9 is the number of months in the human gestation period, and is thus also representative of Initiation; the process by which the adept is born into a new way of life and Being through the rebirth facilitated by Magickal ritual or ceremonial drama (such as those historically exemplified in the Eleusinian Mysteries or the Scottish Rite's use of Constantine's play). Perhaps the most well-known of these examples is provided in the Blue Lodge of Craft Masonry in their legend of Hiram Abiff, the architect of Solomon's Temple.[91]

---

[91] Every Mason becomes him in ritual form, is then killed for keeping his oaths, and then raised from the dead by the grip of the lion's paw into a new life.

This initiatory process can be facilitated by the practice of the LPR as well, for it is a way by which an individual may enjoin the Path of Return through self-initiation as a solitary practitioner (or "solitaire" in Wiccan terminology). While contrary to some traditional teachings, I assert that the entrance into a formal Magickal order or coven, for all intents and purposes, is unnecessary if the aspirant cannot find a reputable and legitimate one in their area. Sources such as this grimoire, and many others extant in occult literature today, will prove efficacious for those of adequate intellect to find their own way without a formal, personal Guru. When the student is ready the teacher will appear; and this may be in the form of books and not an actual person. Truth be told, we are all guided by forces from beyond the tangible world, and the Masters of the Other Side are always there to help and guide. Such is what Christ prophesied when he said in the last days, all that was secret (occult) shall be known. (*Luke* 8:17).

The number 9 is unique in arithmetic, as the sum of the digits of any multiple thereof will always add back to 9. This is a mathematical representation of the spiritual Truth that all things come from One Source, and to it they also return. As 4 + 5 = 9, the Hermit is also, like the Buddha, the son (or sum) of the union of Empress and Emperor grown into full spiritual maturity, as pictorially indicated by his advanced age. This Hermit is a symbol of deep significance and vast meaning. In conquering the climb up this steep mountain, like Hillary on Everest, he is the personification of the enlightened saint and sage. He is the Supreme Magus, the White Wizard, the Sri Yogi, the Great Guru. He has attained Samadhi, Moksha, Gnosis, Nirvana, Kensho/Satori, At-One-Ment; true freedom. He has ascended the Holy Mountain and stands upon its peak. In the LPR this mountain is the North element of earth. There he stands as the link between Heaven and Earth, between Spirit and matter, between God and Man. He has become the great umbilical cord as discussed in Key 6, The Lovers.

The Hermit holds a lantern containing the Hexagram as a guiding light to the others below still in ascent up the various paths that reach the summit of the Holy Mountain. In other words, he has subjugated the forces of the Macrocosm, and harnessed them as a tool through God's grace, enlightened

Wisdom, and the force of Will, and utilizes this light to teach others through his own example; to assist in their ascent back to the top of the peak; to de Chardin's Omega Point. As the Buddha said:

> "As a man of discernment, standing on a rocky eminence, beholdeth those who are below and in distress, so doth the sage, who by his wakefulness hath put to flight his ignorance, look down upon suffering mankind from the Heights of Wisdom which he hath attained."
> (*The Dhammapada*, vv. 28-29).

He is solitary, but not alone, as he symbolizes the Oneness of the individual self with all of creation and the Creator. His staff represents the power of Will and God's guiding Wisdom, but it is also traditionally ascribed to the wheat shaft, as in Masonic lore; an emblem of the seasonal rebirth of crops which mirrors the process of both reincarnation and the birth of the New human (homo novus), of the New Creature (homo spiritus – the spiritual person) through the occult secret of rapidly accelerating our own evolutionary process by being conscious co-creators of ourselves with God. As the philosopher Wilhelm Hegel first discovered, and later elaborated upon by Integralist Ken Wilber (as well as the great "ecologian" Thomas Berry): we are evolution, we are the Universe, become aware of itself! (Wilber, 2000; Berry, 2000).

The Mahayana teaches that this process is known as the Short Path, as such a goal can be attained in a single incarnation. Likewise, as demonstrated throughout this treatise, it is to this glorious end that the LPR is aimed, and to which all of our Magickal usage should aspire. Even Crowley (1970) asserted that the true purpose of Magick is to spiritually draw the Magician in a vertically straight line and that any deviation from this goal is Black Magick; for which he unfortunately and readily prostituted his genius, and in which he often engaged. Let his example stand as a stark warning to all Seekers of the Light; that when left unbridled, genius and madness can go hand-in-hand if we be not on our ever-present spiritual guard.

The Hebrew letter assigned this Trump, Jod (ʼ), means hand. In our context this refers to the hand of God that guides all of humanity and all of His creation. The Hermit's hood upon his head is in fact a stylized Yod, showing God's hand in guidance through our minds. This is a significant lesson granted the Hermit through his attainment of the peak. He has come to realize that, as John Bradford coined, "there but for the grace of God go I." Or as the Nazarene taught, "I can of mine own self do nothing. . .but the will of the Father which hath sent me" (*John* 5:30). Even Islam's very definition shares this idea, as "surrender." We must come to surrender to Allah's will and become his hand, his instrument, for his Will on Earth; A Will of Love, Peace, Harmony, and Tolerance.

<u>10 – Wheel of Fortune – Kaph</u>:    At number 10 we have completed our examination of the Tarot Trumps of prime importance in relationship to the LPR. At 10 we have likewise completed the Pythagorean decad, the Sephira on the Tree of Life, and all of the inherent symbolism attributed to 1 and 0 as previously explained in the creation of the Universal Mandala. Like the figure created by the execution of the LPR, this Key is obviously representative of the Universal Mandala as well.

In its center we see the Dharmachakra; the Cross in the Circle; the Sign of Entropy; the Great Wheel of Life. In its corners, as evidenced by the four sacred Animals, we see the formula of the Tetragrammaton, the four elements, Archangels, and directions. This Trump, though deceptively simple in appearance, is a Pantacle holding supreme esoteric significance as it comprehensively encompasses the Wisdom and cosmology of the occult sciences like the design created by the LPR. It is also remarkably similar to the personal sigil of Madam Helena Blavatsky, founder of Theosophy, and the seal of the Hermetic Brotherhood of Luxor, from which they both most likely drew this Key as their artistic inspiration.

The Hebrew letter assigned this Key is kaph (כ) meaning a closed hand or fist. Like the action of a grasping hand it shows possession and control. Magick, in this sense, like a tool or weapon, must be firmly grasped to be effectively wielded. Kaph can also be considered the Hebrew equivalent to the Mandarin Chinese words Quanfa and Qinna.[92] Though ascribed as the name of the striking art of Kung-Fu, Quanfa literally denotes "clasped Dharma hand" showing the figurative idea of grasping the Buddhist law. And though assigned to the grappling art of Gongfu, Qinna denotes "to seize and control," figuratively illustrating the fortitude we must exercise over our lower passions if we are to go beyond the condition of natural homo sapiens and gain the spiritual prize, the ascendency we seek.

In this Trump's outer circle we see contained letters that spell out the word ROTA, meaning wheel, and thus expressing all of the symbolism intrinsic to this figure that we have previously and exhaustively examined. By rearrangement of these letters, the Key also expresses a few other pertinent words. It can be made as TAROT, the pictorial key to the Universe and the subject of this section. It can be seen as TORA, Hebrew word for the Law, seen upon the High Priestess' scroll in Key 2; concomitant with the Buddhist word Dharma, and one of the Taoist meanings for Tao – all expressing the idea of the Universal Law underlying all things. It may also be read as ATOR, signifying the Egyptian goddess Hathor, personification of Nature; the Great Cow from which all our milk comes.

Upon the top of the wheel is the Sphinx, displaying the formula of the Baphomet or Tetragrammaton. Beneath him is

---

[92] The author is a 4th degree black sash, assistant master, in Kang-Nei-Chin Chung-Kuo Ch'uan Shaolin Kung-Fu which incorporates both Quanfa, Qinna, and P'ing (weaponry) systems in its curriculum.

Mike Benjamin

**Madam Helena Petrovna Blavatsky (8/12/1831 – 5/8/1891):
founding member of the Theosophical Society.**

**Personal Seal of Madam Helena Petrovna Blavatsky.**
*"There is no religion higher than truth."*

**Seal of the Hermetic Brotherhood of Luxor.**

the Egyptian god of the dead, Anubis, in rotation upon the wheel, showing the process of life, death, and rebirth – the formula of IAO. Next to him is the wavy, undulating serpent expressing the properties of the Astral Light. Within the circle are the Alchemical symbols of Salt, Mercury, and Sulphur, or body, mind, and spirit, in conjunction with the Astrological symbol for Aquarius, the age in which humanity now lives. In this glyph we see all of the LPR's and Universal Mandala's lessons summarized together in a single magnificent scene! The profundity of this Key cannot be overemphasized.

Before we conclude this exposition, a further lesson for the Magician regarding the productive use of Tarot must be made. The Keys of the Major Arcana are potent Archetypes that can be fruitfully used for meditation as visual mediums to be gazed upon, as well as for an exercise akin to the Golden Dawn's practice of "Assuming the God-Forms." In this Magickal act the Magician is to meditate in such a way that they are literally assuming the form, transforming their own self-image, into the god envisaged. As applied to the Tarot, the Magician utilizes this same practice to simply **become the Key**. The quote that follows is taken from Dr. Regardie's (2004) *Tree of Life* about this practice, but where the term "god" has been used, I have simply replaced it with "Key" standing for any of the Tarot cards of the Major Arcana's deck. It should be also noted that the Mahayana system, especially in its Tibetan forms, utilizes an identical process applied to the deities of their pantheons as artistically expressed on their Mandalas. The student is well-advised to apply this discipline.

> ". . .(the Magician) should familiarize himself with the shape and form of the (Key), the postures in which the (Key) is usually portrayed, the gestures customarily employed, and (its) colors. . .With all of these facts in memory, the student should proceed to the more difficult phase of the work which consists of the application of the Imagination and the Will, trained by his former practices. In his working. . .he should endeavor to construct before his mind's eye a perfect image or mask

of the (Key). The form must stand out boldly and clearly in the vision of the Imagination, gigantic, resplendent, and irradiating. . .These details should then be applied to the simulacrum held firmly in the mind, until it is seen before the living soul as a dynamic image...an image in which abides no trace of imperfection. It is a tremendous task of creative imagination, and an arduous one. But day after day it must be continued with ardor and devotion, until the sacred task is consummated, and, complete and glowing, the (key) stands forth. . .With this image held firmly in the Astral Light, (he) should endeavor to envelop his own form with the shroud of the (key) and then to unite himself with the Form enshrouding him. As (Eliphas) Levi has already been quoted as saying, the Astral body will assume the form of any powerful thought which the mind evokes. This Astral effigy of the (Key), previously but an image external to the body. . .should now be arranged. . .as a figure around his own astral form until they coincide, his own Body of Light being changed and transmuted into the Body of the (Key). Only when (he) actually feels the superb influx of spiritual power, the acquisition of the. . .force and energy and spiritual illumination, only when he knows in the intuition of the (Key) trance that the identification has been accomplished, is the task of creation complete... Simultaneously with the process of unification with the Body of the (Key) it will prove of no little assistance if an invocation is recited... chanting praises to the (Key), delineating the nature and spiritual qualities of the (Key) in speech. . .With the recitation of each point of the invocation. . .a strong realization in thought of the words should be obtained. . .the astral form of the (Key) should be seen and actually felt with the senses to emit a refulgence. . .the process of the identification with the Astral Form should be accomplished and realized as vividly as possible. . .By infallible signs within his own consciousness, the quickening of a new life, (he) will. . .know that success does crown his effort. In him, and in his soul, the (Key) will seek his eternal dwelling place. Within the heart will be a sanctuary and a serene habitation of a tremendous spiritual force, a... consciousness which throughout all duration will live in him, transforming the child of the earth. . .Within himself latent unfolding spiritual faculties will be felt, and the faint memory of experience gained in time long since past and dead will gradually arise to illuminate the mind and pulse anew in the heart, expanding the horizon of consciousness." (pp.254-258).

In conclusion, the practitioner of the LPR must take time to meditate upon and contemplate the first 11 Keys of the Tarot outlined above. It is also highly suggested that any student of Magick, or any branch of the occult, make ample study of the Major Arcana in general. While my bias has always been towards the BOTA deck and interpretations, and to a lesser extent the Thoth version (despite its inadequacies as previously stated), the aspirant must seek the version to which they feel the greatest affinity, whatever the source. Dozens of legitimate variations of the Tarot are now extant throughout esoteric literature and one can surely be found that resonates with each individual. While the student will find much profit in sampling a variety of deck types, aspirants are strongly encouraged to settle upon one as their base foundation for mastery. Without this a congruence will fail to be established in your studies; there will be no roots or trunk to the branches and leaves you wish to grow.

The student is also earnestly warned to beware of the deception, charlatanism, fraud, ignorance, and broad generality used by many of those (but not all) who claim Divinatory use of the Tarot. Such is, as Levi warned, the gypsy perversion of the Deck's true usage, and such manipulation of it for these purposes is dubious at best. Such suppositions, while possible within the realm of psychic phenomena and Second Sight, raise obvious questions about the space-time continuum and freewill which are far beyond our present inquiry. This utilization of the Holy Tarot for fortune telling must be judged with utmost cynicism, scrutiny, discernment, and skepticism if one is not to be easily played as a rube and made a fool. Tarot's secrets reach infinitely beyond those who set up booths at carnivals or advertise in the Yellow Pages.

Know, ye student, that the Major Arcana of the Tarot is the all-encompassing Hieroglyphic Book and Quintessential Key to unlocking the secrets of God, humankind, and the Universe. Let us quote at length a significant survey of prominent occultists' insights regarding the importance of Tarot to the aspirant as shared in the BOTA handbook, *Highlights of Tarot:*

> Judge Thomas Troward. . .writer on Mental Science wrote, "Among such records explanatory of the supreme mysteries three stand-out pre-eminent, all bearing witness to the ONE TRUTH, and each throwing light upon the other; and these three are the Bible, the Great Pyramid, and the TAROT."

> The eminent Russian philosopher, P.D. Ouspensky. . .says, "There are many methods of developing the 'sense of symbols' in those who are striving to understand the hidden forces of Nature and Man and for teaching the fundamental principles as well as the elements of the esoteric language. The most interesting of these is the TAROT.

> "The Tarot represents a summary of the Hermetic Sciences – the QABALAH, Alchemy, Astrology, and Magic with their different divisions. All these sciences really represent *one*

*system* of a very broad and deep psychological investigation of the nature of man."

Free Masonry is one survival of that ancient psychological system, although all too few Masons realize what a treasure they have inherited from the past. But their great leaders know. Consider these words of General Albert Pike, during his lifetime Grand Commander of the Southern Jurisdiction of the Scottish Rite. . .

"He who desires to attain to the understanding of the Great Secret. . .must follow, to class his acquisition of knowledge and direct the operation, the order indicated in the alphabet of the TAROT." These words are given added significance when you consider that the essential meaning of the Grand Word is MAN, and that the Great Secret is the power of controlling the hidden forces of man's inner life.

Eliphas Levi, one of the most profound students of occult science, wrote, "The TAROT is a book which epitomizes all sciences, while its infinite combinations can solve all problems; a book which speaks by evoking thought; the inspirer and controller of all possible conceptions; the masterpiece, perhaps, of the human mind and undoubtedly one of the finest things which antiquity has bequeathed to us."

In another place he says, "The TAROT is a veritable oracle, and replies to all possible questions with precision and infallibility. A prisoner, with no other book than the TAROT, if he knew how to use it, could in a few years acquire a universal science, and would be able to speak on all subjects with unequalled learning and inexhaustible eloquence. The oracles of TAROT give answers as exact as mathematics, and as measured as the harmonies of Nature. By aid of these signs and their infinite combinations, it is possible to arrive at the natural and mathematical revelation of all secrets of Nature. The practical value of the TAROT is truly and above all marvelous.

In still another place Eliphas Levi says, "The TAROT is truly a philosophical machine which prevents the mind from going astray, even while leaving it its own initiative and freedom; it is mathematics in their application to the absolute, the alliance of the real and the ideal, a lottery of thoughts, all of which are rigorously exact, like numbers, in fine, it is perhaps at once the simplest and grandest thing ever conceived by human genius."

It is known that Madam H.P. Blavatsky was at one time searching assiduously for a pack of TAROT cards. Certain it is that she was one of the greatest expounders of the doctrine embodied in the TAROT, and her penetrating and unusual books, *The Secret Doctrine* and *Isis Unveiled* prove her profound knowledge of the symbology used in these KEYS. (Case, 1989, 11-14).

**P.D. Ouspensky (3/4/1878 – 10/2/1947): Russian mathematician, author, and philosopher; Gurdjieff's greatest student.**

**G.I. Gurdjieff and friends (1/13/1866 – 10/29/1949): founder of the Fourth Way School and Sacred Dance.**

# The LPR as Yoga

The previous sections of this grimoire examined the LPR as both an act of art resulting in the creation of what we have termed the Universal Mandala, followed by an analysis of the ritual through the application of the first 11 Keys of the Tarot's Major Arcana. The sections to follow will deal with the LPR as analogous to the principles, processes, and goals of the seemingly unrelated disciplines of Hindu Yoga and Martial Arts. Upon surface examination these two disciplines may seem in stark contrast; the former being founded upon the pacifist religious traditions of Indian Brahmins and Yogins, while the latter is the evolutionary development of the fighting techniques and moral precepts of Asian Sifu and Sensei. In these contrasting viewpoints of the Priest and the Warrior, we find the duality of Archetypes universally intrinsic to human society collectively, as well as human personality individually. In them we also see the polarity inherent in the functions of Nature Herself. In one we find represented the ideas of peace and life, and in the other, destruction and death.

In this comparison of the Sage and the Soldier we will discover how necessary a healthy balance is between these Archetypes in the psyche of a fully integrated Magician. Ultimately, the occult aspirant should come to realize that these two Archetypes are but two sides to the same coin; two bars that make the same Cross; two edges upon the same sword that cuts both ways; two halves which must be harmonized for total wholeness of being. These Archetypes represent the Universal Duality, the Kosmic Polarity, the Surya and Rayi (sun and moon) of Yoga, the Yin and the Yang. In Magick we see these forces manifested as attraction and repulsion; attention and intention; as creative evolution and entropic destruction; as life and death. Such are the aspects of all the Universe as manifested in the prime substance of all things; the Magician's tool or weapon; their clay or paint – namely, the Astral Light.

Just as art can be understood as a spiritual or Magickal endeavor to the dedicated artist, so is the exercise of Magickal ritual, like the LPR, artistic to the Magician. The attitude for both is identical: one of deference, reverence, fervor, focus, and commitment. The aspirant must possess what Yoga calls Shraddha (determined seriousness) and Dhiras (unflinching commitment) combined with Brahmacharya (self-control) in order to apply proper Abhyasa (effort of practice) and to control one's Sraddha (selfish desire). Together these constitute the Yogic ideal of Ksatraysa Ksatram, "the essence of the fighter's power."

Beyond its symbolic and artistic qualities, as previously discussed, the LPR is obviously a deep and profound method of moving meditation and spiritual supplication. As Crowley (1996) says in *Book Four*,

> What is the state of either prayer or meditation?
> It is the restraining of the mind to a single act,
> state, or thought. . .It is by (this) freeing (of) the
> mind from external influences, whether causal
> or emotional, that it obtains the power to see
> somewhat to the truth of things. (p. 48).

In Buddhist phraseology, what Crowley is saying is that through such practices as prayer or meditation we are freed from our state of Avidya, from ignorance, and in so being, we see beyond the Maya (illusion) within which normal Man is ordinarily bound. What is this illusion? Simply stated, it is the error of thinking that we are separate, isolated, mortal beings apart from everything else. In Yoga, this conception is called Dvitiyam Iva, "separateness as it were." And this is the cause of all suffering, of Dukkha. The Vedas teach, "Bhrdadarshanam eva hi antarkaranam;" for seeing things as separate is the sole cause of otherness. Or as the Zen aphorism similarly states, "Between self and other resides all the suffering of the world."

As we have superficially investigated in this modest tome, this "truth of all things" that Crowley suggests above; this implied correct understanding of the true nature of reality; is based upon what we shall hereby term as the PARADIGM OF UNITY. **This paradigm advocates the comprehension that God, the Universe, and Humanity are essentially One; with the latter two being hierarchically evolving processes from the former. It is the understanding that the Each is the All, and**

**the All is in the Each.** Such a cosmology, if that is what it can be accurately called, acknowledges that there is an interrelationship, an interdependence, between EVERYTHING, from the farthest quasar to the nearest lilac bush. Science fully confirms this paradigm by teaching that every molecule in our bodies was created in the first few nanoseconds of the Big Bang. Every Terran molecular composition, from humans to diamonds to trees to fish, came from the explosions of star novae eons ago, light years upon parsecs away. In our veins runs a lifeblood with the same salt content as that of the seas, out of which our primordial fish-lizard ancestors first crawled. I wave my hand and such dissipation of the air around me reverberates to the farthest reaches of the Galaxy. I throw the proverbial pebble into the pond and onward go the ripples. Such seemingly paltry actions, exercised by Will alone, literally change the constituency of the entire Universe. Such is the premise with which all Magick works as a spiritual technology. These illustrations highlight the UNITY PARADIGM; the common Oneness of all things; the yoke of our existence.

I utilize the word "yoke" intentionally here, for as mentioned earlier, it is etymologically derived from the same Sanskrit root as the word Yoga, both meaning "Union." While an examination of all the different types of Yoga that have evolved over the centuries is beyond the span of this work, we will instead briefly survey the foundational aspects of this discipline, its use of meditation and movement, as contended by such proponents ranging from Pantanjali to Crowley. Not only in Hinduism is such a discipline espoused, but throughout all spiritual paths amongst all times and places have such methods been utilized under different descriptions and emphasis.

In its seated and silent form of meditation, for example, Yoga has been performed in systems ranging from Buddhist Ch'an[93] and Zen, to the desert solitude and stillness practices of the early Coptic Christian fathers in Egypt. Even Christ metaphorically alluded to the process of meditation, ". . .when thou prayest, enter into thy closet, and when thou hast shut thy

---

[93] Founded by the Indian Buddhist monk Bodhidharma, called Daruma in India, and Tamo in Japan, during the 5th or 6th centuries C.E. at the Shaolin Monastery in China. He legendarily tore off his own eyelids and stared at a wall to achieve enlightenment. He is also credited with inventing Shaolinquan (gongfu).

door, pray to thy Father which is in secret." (*Matthew* 6:6, King James Version). This is the closet of the mind, and shutting the door is the process of ceasing the registry of the senses and the flow of thought; the two prime components of all meditation. In doing so, as the Tibetans teach, one comes to know the mind in its natural state, or in what they also call its "nakedness."

Perhaps the simplest, yet starkest example of Yogic meditative insight taught in a non-Hindu work comes from the Old Testament's Book of Psalms. Legendarily attributed to King David, he says, "Be still and know that (the) I Am is God." (*Psalm* 46:10, King James Version).

In its moving and stretching forms (like the Hatha system), Yoga can be seen as a background influence upon everything ranging from Taoist Qigong and Tai Chi, to the whirling dervishes in Sufism, and even in the Fourth Way School's sacred dances founded by Gurdjieff. In each, the discipline of the body, through motion, is enforced through the Will of the mind. The proper usage of the life-force is likewise emphasized by the primacy placed upon proper breathing.

In all these expressions their ultimate purpose is to achieve awakening of the individual from their slumber of spiritual ignorance. Thus, in their ideal perfected form, Yoga and the LPR are both designed to catalyze the attainment of union between the individual practitioner and All That Is. This union is often termed Moksha (liberation) or Samadhi (union with the Lord) in Yoga and is expressive of their famous aphorism "The Atman (indwelling self) is one with the Brahman (God or the All Self)."[94] This idea is also expressed in

---

[94] In the Hindu pantheon, though extensive and elaborate in its polytheism, all gods spring from the One All-Mighty God, typically called Brahman, but also referred to as Parusha, Ishvara, and other names. The gods are thus subdivided personifications of Archetypal and natural forces. The great secret of all Hindu paganism, it seems, like the ancient Egyptian variety, is that there is only one God. As the Hindus say, all gods are one. This lesson is but an amalgamation, or conglomeration, of the four main but differing cosmologies of Humanity – Monotheism, Paganism, Pantheism, and Panentheism. In Monotheism, there is only one God separate and transcendent from the Creation, but who often intervenes with a Divine hand. In Paganism there are many gods in this world and in the heavenly other-realms, each assigned its own sphere influence or area of power. In Pantheism, the sum total of the Universe itself is the only God that exists. And in Panentheism, the Divine is present in the Each, and as the All, but still remains distinct from the Creation, being both immanent and

the equally recited adage, "Tat twam asi" or "Thou art That." In the LPR or Western Magick, this attainment, as we have cited, is termed the 5 = 6; the reconciliation of the Microcosm with the Macrocosm, or also the accomplishment of the Great Work. All these verbiages express the same goal in but different cultural terms relevant to the systems from which they originated. Let not these differences confuse you, but instead seek the perennial meaning behind them all.

Let us now briefly explore some of the affinities between the LPR and Yoga. In so doing we will look at some of the basic pretexts of the Yogic philosophy. While no means exhaustive, such a foundational examination will better exemplify the obvious analogies between our subjects. The student is strongly urged to make a serious study of any one of the myriad of translations of the foundational textbook on Yoga, namely Pantanjali's ancient *Yoga Sutras*.

Tantra: The word Tantra simply denotes the techniques utilized in Yoga. This term has fallen into an erroneous definition in the Freudian West where it has become synonymous with sexual Magick and other occulto-erotic practices. While it is true that some methods of Tantra are sexually based, Tantra is far from exclusively so, with the majority of Tantric practices being non-sexual. In fact, throughout a preponderance of Tantric teachings (from not only

---

transcendent simultaneously. In the practice of the LPR, the cosmology held by the practitioner is completely irrelevant, even if one be an Atheist or Agnostic, as were (surprisingly to most) both Crowley and Regardie! How one will view the form and function of the ritual will be flavored though their own particular cosmological lens, but will not affect the results thereby gained.

Furthermore, when approached from an Integral perspective, all cosmologies hold some truth while no single one holds it all. Perhaps an amalgam of them comes closest to the actuality of reality. Monotheism acknowledges the Unity, the Oneness of Divinity. Polytheism perceives the manifested Many in their varying Divine aspects. Pantheism sees the visible, tangible God as the Universe, as the All, as immanent. Panentheism comprehends a distinct, transcendent aspect of this same immanent God at exactly the same time. Nihilism relates the ultimate unanswerable mystery of existence by arguing that nothing really matters. Atheism transmits this same unanswerable Mystery as incomprehensible, and thus, unreal. Agnosticism shares this Mystery as but a possibility that cannot be known. In each of these views is hidden one component of the truth, while any one alone falls short of unveiling the whole answer. In their combination exists the grand solution.

the Hindu but also the Buddhist systems) the exercise of chastity is emphasized as a spiritual discipline. This emphasis is not based so much upon any moral dicta, but instead upon the fact that the sexual energies of the body, rooted in Kundalini, need to be harnessed and sublimated towards spiritual attainment and not frivolously wasted in carnal pleasure fulfillment sought through physical desire. This is, rather, one of the primary areas of human instinct that must be harnessed and redirected for further spiritual development to occur.

The student is advised to study the preeminent work on Tantra from the Hindu culture – *The 108 Exercises of the Vigyam Bhairav Tantra of Shiva*. The version with commentary provided by the late Guru Osho (1974) is of noteworthy value in this regard. This Tantric work, purportedly 5,000 years old, was legendarily authored by the god Shiva Himself and is alleged by its proponents to be the extant root source in the world's various religions of all meditative, contemplative, and visualization techniques for attaining enlightenment. In it, as we have argued above, sexual Tantra is a relatively minor concern with only a handful of techniques from its 108 exercises constituting any sensual practices. The student of this work is not taught by the Guru to utilize all 108 methods, but is, rather, instructed to experiment with them all in order to find the one or the few that particularly resonate with their own specific personality and constitution, and then to focus on those alone. Here, it is said, will be the ones that will work.

We may likewise categorize the LPR as being Tantric by this definition; Tantra being simply any spiritual technique or practice designed to facilitate the student's awakening from the standard human condition of illusion and ignorance and liberating them from the ensuing byproduct of suffering.

Asana: Asana refers to the proper bodily posture assumed by the Yoga practitioner in meditation to foster the proper flow of prana through the body (kundalini through the chakras) and the proper mental state of tranquility. Perhaps the most famous of these is the seated "lotus posture," though many others are also used. For the same reasons, in the LPR such an assumption of proper bodily form, sometimes static, sometimes moving, is equally crucial to its Magickal success. For example, one must utilize a firm and upright spinal position reminiscent of the erect phallus and its creative emanating energies when vibrating the Divine Names or when taking the form of the cross in the declaration of the Great Work. In the tracing of the Pentagrams, and encircling flaming ring with the dagger, exact form and proportion and precise symmetry must be achieved in the arm's motions. In whatever action being taken in the ritual's performance the Magician must strive for perfection in the physical shape and alignment of their form. This will work to facilitate the free flow of air through proper deep breathing and will thus help create the vibrant vocalizations being carried to the ends of the universe. Correct physical alignment of posture will also support the cascade of Magickal current (prana, Qi) necessary for any execution of Magick. Sloppy or slothful posture will not promote success in the operation but will stifle the energies needing to be harnessed and directed. The body's form, in short, must reflect the will and intent of the Magician; one of strength, one of focus, and one of complete self-control. As without, so within.

Prana: In the Yogic scheme, the life-force or energy is explained on both the Macrocosmic (Universal) and Microcosmic (individual) levels. Universal energy, or the life-force manifested on the Kosmic scale, is referred to as Prakriti and corresponds to our Western Magickal conception of the Astral Light as created with the FIAT LVX. Both are the prime substance, or what Alchemy calls the First Matter, from which the Universe is constructed. It is the common building block of all time, space, energy, matter, and thought in their most fundamental forms. It is the "Planck unit," if you will, of String theory or Quantum particles, to use a scientific hypothesis for contrast.

From a scientific perspective, this Universal Energy can be demonstrated by such measurable forces or phenomena as light, heat, electricity, magnetism, and gravity. It is likewise seen in the fusion process of stars and their emission of electromagnetic radiation (EMR), and in the bi-polar planetary magnetism of the earth. EMR, as science tells us, is the fuel of life. This Prakriti comprises all forms of matter in the Kosmos as well, simply by the differentiation within its vibrational frequency; solidity versus subtlety being but a difference in its energetic rate of vibration. The revelations of physics in this modern age have again proven but an echo of ancient Yogic (and Buddhist) principles in concluding that all matter is an arrangement of energy particles, and that what seems to us as solid forms are but sub-atomic compositions of, paradoxically, mostly empty space – of nothing, of the Void (Shunyata).

Prakriti, however, when referred to in its individualized form manifest through the life of plants and animals, is known as Prana. Prana is the breath of Brahman; the vehicle of the soul, called the Jiva or Jivatman. It is always associated with the concept of wind or air, as well as blood. In plants this is manifest in the process of photosynthesis and is stored within their sap or nectar. In animals this is manifest through our respiratory and circulatory systems, as well as in the production and use of acetylcholine through the processes of digestion and cellular metabolism. Like the Sun, our bodies too emit energy in the form of heat and light, seen by clairvoyants in our auras. Like the Earth, we too are bi-polar magnets emitting the forces of attraction and repulsion in our personal gravities. For astute students, here lies another secret, another hint, to the application of practical Magick.

While both the ancient esoteric and the modern exoteric viewpoints have arrived at a consensus on this concept of energy as the basis of all things, there still exists a fundamental difference in their perceptions. The esoteric, unlike the exoteric, acknowledges that through certain spiritual disciplines (like Yoga in the East or Magick in the West) humans can come to amplify this energy, be more personally sensitive to it, and individually utilize it for their own ends. By use of mind and body, by use of breath and Will, humans can learn that they are a channel and transformer of Prakriti into Prana, and thereby use it for various White or Black purposes. Positively, it may be used for health and healing, for spiritual awakening, and other altruistic goals. Negatively, it can be used to hurt and harm, to manifest personal power, and other selfish ends. Through the use of Yoga, just as with the LPR, the practitioner must utilize their own Prana, and the Prakriti of the Kosmos (the Astral Light) for reasons corresponding only to such White purposes as stated above. Likewise in the LPR, just as in Yoga, this life-force, whatever name we assign it, is used as the substance for the tracing of the Pentagrams, the formulation of the Flaming

Ring, the establishment of the Archangels, the vibration of the Divine Names, the visualization of the Hexagram, and so forth.

Yama: While on some levels denoting morality, the Yogic concept of Yama also pertains to the practitioner's control of their physical, mental, and emotional faculties. As a "thought exercise," and as a ritual act of Magick, the LPR is one of the most comprehensive ways contained in such a brief exercise that Yama can be both applied and strengthened in the aspirant. Just as with the intellectual faculties that are improved through reading or study, or even the athletic building of muscle through lifting weights, Yama is developed through the employment of spiritual exercise, of which the LPR represents one of the paramount examples in Western Esotericism.

Pranayama: In Yoga, Pranayama is the willful control and regulation of Microcosmic life energy (Prana) and its harmonization with Macrocosmic energy (Prakriti) for the purposes of improved health and well-being and for the goal of achieving liberation and awakening. These techniques are characterized in Yoga by special mental visualizations, proper breathing, and postures designed to facilitate such ends. This is identical to the usage of precise motions, visualizations, and vocalizations as exhibited in the LPR.

Yoga's use of Pranayama for the purpose of achieving spiritual liberation is also facilitated on bodily and subtle levels by the awakening of Kundalini, the coiled serpent energy located in the base of the spine, and its sublimation upwards through the Nadis, or energy meridians, (analogous to the Taoist Jingluos), through the ascending Chakras (analogous to the Taoist Dan Tiens). These Nadis intertwine as they rise upwards through the Chakras. This same theory has been emblematically preserved in the Western esoteric traditions by the symbol of the Caduceus held by the god Hermes. As the messenger of the gods, this wand, consisting of a red and blue serpent interlaced, is his tool for bringing humanity their Divine messages. In another Greek allegory, it was these same red and blue serpents which Hercules wrestled apart and slayed as a babe in his crib.

This same concept of energy channels and centers is mirrored in the LPR by the use of the Qabalistic Cross and the drawing down of the Divine White Brilliance through the

Middle Pillar, from the Macrocosmic Kether to the individual Kether, and down through the bodily Sephira. This path follows the following route: forehead (Kether); to Daath down the nape of the neck; to Tiphareth in the heart; out to the left and right Pillars of Severity and Mercy in equilibrated balance; to Yesod in between the hips; to Malkuth in the soles of the feet; and then back up again to create a perpetual circuit or orbit of energy (analogous to the Taoist Great Circulation). This rising and falling orbit of energy, subsequently utilized for the LPR's horizontal projections, is represented in Qabalah upon the Tree of Life as the Descent of the Flaming Sword (or Lightning Bolt) and the Ascent of the Winged Serpent. Thus, the Tree is grown in both directions; its roots down and its branches upward.

*The Emerald Tablet of Hermes* (8th Century C.E.) hints at this practical use of energy when it states in its 8th precept: "Use your mind to its full extent and rise from Earth to heaven, then descend to Earth and combine the power of that which is above with that below." [95] This energy is then projected outward horizontally into the Universe, to the four quarters, and is used to manifest the Pentagrams, Flaming Circle, Archangels, and so on. Also note that this merging of the vertical energy orbit with the horizontal one is another manifestation of Cross symbolism. In this schematic we see a more complex and encompassing Magickal version of Yogic Pranayama as applied in the LPR. With its rising and falling circuit and the energy projection cast out and then reabsorbed at the ritual's finale, the energy flow created in the LPR proves more comprehensive and more difficult to master than the simple rising Kundalini path advocated in Yoga. However, in being more comprehensive and difficult, its ensuing results, in this aspirant's humble opinion, prove superior to Yoga's practice.

The lesson unveiled through the Pranayama created by the LPR is one of great practical importance in advanced Magick. The horizontal extension of the vertical current of force is both the medium of the Magician's Will and the stimulus of occult effects upon environmental reality. It is a channeling of the vertical orbit of force drawn down (invoked), received from the One Source, from the Grace of Godhead. It is then

---

[95] From the author's own personal, unpublished translation.

transformed through the Magician, through the center of his/her Universe (him/herself), and is thereby being used for calculated effects in and upon the world. This vertical orbit is then extended upwards again in sign of reverence, awe, and love to the Ain Sof Aur from which it came. In more poetic terms, the vertical orbit is the Nile, while the Magician is its locks and dam. The Magi's Will becomes the canal leading therefrom, just as the horizontal current is the tributary irrigating and giving fruitful bloom to the once barren surrounding fields of dry dirt and blowing Egyptian sands.[96]

Mantrayoga: Mantrayoga is the form of Yoga in which the practitioner augments the processes of Asana and Pranayama by the repetition of the rhythmic vocalization of scriptural phrases or names of god(s) timed with the exhalation of breath, or, in contrast, by simply repeating the words internally in the mind without vocalization. This word or phrase is the Mantra. In many schools the mantra is individualized for the particular student, being given to them by the Guru in secret, with no one else being allowed to know what it is. Mantras are often selected scriptures from the *Vedas* or *Upanishads* or are names of beneficent gods like Ganesha or Krishna.

The purpose of the mantra is threefold. One, the sound and repetition of the Mantra assist the aspirant in drowning out all superfluous thoughts and external distracting stimuli from both the environment and body, bringing the mind into sole focus upon the meditation. It therefore assists the Yogin in achieving one-pointedness of mind, pure focus, unsullied concentration. In this way it can be said to be a form of auditory Dharana, to be explained below. That is to say, what Dharana does by focusing the mind by an optical process, so do Mantras concentrate the mind by the use of hearing via a repetitive sound (i.e. the name, phrase, etc.).

Two, the sound vibrations established are also believed to have a helpful or favorable effect upon the aspects of external reality, upon some facet of the world, as they expand out into the Universe due to the subject from which they are derived (i.e.

---

[96] The reader is again advised to study the charts presented in Appendix B of this work for a thorough comparison of various systems' energy-center models.

a loving god or holy scripture). Most often it is taught that Mantras, in this function, allow control or usage of some class of spiritual being. Dr. Evans-Wentz (1968) footnotes in his *Tibetan Book of the Great Liberation* such an explanation:

> Each living thing, in all states of existence, possesses a bodily form attuned to a certain frequency of vibration. A mantra is a syllable or series of syllables of the same frequency as the thing or being (usually an invisible spiritual being, god, or demon) to which it appertains; and an expert magician who knows the mantra of any deity or order of lesser beings can, if intoning it properly, invoke the deity or dominate the lesser beings. (p. 141, footnote #1).

Three, and this is the most significant purpose from an occult view, **the vibrations of the Mantra are meant to cause a direct change upon the human organism.** Just as when a vibration of particular notes, when applied to a plate of sand, will cause the sand to shift into particular patterns, so does the mantra act upon the chemical composition of the brain **affecting alterations in certain glandular and cellular structures.** The result is an awakening of an area in the human brain that otherwise lies dormant in the common person, accelerating the evolution of this particular organ, and giving birth to a new individual via the genesis of a different species. This secret has been poetically hinted at elsewhere in this work, and due to sacred Oaths, as much as I can give regarding this Mystery has been given. The exceptional aspirant will here have enough with which to work to be fruitful in this issue, but I will reiterate these clues in poetic form:

> In the cradle of Jesus deep within,
> In Bethlehem, the house of bread,
> A baby's meal, the mammal's making, the chyle is absorbed.
> The snake climbs high
> From lotus to lotus, wheel to wheel
> Riding songs to God and His visions,

> Knots untied and sickness healed.
> As the tide that crashes upon the shore,
> Makes the seed of the pine grow to be more –
> The new sand born, crystallized behind the eyes.

This resultant goal is identical to the purposes of all Alchemy, of transmuting the base lead into gold, and having our outcomes championed through the dedicated practice of the LPR. **(A further hint for advanced aspirants: Note that this process is also related in the Major Arcana by the combination of Keys 14, 13, 12, 9 as well as 17, 16, 18, 19, 20, 21).** To this end, the reader is again strongly directed to the BOTA curriculum of Paul Foster Case originating from the guidance of the Ascended Master R.[97] In this regard, one is advised to pay especial attention to BOTA's lessons concerning Spiritual Alchemy and the Great Work.

The parallels between the Yogic application of sound via Mantras and sound as used in the LPR should be obvious. The vocalizations of the LPR within the Qabalistic Cross, but especially within the vibration of the Divine Names, hold the same exact functions and purposes as those elicited from the use of Mantras. The four Tetragrammatons are, in fact, nothing but Westernized Mantras of the Qabalistic-Hermetic-Magickal

---

[97] This is of specific pertinence to Americans, as the Count Rakoczy is the particular Divine Ray put in charge of overseeing the spiritual guidance of this great nation, and from whom the great experiment in human freedom was catalyzed within the founding fathers. Whether this great political experiment will ultimately work and prove permanently fruitful or instead show America fallen into a tyrannical culture is yet to be seen, especially considering the current troubling spiral downward being taken by America into a fascist (corporate controlled), surveillance-based, imperialist war-mongering, militarized police state. The fact that (at the time of this writing) the executive administration of Barack Hussein Obama is completely antithetical to the very legal foundation of American government, namely the U.S. Constitution and the Bill of Rights, via totalitarian executive orders and legislation (i.e. the NDAA, the National Resource Preparedness Order, Patriot Act 2, Obamacare, etc. etc.) lends itself to a frightening outcome for a nation that was once the bastion and model for world liberty. Alas, this is a separate topic to be taken up by political scientists now as well as historians in the future. Beware what comes, all ye patriots, as the time for readiness draws ever nigh! Let it suffice to say, that in addition to being a devout occultist and dedicated martial artist, the author is also an avid "truther" and "prepper." The interested reader is referred to the author's political essays upon his dojo's website (closequarterskempo.com).

tradition. The vibratory frequencies established by these recitations create not only patterns that reverberate via the Astral Light so utilized, and upon the Astral Plane (i.e. the Buddhist Bardo), but also ripples of force that extend throughout the material plane of the Universe (the Qabalistic Assiah, or the Buddhist Nirmanakaya) and throughout the ascending strata of all existence (i.e. the Qabalistic Yetzirah, Briah, and Atziluth; or the Buddhist Samogkhakaya and Dharmakaya).

These vibrations also possess the identical rationale as the Yogic Mantra as they are meant to stimulate the genetic alteration of the human organism; to accelerate the biological evolution of the species beyond the normal velocity carried out by Nature's time frame. The Divine Names, like other Words of Power within Magick or Yogic Mantras, possess intrinsic power in the way they stimulate the mind of the orator by automatically invoking images and their associated meaning. As prominent occult scholar Richard Cavendish (1983) explains,

> In magical theory the 'real' name of a god or an
> idea contains the essence of that god or idea,

> and therefore enshrines its power. Using this name turns on this power automatically, in the same way pressing the light switch turns on the light. (p. 123).

Thus, the Mantra or Magickal word must be understood as both sacred and alive, like the breath that utters it.

As food for thought, however, in our final analysis of Mantras, we end with the important contrast provided by Dr. Evans-Wentz (1968), "Words being, as the Buddhas teach, merely sangsaric means of expounding the Dharma, it matters not how they are written or spoken so long as they contain the meaning intended, and thus assist mankind to attain the Great Liberation" (p. 163).

Dharana: Dharana is the practice of controlled visualization of particular object, symbol, hieroglyph, or artistic rendering of a deity within the Mind's Eye, within the Imagination. The purpose of such an exercise is to absorb the essence or intrinsic power that the chosen object possesses. Crowley (1991) explains that Dharana is the ". . .actual restraint of the consciousness to a single imaginary object chosen for that purpose" (p. 71).

What the Mantra is to sound and hearing, the object of Dharana is to light and sight. Or by analogy of Tarot, the Mantra is to the Hierophant what Dharana is to the Emperor. Just as the Mantras cause a change in the genetic constitution of the human organism via sound wave, so does the exercise of Dharana foster such organic growth as well through the use of Light and quantum particle.

In the LPR, Dharana is manifested in the various visualizations in the creation of the Universal Mandala. In addition to the bio-physical and genetic modifications created in the organic homo sapien structure (as hinted at earlier), these images in Dharana and sounds within the Mantras, as we have seen, act directly upon the mind of the Magician and perform the purpose of expanding the horizons of human consciousness. Only in the harmonization of the above ingredients, in the perfection of Asana, Pranayama, Mantrayoga, and Dharana, whether in the application of Yogic or Magickal forms, will Dhatu Prasadat (stilling of the constituents of the senses) be attained and the following results of Pratyahara and Dhyana come to fruition.

Pratyahara: While the above components of Asana, Pranayama, Mantra, and Dharana comprise specific Tantra, Pratyahara differs in that it is one of the goals of this formulated process whether achieved through Yoga or the Magickal processes of the LPR. Attaining Pratyahara achieves two abilities within the practitioner. One is an absolute inhibitory control over all thoughts and emotions. Intellectually, this allows acute concentration on and analysis of anything the superfluous stimuli and contraindicated negative thought patterns may be eliminated by Will alone. Likewise, the adept is able to control and channel emotional energies for purposefully designed ends. He is able to perform the miracle of transforming the demons of hate, fear, lust, envy, avariciousness, and prejudice into the opposing deities of love, courage, control, respect, altruism, and tolerance. The person who has achieved Pratyahara is thus vastly different from others in that they are the master of their mind and feelings, and are not, as are the preponderance of our species, a slave to them.

To make a fundamentalist analogy, Pratyahara can be seen as the spiritual ability to resist temptation and deny sin. In a Buddhist sense it can be seen as the overcoming of sorrow by the denial of desire and fear. It is hitting, rather than missing, the mark.[98] It is a source for increased happiness, for as the threshold of desire is lessened, so is the horizon of joy expanded. It is a source for improved peace, for as the bar of fear is lowered, so is tranquility heightened. As Sri Ramana Maharshi (2008), the great 20th century Indian sage, taught, "All scriptures, with one voice, declare that control of the mind is absolutely necessary for the attainment of salvation. Hence, control of the mind is the goal to be aimed at." (p. 142).

Along with these beneficial outcomes, Pratyahara affords the adept the ability for deep introspection, accurate reflection, and critical self-analysis unsullied by the erring self-justification inflicted by our usual egos. Though a Yogic teaching, perhaps

---

[98] The true and original meaning of "sin;" to miss the mark; to not achieve what one has aimed for.

Pratyahara, with a little literary free license, can be best epitomized as the unified attainment of the following trinity of virtuous instructions provided to us by Western antiquity:

> As Socrates said, "Know thyself."
> Cicero said, "Control thyself."
> And as Jesus taught, "Give thyself."

Know, control, and give yourself. Such is the lesson of Partyahara as achieved through the Tantras of either Yoga, or its Western counterpart, White Magick.

Dhyana: Like Pratyahara, Dhyana is a sought-after goal of Yoga or Magick, as manifested from such practices as the LPR. This next progressive step in consciousness-attainment is characterized by a loss of the sense of space and time, of duality and causality, and a uniting of subject and object. In the LPR such a state is experienced, once perfected practice is gained, with the Magician uniting as One with the Universal Mandala created. In this state, he or she becomes the Universal Mandala and all it symbolizes. The Kosmos for them becomes no less than the extension of themselves; their environment becomes their expanded body; and the Universe's space their consciousness, the emptiness upon which all of reality unfolds. This can be likened to the understanding of the Magister Templi who comprehends the Truth that they are not within the Universe, but the Universe is, in Truth, within them; the Advaitic principle that you and it are not two but One!

This attitude is expertly elucidated by the Western Guru, Dr. Wayne Dyer (1999), himself inspired by the practice and mastery of Yoga. In one of the most seminal works ever written in the modern era on the subject we are calling Magick, in his incomparable *Manifest Your Destiny,* his third principle states,

> You are not an organism in an environment. You are an enivronorganism. . .it is absolutely impossible to describe ourselves as separate from our environment. . .there is absolutely no difference between you and your environment. You are your environment and. . .your environment is you. . .your environment (is)

your extended body. . .you are not separate
from the external world you see. . .You cannot
be. . .independent of your environment. . .It is
an extension of yourself, just as you are an
extension of the environment (p. 47).[99]

In this spiritual state, the normal confines of our limited intelligence are vastly extended and greatly expanded. The restrictions of our consciousness imposed by modernization, inflicted upon us by countless generations of cultures immersed in selfishness and aggression, have inevitably separated us from our One Source (call It God), and His/Her Creation. This is the true meaning behind the allegory of the fall from Eden. Dhyana is a return to this state of connection with All That Is.

Dhyana is not so much an attainment of new powers or faculties, however. It is more a reawakening, an "Anamnesis" (a remembering), of what we have long forgotten about ourselves. It is recalling sensitivities lost to many, buried deep within, but manifested in all times and places by personas we have capriciously called Gurus and Sages, Shamans and Seers, Wizards and Witches, Prophets and Mystics, Buddhas and Avatars.

Dhyana is also characterized by the mental ability to unlock a veritable unending stream of information, a continuous train of knowledge, from the object being visualized or meditated upon in Dharana. In the LPR, each symbol individually projected can serve this Dhyanic function as can the Universal Mandala taken as a whole. Appendix A of this grimoire is a meager example of this type of flowing, fluid, correspondent data implied by the imagery and formulae of the LPR, that can be accessed by the dilated state of consciousness known in Yoga as Dhyana.

Samadhi: Like the prerequisite stages of Pratyahara and Dharana, Samadhi is the next rung in the ascending ladder of consciousness fostered by the processes of both Yoga in the East and Magick in the West. If we examine the etymology of the word, "Sam," from the Sanskrit, is a prefix meaning "together

---

[99] This same truth was also proposed years prior to Dr. Dyer by the spiritual Master and Western Buddhist Alan Watts.

with." "Adhi," from the Sanskrit, denotes "the Lord," as in God or Divinity, and is the linguistic root to the Tetramgrammaton ADNI in Hebrew. Hence, Samadhi can be understood as "being together with the Lord," or "union with God." Crowley (1991) describes Samadhi as when ". . .the Many and One are united in a union of existence and non-existence" (p. 72). This can likewise be considered a precise definition for the Buddhist concept of Nirvana. In Western Magickal terms relevant to the LPR we can recapitulate this concept by saying Samadhi is the Fulfillment of the Great Work, the achievement of the 5 = 6; it is Gnosis and At-One-Ment. It is the annihilation of the false in the real, of the little ego into the Big Self.

This state can be experienced briefly, as but a temporary glimpse of Truth and Reality, in meditation, ritual Magick, or other Tantras. This impermanent, fleeting experience of Samadhi is known in Zen as Satori, and is personified in Tarot by The Tower. However, these temporary moments of Samadhi, when eventually experienced enough times or in sufficient intensity, act together as a "critical mass," so to speak, ultimately leading to the explosion into this state of ascended consciousness as a permanent, unending condition, called Kensho in Zen.

In Yoga this is referred to by various terms. As Moksha, the most common of these terms, it denotes liberation or salvation. It is called Sahaja when the meditative state of enlightenment continues uninterrupted in the changing world. It is also called Muktika or deliverance; and the achievement of Sabdabrahman, ultimate reality; or attaining Svaraj, freedom.

Such a transition of consciousness is also expressed in Yoga by the Mahavakyas – statements of truth or realization. These include Tat Twam Asi (Thou art That); Isa Vasyam Idam Sarvam (All This is filled with the Lord); Ayam Atma Brahman (the self is God); Prajnanam Brahma (consciousness is God); So' Ham Asmi (That very Self am I); and the grand statement which Jesus was condemned for blasphemy by the Pharisees, and to which exoteric Christianity has misunderstood ever since – Aham Brahmasmi (I Am God).[100]

---

[100] Jesus did not reserve this declaration for Himself alone. No. He did not purport Himself the grand exception to all mortal others, but declared Himself as the great rule for all others to realize. As He stated, "Is it not written in your

By Tarot analogy it is personified in various Keys, each with a slightly different meaning, but all holding, amongst other lessons, this idea of permanent Samadhi. These Trumps are The Hermit, The Hanged Man, The Sun, and The World. The Hermit and The Hanged Man represent this attainment in the individual. The Sun, shining above the reborn children symbolic of regenerated, evolved humanity, shows this attainment throughout our whole species. And The World shows how this evolution of humanity could thus affect our planet, and even the Universe, *in toto*.

This entire Yogic process outlined above can be easily summarized for brevity and comprehension. By Pranayama impurities of the body are cast out; by Dharana, mental impurities are eliminated; by Pratyahara the impurity of attachment; and by Samadhi is obliterated everything that veils the soul's singular and supreme Lordship over all.

In conclusion, it is readily admitted that my above attempt to synthesize the teachings of Eastern and Western esotericism, or of Yoga and Magick specifically, is not necessarily novel. Such a synthesis of Eastern and Western teachings has been dealt with by far greater minds of the past such as Eliphas Levi, Madam Blavatsky, Alice Bailey, Dion Fortune, and Aleister Crowley. This fusion has even been covered by the philosophical genius Aldous Huxley (1970) through his origination of the *Perennial Philosophy* (as first covered in his masterpiece of the same name). It has been comprehensively dealt with by the unprecedented anthropological and psychological work of the spiritual prodigy Ken Wilber and his philosophical school of Integral Methodological Pluralism (or simply, "Integralism") which he founded, and with which I identify my own belief system. Nevertheless, these areas summarized above, despite the superficiality of my examination, still represent a vital outline of the basic processes that must be comprehended as analogous to the form and function of the LPR. Without them, this seminal

---

law, 'I have said – Ye are gods"? (*John* 10:34). And elsewhere he furthers, ". . .I am in the Father, and you in me, and I in you" (*John, 14:20*). Remember too, as the stoic and wise emperor-philosopher Marcus Aurelius taught, ". . .it is very possible to be a divine man and to be recognized as such by no one. Always bear this in mind" (cited in Eliot, 1969, p. 252).

Western Magickal ritual's meaning will be but dim in the eyes of the aspirant and will fail to glow with the full flame of which it is capable in casting light upon our walk down this world's shadowed path.

# The LPR as Analagous to Karate Kata

As far as historical and anthropological research currently reveals, the ancient martial arts Masters of Asia were the first warriors to develop a unique method of individual training for the preservation of fighting techniques and strategies, called in Japan and Okinawa, the Kata.[101] In most cultures of the Orient, nearly all traditional martial arts utilize some version of

---

[101] Kata is the term utilized for such "forms" in Japanese and Okinawan martial arts. In Chinese martial arts they are known as Tao Liu, Quan, and Kuen; in Korean forms Hyung; in Indonesian, Djuru and Langkha; and in Filipino they are called Anyos. Note that these practices are represented by both unarmed and armed (weapons) types. For pictures of the author and his Sifu displaying movements from Okinawan Kata and Chinese Tao Liu along with their applications, see Michael Benjamin's "The 4 Stages of Development in Gong-Fu," *Inside Kung-Fu Magazine* (January 2004, pp. 98 – 102, & 104).

"forms," with literally hundreds of them being extant throughout the martial systems thereby represented. While not a universal rule, most of these forms are based in part, or wholly, on movements or tactics which their originators gained from observing the predatory behavior and fighting methods of various animals. The most typical of these are the tiger, snake, eagle, crane, monkey, and mantis with mythological animals also represented such as the dragon and phoenix.

While many countries and martial arts systems utilize this training method under different names, for purposes of brevity, we will be referring to the use of Kata in one of the most renowned and familiar types of martial arts in the world, namely Karate. Usually translated into English as "forms," Karate Katas are a prearranged set of combatively oriented calisthenic movements designed to be performed in exactly the same way every time. To an observer, the Kata appears as a "fighting dance" in which the Karateka (practitioner) engages multiple invisible enemies in self-defense by exercising a set of stylized movements through punches (tsuke), strikes (uchi), blocks (uke), kicks (geri), and stances (dachi). The footwork utilized in so doing traces a specific performance line or pathway upon the ground, called in Karate its Enbusen.

The intended effects upon the dedicated Karateka (practitioner) are many. One, it is meant as an exercise designed to build physical strength, balance, power, precision, and speed for the execution of Karate technique. It not only builds the power of the musculature, but the respiratory and circulatory components of athleticism as well.

Two, it is meant as a mental exercise to build the student's memory, foster focus and concentration (Kimei), and to develop the mind's ability to flow as manifested in the proper flowing physical motion within the Kata (Nagashi). By memorizing the Kata and through repetitive practice, the Karateka strives to ingrain its performance into their muscle memory so that it can be executed as flawlessly and naturally as a reflex. In perfecting this Kimei and Nagashi, the Karateka learns to manifest the mental state of Munenmoso No Heiho (to be free of all useless thoughts).

Three, the Kata hides meanings as its movements are often symbolic, reflecting multiple levels of actual combative applications (Bunkai) that are not readily apparent to the untrained eye and must be revealed to the student by the Sensei (instructor). There are also secret meanings and techniques assigned to many of these movements known as Himitsu (hidden hand). These are often motions that appear as either strikes or blocks, or seem completely nonsensical, but actually possess clandestine grappling applications (Torite) and/or sureptitious nerve point attacks (Kyoshu-Jitsu).

Four, by being taught and performed in exactly the same way for centuries, the Kata provides and sustains a Karmic link through time and space between its living practitioners and the ancient Karate Shihan (Masters). In other words, it creates a current or chain of force linking all of its exponents back to the particular Kata's founder. The purpose of Kata, therefore, is to build all facets of the student's being – body, mind, and spirit.

In addition to these purposes, Kata is also designed to exercise and build the practitioner's internal energy, or life force, called Ki in all Japanese and Okinawan based martial arts, Karate being no exception. Ki is believed to be centered in the Hara (belly), at the point one to three inches below the navel called the Itten (the Microcosmic Yesod of Qabalah and the Dan Tien of Taoism). Regarding this center called the Hara, the learned martial arts scholars Oscar Ratti and Edelle Westbrook (1973) expound the following insights pertinent to this spiritual examination:

> The concept of the Center is ancient (and) complex. . .Its dimensions range from the cosmic or universal to the particular or individual reality of man – the latter embracing him as a complex and delicate balance of physical, functional, mental, spiritual, and moral components of factors. . .The theory or idea of a Center begins with the observation of man's chaotic reality, his confusion, his sorrows. These are attributed to his ignorance, which renders him easy prey to inessential phenomena, to 'shadows' which, eventually, turn him. . .against himself, against his fellow men, against the world. In an effort to

counteract the effects of man's deadening and enslaving dependency upon the multiple and confusing variety of existential phenomena, the men of wisdom. . .sought to perceive the substance or essential Center of existence – the Center where the many become one, chaos became order, the particular became universal, death or stillness became life or motion, dazed and pained blindness became clarity, the unintelligible became intelligible. This Center could be found everywhere and in everything; in cosmos, in nature, in all forms of life – in man and his creations. According to Asian modes of thought, man's true Center found its first, physical expression in his lower abdomen. The Japanese word Hara, in fact, is literally translated as 'belly' and, in the Japanese version of the theory which re-echoes throughout all Asia, this area is the Center of life and death, the Center of consolidation. . .and of development. . .of a man's entire personality. This holds true on all levels of his existence, beginning with the physical, then progressing upward through the functional to the mental and spiritual dimensions. . .Every major doctrine of enlightenment. . .refers to this center and relies upon it for the achievement of its final aims. . .the Hara, through centralization at a point of mutual welfare encompassing man and his fellow man. . .reaches the cosmic dimension of centralization at a point of maximum integration, balance, and harmony of mankind with the natural order on earth and the universe at large. This point was the main theorem of ancient Taoism. . .The true Center... was the product of a successful fusion of these various Centers which were only apparently different (that is, differing in outer form and manifestation) but which were intrinsically identical in ultimate substance. And the first

> characteristic of a successful fusion was harmony, peace, fulfillment – with the self, with the other, with reality as a whole." (pp. 377-378).

In addition to its physical movements and mental concentration, Karate also emphasizes the proper use of breath to the end of augmenting and intensifying Ki. The use of the previously explained Total Breath assists in this by enhancing the intake of oxygen through the respiratory system which in turn enhances the fueling of the circulatory system that is running the body's muscles via blood, thus providing greater power and endurance.[102] Such breathing likewise enhances the metabolic utilization of caloric energy in cellular respiration, thus boosting the output of acetylcholine – the biochemical source of bodily energy.

The correct implementation of Total Breathing timed to the tempo of the Kata movement is taught as essential to this

---

[102] The ancient *Yellow Emperor's Classic*, one of the first textbook sources on acupuncture and Taoist medicine teaches, "Where blood goes, qi goes." Likewise does the Bible teach, "For the life of a creature is in the blood. . ." (*Leviticus,* 17:11). From an occult perspective, this is precisely the premise that physical vampirism and much of Black Magick operates upon. While it is vehemently professed that occult aspirants avoid all such practices, for informational purposes only, the student is directed to see Crowley's (1996) poem "Mulberry Tops" in the *Book of Lies* where he muses, "Black blood upon the altar! And the rustle of angel's wings above!. . .The blood is the life of the individual: offer then blood!" Real cheery shit to read to the kiddies before bedtime. How this man considered himself marked with the signs of the Buddha shows only his utter delusions of grandeur; a man truly in the grips of a narcissistic/histrionic/sociopathic character defect, despite his unarguable scholarly, occult, and writing genius. This is why, that while Crowley **must** be studied by any student of Magick for his unarguably lofty contributions to this field, he must be studied **carefully** and with **great caution**, just like when playing with fireworks, or when arming explosives, or when handling a loaded gun. To fail to do so is to risk ending up like poor Jack Parsons, figuratively on the mental and moral level, or literally on the physical level – incinerated! See also, Crowley's (1970) *Magick in Theory and Practice* (ch.XII). Note that Crowley's reference therein regarding the sacrifice of male children is a metaphoric blind in which he is actually referring to his homosexual sodomy penchant. And lastly, see also Crowley's (1994) snide remarks on Black Magick and the eating of raw oysters and Himalayan sheep's meat in his letter "Vampires" in *Magick Without Tears*. For extensive historical examination of the phenomenon of Vampires, see also Summers (1991).

goal. As part of this process the Kata is performed with the execution of gutteral screams exclaimed at particular timed moments. In addition to such functions as scaring the enemy and tightening the body to absorb blows, the use of these vibratory-like vocalizations called Kiai (spirit yells) at specific places within the Kata is meant to display the emission of Ki in the movements performed.[103] Taken together as a whole, this combination of movement coordinated with proper breathing displayed through the vocalizations creates what the Karateka[104] calls Kokyu Chikara (breath power). By the fluid display of Ki through Kokyu Chikara achieved in the physical movements of the Karate Kata, and by their use of Kiai, the Karateka achieves what is called Ki No Gashi (flow of energy). In ancient times, and even today amongst a few true Karate Masters, incredible feats of strength and power, like absorbing blows to vital parts of the body such as the throat and testicles, and the breaking of stacked bricks, tiles, and boards (Tamashiwara), were accomplished by this use of Kokyu Chikara, Kiai, and Ki No Gashi.[105]

---

[103] Musashi says in the *Gorin No Sho*, "The voice is energy" (cited in Harris). This is more than martial metaphysics and holds scientific validity. Total Breathing combined with Kiai creates not only sound waves or vibrational patterns, but increases the amperage of static electricity throughout the windpipe and chest cavity by the friction of the breath combined with the stimulation of the vocal cords by the central nervous system's willed electrical impulse.

[104] A practitioner of Karate.

[105] I have personally witnessed non-fraudulent demonstrations of Okinawan and Chinese methods of Sanchin and Iron Vest (respectively) in which the Martial Master receives full-force blows to the most delicate areas of the anatomy, such as the testicles, throat, and ribs without incurring injury. Rodney Sacahrnoski, *Soke* of the Juko-Kai Kokusei Remmei Martial Arts Federation (under whom I personally trained in the 1980's in Iaijutsu/Kenjutsu, Kobudo, Jodo, and Kijutsu) is world renowned for training people in this art that he calls Kijutsu (some his most accomplished masters in this art having taken baseball bat strikes to the windpipe without being hurt). Some members of China's official Wushu team surpass even this, placing sharpened spear points to their throats and bending the shafts until they break! Or, one step further, lying on sharpened swords across their throats and stomachs while having cinder blocks broken over their backs with sledge hammers (all without a drop of blood being spilled!). Some Japanese Masters of Tamashiwara and Chinese masters of Iron Hand not only use their internal energy to legitimately break vertically stacked materials like bricks and rocks with strikes, they can also do so to horizontal stacks (set up like books on a shelf) or perform "selective breaking" in which a tile or board in the middle of a stack is singularly broken without smashing the

While the analysis of Karate and Kata is an immense and separate thesis beyond the focus of this work, the aforementioned basic premises outline some of the more fundamental, yet crucial aspects of the proper execution and comprehensions of such practice. Though a martial endeavor, in these basic Kata tenets we find analogies that prove identical to the purpose, form, and function of the LPR. As we shall see, the LPR proves nothing short of a Magickal Kata par excellence (as a spiritual ritual, that is, and not as a martial artistic exercise).

Like the intended effects of Kata upon the dedicated Karateka, the committed Magician practicing the LPR can expect very similar if not identical results upon the fabric of their being. One, while not nearly as athletic an endeavor as Karate Kata, the LPR is still, in part, a physical exercise due to its movements and gesticulations. It will not, however, necessarily build physical strength, balance, power, or speed like Kata. Its effect, rather, will be to develop the precision in motion necessary to execute it properly, as for example, in creating the exact geometric tracing of the Pentagrams. Such practice assists in enhancing the Magician's mind-body connection as manifested through physical coordination.

Two, just like the Karate Kata, the LPR is meant as a mental exercise that requires use of the student's memory, the application of emotional control and mental concentration, and the proper flow of physical motion within the ritual that should become as natural as a reflex. Like the Karateka, the Magician must learn to exercise a mental state free of all useless, superfluous thoughts, to be entirely focused upon the ritual, with their Will being one-pointed. Like the Karate concepts of Kimei and Munenmoso No Heiho, Crowley (1994) calls this focus in the practice of the occult arts as the Beta mode of concentration. As he explains, "To train the mind to move with maximum speed and energy, with the utmost possible accuracy in a chosen direction, and with the minimum of disturbance or friction. That is Magick. . .Magick is wholly outward" (p. 139).[106]

---

ones surrounding it. Such ability when applied minimally to a person's chest can leave a bruised handprint on his back, or when applied with lethal intent, can be used to rupture internal organs.

[106] Crowley (1994) also explains what he calls the Alpha type of concentration, which is related to Yoga, just as Beta is related to Magick. He states, "The rules,

Three, the Kata hides meaning in its often symbolic movements which are representative of combative applications (Bunkai) not readily apparent to the untrained eye. By necessity they must be revealed to the student by their Sensei. Similarly the LPR possesses vast strata upon strata of interpretation. This interpretation is unlocked by the personal inspiration and understanding gained by the ritual's habitual practice; by the study of primary occult sources that provide analysis of the ritual; and by the insights directly provided by one's Magickal Master or spiritual Guru. This very tome is based on all three types of resources. However, note that the first source (personal inspiration and intuition) is always the most fruitful as this knowledge is arrived at through the exercise of one's own efforts and the insight and ensuing realizations born of the process. To be taught or told by another, or to learn by a book, while very helpful, will never prove as beneficial to the aspirant on the Path of Return as does the knowledge you gain through your own efforts.

Four, performed in exactly the same way every time, the LPR provides and sustains a Karmic link between all previous performances of the ritual by the Magician. And just like the link established between the Karateka and the ancient Shihans by exercise of the Kata, the persistent performance of the LPR establishes a Karmic link in the living practitioner to the previous Magicians who have also dedicated themselves to its exercise. Both work to create the same type of current or chain of force linking all of their exponents back through time and space. The LPR, therefore, just like Kata, builds all facets of the student's being – body, mind, and spirit.

Furthermore, just as all Karate Katas hold some type of symbolism (such as animals),[107] whether in whole or in part, so does the LPR possess such symbolism. As we have seen in the creation of the Universal Mandala, and in the Tarot analogies as

---

strangely enough, are identical in both cases. . .Yoga merely goes a step further. In Beta you have reduced all (mental) movements from many to one: In Alpha you reduce that one to zero. . .To Stop the mind altogether. That is Yoga. . .Yoga is wholly inward" (p. 499). By Tarot analogy, we could say that the Magician is reduced to the Fool. Or, by action of the Star, one becomes the Hanged Man.

[107] For example, stances typically utilized in Karate Katas include the Horse, the Cat, and the Crane. Some Katas also, in part or in totality, are based upon an animal, such as Seisan and Chinto, which draw from the crane.

so applied by use of Key 10 (The Wheel of Fortune) and Key 21 (The World), the LPR utilizes the Four Sacred Animals as symbols applied to the Four Directions, the Tetragrammaton and Four Elements.

Lastly, just as the practice of Karate Kata stresses the importance of developing Ki and the Itten, as we have examined, the exercise of the LPR utilizes the same internal energy through the energy-channel system of the body. We have also seen the importance and primacy of the Center in martial arts and how this same lesson is identically applicable to the form and function of the LPR (with the Magician themselves being the Center of the Universal Mandala). Qabalistically speaking, the Magician, as this Center, becomes the fifth point of the four directions; the crown of Spirit, the Shin upon the Yod He Vau He; the Crown of Spirit upon the four elements of the Tetragrammaton, raising it to the Pentagrammaton; Jehovah to Yeheshua; God in Man; the Cross to the Star!  What Kokyu Chikara and Kiai are to Karate Kata, so is the vibration of the Divine Names and Declaration of the Great Work within the vocalizations of the LPR. Likewise, the projection and visualization of the Universal Mandala within the ritual is nothing less than the Kata concept of Ki No Gashi as Magickally applied!

When we understand these premises of Kata, important insights are gained in comparing this Karate practice to our subject of the LPR. While we have likened the LPR to Deepak Chopra's (1995) concept of the "thought exercise," as we have seen, the LPR is likewise a Magickal Kata reflecting many of the same functions and goals as its Karate counterpart. Both augment physical and mental development in the practitioners. Both hold symbolic and multi-level meanings within their movements. And both intensify the student's intrinsic personal energy while also establishing a concentrated link to Universal sources thereof.

Ultimately, these preceding metaphors applied to the LPR, based on Art, the Tarot, Yoga, and Karate, are nothing more than poetic, symbolic aids to assist the student in gaining deeper insight and further understanding of the principles, meaning, and applications of the LPR. If these attempts have not clarified, but confused, not illuminated, but darkened our exposition, then cast them aside! Through thy own practice and dedication, understanding will blossom on its own just as a seed becomes a sprout and then a flowering bud. If nothing more, the previous examples should at least suggest to the student the spiritual profundity hidden within the LPR's seeming technical simplicity. So Mote It Be, brothers and sisters – So Mote It Be!

# Chapter 4: Conclusions

*"All that we are is the result of what we have thought;
it is founded upon our thoughts,
it is constituted by our thoughts."*
-Buddha, *The Dhammapada.*

*"As a man thinketh in his heart, so is he."*
-*The Book of Proverbs,* 23:7.

*"The Samsara is no more than one's own thought. With effort one
should therefore cleanse the thought. What one thinketh, that doth one
become. This is the eternal mystery."*
-*Maitri Upanishad.*

# Formal Applications of the LPR

I hope to have proven that the Lesser Banishing Ritual of the Pentagram as taught in the formal curriculum of the original Heremtic Order of the Golden Dawn is the quintessential, prototypical Magickal practice of the Western esoteric and occult tradition. In this examination we have drawn extensively from wellsprings both West and East in arguing this thesis, thus showing the perennial, universal essence of its content and meaning. Through metaphors ranging from spiritual to warrior endeavors, insights into the vast nature of this ritual's function have been allotted in order to relay pertinent understanding to individuals whose background experience is bound to vary and who possess a variety of personality types. It is now left to convey a few brief comments on the formal applications of the LPR which can be separated into two basic categories: the psychological (or cognitive) and the Magickal.

# Psychological Applications of the LPR

Much information can already be garnered from the foregoing chapters with regard to the impact this ritual has upon the intellectual faculties of the human. This very grimoire is, in and of itself, little more than the result of dedicated practice of the LPR and the resulting intellectual effects it has had upon the author in fostering the insights provided, coupled with a *bonne bouche* of historical research. Therefore, in summary, little more will be added regarding the LPR's function upon Man's psyche than this tidbit of added data.

Again, comparing the LPR to a "thought exercise," like any workout, the parts utilized in so doing gain greater strength. Just as muscles become stronger in lifting weights, so does the brain become stouter and more robust by using it, because it can, like muscles, atrophy and weaken if not regularly put through the paces. Thus, as a thought exercise, regular practice of the LPR strengthens one's ability to think; it enhances the cognitive, or executive functions, of the practitioner's psyche, improving the health of the brain area associated with these mental functions. It would be useful for scientific researchers to carry out replicable experimentation combined with quantifiable evidence to test whether or not the habitual practice of the LPR improves the human I.Q. It would be interesting to learn if it might even have the ability to stave off the effects of certain types of cognitive dysfunctions associated with aging; for example, minor issues like the progressive loss of short term memory, or even severe medical problems of the psyche, such as the onset of dementia. Though only anecdotal, I believe that such hypotheses would be proven affirmative.

Despite all of the jargon and theories surrounding the function of the human psyche, with regard to the thought process, an outline can be conveyed with great brevity. Similar to the Hegelian dialectic, all mental processes can be summarized as being of only two varieties. These are reflected in Alchemy by the Latin adage, *"Solve et coagula. Coagula et solve."* Or as Crowley (1994) explains in a tone redolent of the Pythagoreans, from *Magick Without Tears:*

> What do we do when we think? There are two operations, and only two, possible to thought. However complex a statement may appear, it can always be reduced to a series of one or the other of these. . .Analysis or Synthesis; or Subtraction and Addition. 1). You can examine A, and find it composed of B and C; A = B + C. 2). You can find out what happens to B when you add C to it; B + C = A. The two are identical. . .but the process is different.

In this simple and brief, yet ingenious statement is revealed not only the entire process of human mentality, but also another perspective of Advaita as psychologically unveiled.

As a thought exercise, the LPR expresses the totality of these criteria of the mental processes in humans. Analysis is initially exercised by reading and memorization; by learning the ritual's steps. Synthesis is then produced every time the ritual is performed; when the analyzed, component parts are put together as a whole. Analysis then follows again as the performed ritual is contemplated by the practitioner to unlock deeper messages and symbolic meaning from it. It is broken apart again to gain further insights. As previously stated, this very tome is but a final synthesis of the analysis gained by the author; that which was learned by the ritual's performances being put together again into the construct of language. The reader of this work has in turn applied further analysis through the act of reading it, and will then form further synthesis in bringing this knowledge together into personal practice. Thus, as an act of language, thought, and Magick all rolled into one book, we hope that Thoth smiles approvingly over the final product!

Life and Death are but plus and minus,
The lesson of Isis, Apophis, and Osiris!
Synthesis and Analysis, Coagula et Solve;
Brahma, Vishnu, Shiva –
Yod He Vau He!

# Magickal Applications of the Ritual

Dr. Gerald Gardener was a man of many hats. He was a famous pistol-toting explorer and accomplished anthropologist in the same vein as Roy Chapman Andrews (the real life Indiana Jones). He was an initiate in the Hermetic Order of the Golden Dawn and proficient occultist. He was the founder and curator of the Museum of Magic and Witchcraft on the Isle of Man. And, as he is now accurately remembered in the subject of esotericism, he was **the** revivalist of British Wicca in the 20th century, rightfully earning him the moniker "The Grand Old Man of English Witchcraft" by which he is now famously known in both Golden Dawn and Wiccan circles. His credentials are truly impressive having achieved in academics, the occult, and adventure no less than Crowley himself. As such, he made an interesting and fundamental distinction between Ritual Magick and Witchcraft applicable to our study of the LPR. Dr. Gardner argues that this distinction is based upon these two systems' complimentary use of the Magick Circle, or what we have termed in the performance of the LPR, the Universal Mandala.

Magick, as he argues, utilizes the Circle generally as a defense. It is a barrier against the potentially overwhelming energy or even outright hostility of elementary, demonic, angelic, or Divine forces being ceremoniously manipulated. To over simplify Magickal theory, the Magician is in contact with and control of external powers against which the Circle acts as an aegis.

Witchcraft, in contrast, uses the Circle as a harness to hold in and center the spiraling energy of their dance-driven, rhythmic rituals. To over simplify Wiccan theory, the Witch feels the power of Nature in and through him or herself, focused and channeled by the Circle. As with flood water, the Circle acts as a canal to direct their internal power.

Dr. Gardner (1991) writes,

> Kabbalistic (types of) magic. . .all have certain things in common, and work by calling up a spirit or intelligence and commanding it to do their will. All the members stand in a circle for protection and are warned that if they leave the circle before the spirit is dismissed they may be blasted. . .The English witches' method is very different. They believe the power is within themselves and exudes from their bodies. It would be dissipated were it not the circle cast...
> to keep the power in, and not as magicians usually use it, to keep the spirits out. (pp. 46-47).[108]

If we apply these two distinct usages of the Magick Circle to the execution of the LPR and its creation of the Universal Mandala, we are provided a deeper understanding behind the dual applications of this ritual. From each perspective, the Magickal compared to the Wiccan, is revealed the dialectic of the LPR's use as either a banishing exercise or an invocative practice. Each

---

[108] Gardner (1991) also says, ". . .use of the circle to keep the power in, were local inventions, derived from the use of the Druid or pre-druid circle. . .It was influenced by the Greek and Roman Mysteries which originally may have come from Egypt." (p. 48).  Note also, in this context, the extensive Egyptian influence upon the Glden Dawn curriculum via MacGregor and Moina Mathers.

procedure is proper to the study and execution of the LPR; one as a weapon, one as a tool.

In the employment of the LPR as a banishing exercise, the Universal Mandala created is an Astral shield that acts as a spiritually defensive barrier. This shield works to protect the operator against the mentally and emotionally depleting energy and negativity associated with ill, depressed, addicted, jealous, manipulating, ignorant, avaricious, hateful, narcissistic, or sociopathic people; and all other forms of human psychic vampirism in general. Classical sources of instruction in this ritual state that it is needed as a preliminary to visiting with or counseling such energetically parasitic individuals (whether they are intentionally so or not) to prevent the spiritually depleting, osmosis-like diffusion of Prana from you to them.

The LPR's application as a banishment also acts to spiritually cleanse the immediate, surrounding environment of most "evil" (or more properly stated, negative and unnecessary; or antithetical and counterproductive) spiritual forces that may manifest in Astral, elemental, or demonic forms in preparation for any prayer, meditation, ritual, or divination. The size of this area being purified is in direct proportion to the expanse, strength, and intensity of the Magician's aura. The Magician's auric circumference, of course, may be inconsistent on a day-to-day basis due to such factors as health, concentration, state of mind, and so forth. But the aura may also be positively affected, and thus expanded, by not only regular performance of the LPR, but by practice of such other disciplines as meditation, ritual work, Taoist Qigong, Yoga, Tai Chi Ch'uan, and any other martial art. To this end, such alternative "cross-training" methods can be beneficial to the Magician's LPR practice due to the favorable effect they have on his or her energetic constitution and in magnifying their aura.

The banishment function of the LPR may also be used as an exorcism-like defense in the action it performs against denizens of the subtle spheres. Such entities include shells (ghosts), poltergeists, demons, vampires, therianthropes,[109] and

---

[109] Popularly known as lycanthropy, this word denotes only human to wolf transformations, as where therianthropy refers to human transformations to any kind of animal. For the quintessential expose on Lycanthropy see Summers (1966) and see also Appendix J.

so on. In short, the Magickal technique utilized in the LPR for banishment is akin to magnetic repulsion and may be likened through simile to the implementation of a Magickal scarecrow.

Invocation is, in complement, the opposite of banishment and is accomplished with the LPR by the tracing of the alternative Spirit Pentagram, instead of the Earth Star as otherwise used. Conversely, the elements imaged in the Stars are manifested in invocation rather than disintegrated as in banishment. With invocation, the Universal Mandala acts as a summons, as a focus to draw Universal and Divine energy into the Magician who stands as the nucleus of the Circle, as the Sun of the symbolic solar system generated by the ritual's projections. The energy drawn in, or called down (depending on your preferred metaphor) is used either as a means to fortify the practitioner's individual aura, or Body of Light,[110] or is directed as energetic current for some other pre-specified Magickal operation. Thus, the technique used in the LPR for invocation is akin to magnetic attraction and may be likened through simile to the implementation of a Magickal lightening rod.

**Dr. Gerald Gardner (June 13, 1884 – February 12, 1864) armed with his ceremonial sword, subjugating a "demon."**

---

[110] In the Tibetan Buddhist systems this is known as the Rainbow Body and is the form of an individual left after death which goes on to temporarily inhabit the Bardo realm before reincarnating into physical manifestation.

The LPR, therefore, through its dual purpose as both a banishment and invocative ritual, illustrates the Magician as both a battery of self-producing Micrcocosmic energy (Prana) and as a focal receptor and transformer of Macrocosmic energy (i.e. Prakriti). As Regardie (1994) states regarding this twin purpose of the LPR, "(The Lesser Banishing Ritual of the Pentagram's) use is permitted. . .that Neophytes may have protection against opposing forces, and also that they may form some idea of how to attract and come into communication with spiritual and invisible things." (p. 281).[111]

In closing, it is necessary to reiterate the following technical considerations regarding the LPR for either invocation or banishment. Beyond the above mentioned applications, as a daily exercise the LPR may be utilized as a solar ritual; invocation in the morning timed with dawn; banishing in the evening timed with dusk. In a complex ceremonial working where the LPR is used as an opening and closing component, the following formula is to be patterned:

1). An initial banishing LPR to purify the area for the main Magickal operation.

---

[111] "The Banishing Pentagram. . .will also serve thee for protection if thou trace it in the air between thee and any opposing Astral force. In all cases of tracing the Pentagram, the angle should be carefully closed at the finishing point." (Regardie, 1994, pp. 281 – 282). Also,

> . . .it is held that the banishing Ritual of the Pentagram alone suffices to secure adequate protection and eliminates all possibility of demoniac possession. . .moreover. . .the Body of Light must be purified, made glowing and glittering, iridescent and self-shining, a solar-organism which emits the radiant light of the Spirit within. It is only thus that he (the Magician) may attain to more fiery and exalted states. . .The means of effecting this purification are the frequent performances of the Pentagram Ritual, thus formulating more clearly and radiantly the thought body. . .
> (Regardie, 2004, pp. 230 – 231).

In its main purpose of strengthening the practitioner's Body of Light, this same efficacy attributed to the LPR above could likewise be said to afford protection against other modern denizens akin to the ancient concept of the demon such as Archons and Annunaki (as popularized by such researchers as Erich von Daniken and Zecharia Sitchin), as well as alien abduction and inter-dimensional entity manipulation (such as those popularized in the works of Bud Hopkins, Terrence McKenna, and Whitley Streiber).

2). An opening invocative LPR to summon and focus the fundamental energies to be implemented in the main operation.

3). The performance of the main ceremony.

4). A closing banishing LPR to close the circle opened and dismiss the energies and entities invited and utilized.

> And in this flux of to and fro,
> A circuit made of come and go,
> Rides the tide of ebb and flow,
> As the Magus sings to high and low –
> So as above,
> As so below!

This ends the formal applications.

# Potential Outcomes of Dedicated Practice

As we have illustrated throughout this work, the dedicated practice of the LPR will eventually produce objectively real results for the aspirant. The section to follow, "Warnings," will outline the possible dangers and potential risks inherent in any occult practice including the LPR, especially by those practitioners of ill disposition in body or spirit; those who be spurred by hate and not love; those pitiful left-hand wretches inspired by such spiritually antithetical motivations as the lust for power or the quest of greed. Here, however, we endeavor to reiterate and summarize some of the basic benefits spawned by the LPR for those who enter it with a healthy nervous and physical constitution, sound intellectual and emotional fiber, and a solid moral makeup.

All of the classical writings of the modern Magi that we have been witness to herein, such as Levi, Mathers, Crowley, Regardie, Case, Gardner and others, adamantly promise and attest to the efficacy of the LPR. Magician and occult scholar Chris Monnastre, a distinguished sorror of Dr. Paul Foster Case's BOTA, and the only accepted personal student of Dr. Francis Israel Regardie, writes that within the LPR, ". . .are the formulae for future practical magical operations as well as it being the engine whereby the candidate is brought to the Light" (cited in Regardie, 1994, p. xxiii).

Crowley (1970) summarized that the basic advantages to be gained from the practice of any magick, the LPR being no exception, are: "1). A widening of the horizons of the mind.

2). An improvement in the control of the mind." (p. 375).

In regard to Crowley's first point, as we have examined, the LPR acts as a "mind expander" in its creation of the Universal Mandala. Furthermore, the Yogic processes intrinsic to the LPR, such as its Pranayamic, Dharanic, Pratyaharic and Dhyanic components, completely fulfill the premise of Crowley's second point. In this dual process of expanding the mind while improving its control, the practitioner of the LPR is affected with such beneficial results as stimulated creativity, improved memory, enhanced organizational skills, enriched deductive ability, broadened intellectual perspectives, and expanded mental flexibility. These are the most tangible fruits harvested from the labor of the LPR that can most readily be applied in the Magician's everyday life.

Biophysically we have discussed how the LPR works as a Will-driven exercise to intensify the body's natural battery-like production and output of Microcosmic energy. We have seen how this is all medically and scientifically validated as shown in the processes of the assimilation of energy through the matter used in digestion and catalyzed on the cellular level through metabolism, circulation, and respiration. We have shown how the proper breathing technique can augment this process in the ritual's vibratory methods by increasing the body's electrical amperage through the central nervous system and how the projected images of the ritual stimulate the mind's intensity of thought. Both of these are but different manifestations of the Astral Light, Prana, Qi, to be guided through the body in the Qabalist Middle Pillar (or in what the Taoists call the Grand Circulation).

We have written of how these processes are all goads to instigating and guiding the needed alterations in the physical and mental apparatuses of the human organism; how these means can foster personal evolution driving it on faster than Nature does by Herself, perhaps even to the level of birthing a new species; perhaps even to the level aimed for in the Golden Dawn's pledge, *to become more than human*. We have investigated how humanity is the Temple of the Spirit, the

Laboratory of experimentation, the Great Athanor, the receptor and transformer of Kosmic energies; and how, in its perfected form, the LPR, like Yoga and martial arts, can result in improved health, strengthened immunity, greater longevity[112] and increased personal power for pursuing what Plato called "the Good, the True, and the Beautiful."

Magickally speaking, we have also seen how the LPR can be used as a spiritual defense against malevolent energies and intelligences, how it can help in manifesting and directing energies for usage in ceremonial workings, and how it may sharpen the practitioner's ability to sense or see the subtler inhabitants of the Kosmos. And while beyond this work's scope to prove, and thus perhaps risking the lapse into a dogmatic assertion, I likewise extend that the committed practice of the LPR will also verify a sharpening of the individual's psychic propensities, whether clairvoyant or clairaudient.[113]

We hereby recap that the Lesser Banishing Ritual of the Pentagram is **the** Magickal practice of the Western esoteric tradition par excellence; that in its perfection it proves no less

---

[112] In regards to physical longevity, many traditions the world over allege that there exist Adepts so accomplished and ascended that they are able to dematerialize and rematerialize their physical form at will (such as Jesus in the West and Padmasambhava in the East) while still existing in their own personal forms either on the material plane or others. The demonologist Merril Unger (1972) documents this phenomenon as attested by Christian missionaries in China who reportedly saw Buddhist monks able to do this from mountain top to mountain top in displays of teleportation (in his fundamentalist work, *Demons in the World Today*). As a fundamentalist Christian, however, Dr. Unger wrongly attributes this power to Satanic forces rather than to Holy Science. Furthermore, some traditions also ascribe certain Masters' ability to stave off the effects of physical entropy or bodily dissolution (i.e. old age and death) far beyond the usual lifespan acknowledged by medical science. An example would be St. Germain in Theosophy, allegedly alive now in bodily form for several centuries.

[113] While it is obviously far beyond the scope of an endnote to prove such assertions that have been dealt with in voluminous documentation elsewhere, I maintain as a paradigm that humans, and many other life-forms (plants to animals) possess forms of extrasensory perception that science is only now beginning to fundamentally acknowledge. This can be evidenced in various examples such as the phenomena of people having accurate prescient dreams, in the shark's electrical-sensing organ called Ampullae of Lorenzini, in farm animals' odd behavior prior to earthquakes, in dogs' ability to smell cancer, and even in my own cats who regularly track and follow objects (or subtle beings?) that I cannot see across the ceiling and walls!

than the Medicine of Metals and the Stone of the Wise. It is, when rightly accomplished, the fulfillment of the Great Work, the 5 = 6, the reconciliation of the Microcosm with the Macrocosm. It is Gnosis and At-One-Ment in the West, and Nirvana and Moksha is the East. It is, as the Great Master taught, the realization that *the kingdom of God is within you*; that you and the Father are One; that the Atman is one with the Brahman.

Can my claims be proven? Can they be denied? Have there not been men of such genius, of such understanding, of such love in our midst that they seem but two-legged reflections of the Divine? Have there not been, like diamonds shining amongst the mountains of coal, Mahavira, Buddha, Lao Tzu, Jesus, Nagarjuna, Padmasambhava, Da Vinci, Eckhart, Boehme, Bruno, Emerson, Thoreau, Aurobindo, Krishnamurti, Maharshi, Tolle, Wilber? Can we really deny our sovereign tie with the Divine? To do so. . .that would be the lie!

Much has hereby been written. The only direction left to give is to try for thyself. Judge not lest ye have exercised the effort. The guarantee is provided that results will be invited. Remember these words of the yogic guru Sri Anirvan from his essay "On Being Oneself":

> Every disciple in his quest is fully aware that the personal discipline he has accepted has a practical aim, which is the complete union of human consciousness with the highest reality. The goal is to transform the mental, vital, and even the physical nature of the being, down to the smallest cells of the body, in order to attain the understanding of the ultimate reality. (cited in Reymond, 1983) .

So in our breath,
From both East and West,
Is the circle trekked
On this, our quest.

# Warnings

When tampering with the human psyche for any reason and by any methodology (psychological, spiritual, or otherwise), effects, whether of beneficial or detrimental character, must be expected to the biological-organic-corporeal component of the mind; that is, the brain, even when one is motivated by noble intentions. Despite the titanic conquests already achieved by medicine, psychology, philosophy, and religion, the mind is still a mystery to most humans and much of its functionality remains incomprehensible. What may prove helpful or healing to one person's mind may be quite disturbing and damaging to another. Not everyone, for example, responds positively to electroshock therapy, while in some chronic cases of clinical depression sufferers have been fully alleviated by it when no other treatments would work. It is true that some people's demons are angels to others. What's trash to you may be gold to me, and all humans, while entirely of the same stock, are still totally different, one from another.

In the history of the Magick and Mystic arts it cannot be denied that many instances exist of students going stark raving mad into total neurotic breakdowns or psychotic episodes as a direct causative result of their occult studies and practices. In many of these, the occult practice may have simply exacerbated a pre-existing or innate condition that had yet to manifest itself, just as drug abuse, alcoholism, or excessive stress can do, thus allowing the illness to emerge in full blown symptomatology. In others, these negative consequences upon the mental health of the practitioner were undoubtedly caused by blatant errors on the part of the student or even from negligent instruction or outright deception by the teacher. In addition, the obvious dangers of practicing intrinsically evil, black, or left-hand forms of Magick cannot be overstated; nor can the risks of attempting methods beyond the student's ability, level, or readiness.

As has been said, Dr. Regardie promoted the admonishment that any potential student of Magick should undergo at least a year of Jungian or Reichian based psychoanalysis to ensure the individual had adequately dealt with all of their shadow material first. This would ensure that they were ready for the potentially perilous power lying dormant in the subconscious that occult training would inevitably release. Crowley (1970), perhaps in uncharacteristically optimistic fashion, stated as one of his opening aphorisms in the prodigious *Magick in Theory and Practice* "Magick is for all" (p. 1). Arguably, however, Magick, like any other esoteric enterprise, is not for most of the general public, but is for an especial minority; for an elite composed of the right-minded. This is only because, at this stage of our species' evolution, Magick is beyond the grasp of most people, not due to a lack of potential as much as a lack of interest; of an apathy towards the subject. This lack of aptitude towards Magick can also be explained as fear caused by a lack of courage in facing and pursuing the unknown, [114] as well as environmentally exacted handicaps such as lack of education, fundamentalist upbringing, superstitious inclinations, or the like. Thus, I would assert, Magick is *not* for all. If it were, this planet would be living in a Golden Age of fatherly Priest-Kings and motherly Priestess-Queens in harmony with the forces of Nature.[115]

While it is my hope that this book will responsibly illuminate some important premises of the practice of Magick and its worldview, there is always the possibility of pitfalls. To again quote Crowley (1970), but this time in complete agreement with him:

---

[114] Legendary horror writer and creator of the Cthulu mythos, H.P. Lovecraft (1965). points out (as the opening line to his quintessential essay, *Supernatural Horror in Literature*), "The oldest and strongest emotion of mankind is fear, and the oldest and strongest kind of fear is fear of the unknown." (p. 365).

[115] Such would be our Utopia, and not, as we are instead, in a corporate-driven, consumption-based cesspool system engaged in the wholesale slaughtering of this planet's biodiversity upon which our very own survival depends, like some cancer or parasite upon its host; and all for nothing but the petty desire of the empty materiality gained for next quarter's dividends and profits! Woe to we who have forgotten the Native wisdom of taking only what you need and leaving the rest as you found it. Hearken this warning all ye seekers of the Light. Regardless of what the ancient nomadic desert author of *Genesis* had to say on behalf of a pissed-off, masculine, Semitic volcano god – we *do not* have dominion over Gaia. It is She who has dominion over us. It is nothing but sheer human hubris, complete madness, to think otherwise. Humanity is not the landlord of the Earth, but simply one of its uncountable, finite, temporary cohabitants. To paraphrase David Brower, we do not own this world. We simply borrow it from our heirs.

This book is very easy to misunderstand; readers are asked to use the most minute critical care in the study of it, even as we have done in the preparation. . .The student, if he attains any success. . .will find himself confronted by things (ideas or beings) too glorious or too dreadful to be described. It is essential that he remain the master of all that he beholds, hears or conceives; otherwise he will be the slave of illusion and the prey of madness. Before entering upon any of these practices the student must be in good health, and have attained a fair mastery of Asana, Pranayama, and Dharana. There is little danger that any student, however idle or stupid, will fail to get some result; but there is great danger that he will be led astray, even though it be by those which it is necessary that he should attain. Too often, moreover, he mistaketh the first resting place for the goal, and taketh off his armor as if he were victor ere the fight is well begun. It is desirable that the student should never attach to any result the importance which it at first seems to possess. (pp. 375-376).

Levi (1997) similarly chides:

You. . .who are undertaking the study of this book, if you persevere with it to the close and understand it, it will make you either a monarch or a madman. Do what you will with the volume, you will be unable to despise or to forget it. If you are pure, it will be your light; if strong your arm; if holy your religion; if wise, the rule of your wisdom. But, if you are wicked, for you it will be an infernal torch; it will lacerate your breast like a poinard; it will rankle your memory like a remorse; it will people your imagination with chimeras, and will drive you through folly to despair. You will endeavor to laugh at it, and will only gnash your teeth; this book will be the file in the fable which the serpent tried to bite, but it destroyed all his teeth. (pp. 33-34).

We earnestly advise the student to heed these ending details:

1). You are warned of the dangers regarding any practical application of Magick as exemplified by such instances as the madness of Cornelius Agrippa, the hazards Levi faced in his evocative work (Levi, 1997, pp. 107, 113-121), the experiences of Tal Brooke (1982) under Sai Babba in India,[116] and the historic warnings of Golden Dawn fraters Sub Spe, N.O.M., Resurgam, and D.D.C.F. in *Flying Roll XXXIV* (cited in King, 1997, pp. 40-42).

2). "Any practical occult work exhausts the operator or takes away some of their magnetism. That is why if you want to realize work of some magnitude you must possess a perfect magnetic balance. Otherwise you would do more harm than good." (Philosophers of Nature, 1996). Extreme examples of such harm could include physical illness, mental disorders, anxiety, hallucination, delusion, and the infamous "Magician's disease" suffered by Crowley, Allan Bennett, W.B. Yeats, and myself – namely, asthma.

3). The LPR acts as a defense that protects, but the Pentagrams used also have the potential to,". . .light up the Astral and make entities aware of you." (Regardie, 1994, p.308). Therefore – **always close the door when you're done having it opened.**

4). Furthermore,

---

[116] Tal Brooke's *Avatar of Night*, though written from a fundamentalist Christian perspective, holds valid warnings for all who would subjugate their own freewill and place it under the domination of any alleged guru. All who claim to be gurus surely are not, and more than less are simply spiritual and monetary parasites using chicanery and half-truths upon others for their own narcissistic, controlling, and material ends. A true guru is a servant to, and not a leader over, their students. They give all to them and ask for nothing in return save their own dedicated efforts towards awakening. Remember to, when approached by new people wishing to become his chela (student), Sri Ramana Maharshi would fittingly respond to them, "There is no guru but Brahman." As a Western correlative, and in similar tone, I am reminded too of Plato's *Apology* where Socrates says, ". . .God only is wise. . .the wisdom of men is little or nothing" (cited in Eliot, 1969, p. 11).

> To the Pentagram, the denizens of the Astral Plane respond in two different and quite distinct ways. . .when faced by the flaming five-pointed Star, formulated by the Magical will, some astral beings will shrink perceptibly, and appear to fade away. Another class of beings, however, will grow and expand to cover the whole horizon with a splendid luminosity and radiance. . .the being which shrivels up in fear of the Pentagram or hastens rapidly away is either a. . .demon or an elementary, and must be treated accordingly. . .the being that does not suffer by the Pentagram and the appropriate banishing ritual is a spiritual intelligence, an Angel, a lofty celestial being to be respected, and loved, and venerated. (Regardie, 2004, p. 361).

5). As an epilogue to any ritual, always re-absorb the projections made in the exercise to prevent any depletion of energy or formation of chinks in your auric armor.

The appendices that follow must be as rigorously assimilated by the student just as the rest of this text.

You have been warned.

> This work is done,
> My breath is gone.
> Sit silent and still
> And awake with dawn!

*"As long as the sky endureth, so long there will be
no end of sentient beings for one to serve; and to
everyone cometh the opportunity for such service.
Till the opportunity come, I exhort each of you to
have but the one resolve, namely, to attain
Buddhahood for the good of all living things."*

-Tibet's Great Yogin Milarepa
(taken from his last great exhortation to his disciples).

*"Go forth and set the world on fire."*

-St. Ignatius of Loyola.

*"You must be your own lamps, Be your own refuges.
Take refuge in nothing outside yourselves. . .
Do not look for refuge to anything besides yourselves."*

-Buddha, *the Nirvana Sutra*

*"Man must amalgamate himself with the Principle that he possesseth
innately. Then, from the manyness that he was,
he will have become One."*

-Plotinus

# Chapter 5: Appendices

# Appendix A – Charts of Directional/Elemental Correspondences

Explanatory Note: The following charts and accompanying illustrations represent a trifling example of the symbolic correspondences inherent in the formula of the LPR, particularly those of the four elements, four directions, and four letters of the Tetragrammaton. Other rituals and systems may or may not possess these same correspondences. The student may observe these seeming discrepancies early on in his or her studies. Not only will differing systems obviously vary, but even grades or stages within the same system will unlock differing charts of strata to such correspondences.

This does not, as may be erroneously thought by the profane, display inconsistency in the subject matter of Magick, but rather, it displays its depth and totality, as the different systems and levels of Magick are capable of providing insights from every possible mental angle or philosophical perspective. An example of this, in comparison to this study of the LPR, would be the fluctuating symbolic correspondences allocated to the Pentagram or cardinal directions in other Golden Dawn-based rituals such as the *Supreme Invoking Ritual of the Pentagram* or the *Hexagram Rituals*. The student should not be surprised or overwhelmed by this apparent magnitude of information in the occult, as the expanse of the occult proves no less than the subjects it studies: namely God, the Universe, and humanity. Likewise is your own growth as infinitely possible as are these indefinite strata.

That which you do not comprehend at this level will be understood later on, if endured with diligence step by step, stage by stage, idea by idea. Any limitation, hindrance, weakness, or ignorance that one possesses can and will, eventually, be overcome. This is but the essence of our own species' survival instincts, as well as the spirit of evolution that is spurred on by adaptation and growth into ever-increasing expressions of depth and complexity. It is, in short, God's Way to present one Mystery to be unlocked, and when conquered, to then veil but another, and another, and another, ad infinitum! Such is the process of Spirit-in-Action; of what has been termed, "evolutionary enlightenment." There is no end in working our way back to God. There is no end on the Path of Return; that is, until Brahman awakes from his dreaming sleep that gives rise to all the worlds.

Because this chart is but rudimentary in scope and by no means exhaustive, the student is encouraged to build upon its contents keeping in mind the importance that the Yogic state of Dhyana will have towards these ends. Just like the Tree of Life itself, all esoteric and occult knowledge continues to grow and expand, as do roots to saplings to trunks to branches to leaves in the wind.

The contents herein are laid out alphabetically for convenience and, where relevant, Gematria equivalents have been added, presented in parentheses after the word.
Excelsior!

## EAST/AIR

ALCHEMICAL SYMBOL: Azoth.
ANGEL: Chassan (1008).
ARCHANGEL: Raphael (311).
ATU OF THOTH: The Fool.
AREA OF KNOWLEDGE/DIVINATORY: Paternal, intellectual, masculine spiritual.
BAPHOMET COMPONENT (per Golden Dawn): Man's face/woman's breasts.
BAPHOMET COMPONENT (Per Levi): Eagle's wings.
BODY APPENDAGE: Right hand.
CARDINAL VIRTUE: Justice.
CHERUBIM OF THE ARK OF THE COVENANT: Eagle.
CHIEF DAKINI OF TIBETAN BUDDHISM: Vajra.
CHINESE CORRESPONDENCES PER GODWIN: East, blue/turquoise, dragon.
COLOR: Yellow.
COLOR PER LAKOTA SIOUX SHAMANISM: Green.
COLOR SCALE: Emperor or prince (white brilliance, bluish mother of pearl, dark brown, deep purple, bright scarlet, rich salmon, bright yellow-green, red russet, very dark purple, four

colors flecked gold, blue-emerald green, gray, cold pale blue, early spring green, brilliant flame, deep warm olive, new yellow, rich bright russet, gray, green gray, rich purple, deep blue-green, deep olive green, very dark brown, green, blue-black, venetian red, bluish mauve, light translucent, pinkish brown, rich amber, scarlet flecked gold, blue black, dark brown, seven prismatic colors/violet outside, pure violet).

COMPONENT OF THE FIAT FORMULA: F.

COMPONENT OF THE INRI FORMULA: I.

DEMON PRINCE: Azazel (115).

DEMON KING: Orions.

DIRECTIONAL EXPRESSION OF ELEMENTAL WEAPONS: Magi (dagger, wand, cup, pantacles).

EGYPTIAN GOD: Hermomphta.

ELEMENTAL ASPECTS:
 -COMPONENTS: Heat and moisture.
 -ATTRIBUTION PER HEBREW LETTER: Aleph.
 -KING: Paralda.
 -RACE: Sylph.
 -WEAPON: Dagger

ENOCHIAN ASPECTS:
 -DIVINE NAME: ORO IBAH AOZPI.
 -GREAT WORD: EXARP.
 -SUPREME ELEMENTAL ANGEL: TAHOELOG.
 -TALISMAN: Air.
 -WATCHTOWER: Air Tablet.

EVANGELIST/GOSPEL: Matthew.

FINGER: Pinky.

FOUR GREAT GUARDIANS OF TIBETAN BUDDHISM: Dhritarashtra

GENII OF ZODIACAL SIGN: Sagras, Grasgarben, Sagham.

GENIUS OF THE QLIPPHOTH: Amprodias (401).

GOETIC DEMON KING: Amayon (798).

GOETIC GREATER RULER /ELEMENTAL KING: Amaimon.

GOLDEN DAWN ASPECTS:
-ADMISSION BADGE: Cubical Cross and Caduceus.
-COMPONENT OF LVX FORMULA AND SIGN: +, the Cross, Osiris slain.
-GRADE: Theoricus.
-LORD OF PATH: 32.

-MYSTIC NUMBER: 36.
-PASSWORD: Eloah.
-SEPHIROTH: Yesod.
-SIGN: The god Shu supporting the sky.
-TITLE: Poraios de Rejectis.
GORIN NO SHO CHAPTER: Book of Wind/Tradition.
GNOSTIC WORLD: Psyche.
GREAT DIVINE NAME: Shaddai El Chai (363).
GREEK GOD: Hera.
HEBREW DIRECTION: Mizrach (255).
HEBREW ELEMENT: Ruach (214).
HINDU TATTVA/COLOR/SHAPE: Vayu/blue/disk.
HUMOR: Phlegm.
INFERNAL RIVER: Cocytus.
JUNG'S FOUR MENTAL FUNCTIONS: Thought/reason.
KERUB OF THE BENEDICTINE OMNIA OPERA: Kerub of Air/Man.
LETTER OF THE TETRAGRAMMATON: Vau.
LEVI'S FOURFOLD REVELATION: The Fall.
LEVI'S FOUR WORDS OF THE MAGUS: To know.
LEVI'S FOUR MANIFESTED PHENOMENA OF THE ASTRAL LIGHT: Light.
LEVI'S FOUR MEDIEVAL PHYSIOLOGY OF TEMPERAMENTS: Bilious.
LEVI'S FOUR PHILOSOPHICAL IDEAS: Spirit.
LEVI'S FOUR PHILOSOPHICAL OPERATIONS OF THE MIND: Affirmation.
MOLECULAR ACTION: Locomotion.
NATURAL PRINCIPLE: Perpetual motion.
NAVAJO SACRED FOOD: Beans.
PATH ON THE TREE OF LIFE: 11th Path between Kether and Chokmah.
QABALISTIC WORLD: Yetzirah (315).
QUALITIES OF THE WARRIOR PER SUN TZU: Swift as wind.
RIVER OF EDEN: Hiddikel or Tigris.
RITUALISTIC MAGICKAL PRINCIPLE: Banishment.
RULER: Ariel (242).
SCENT: Galbanum.
SENSE: Smell.
SPHINX (per Golden Dawn): Man's face/woman's breasts.

SPHINX (per Levi): Eagle's wings.
SPIRITS OF ZODIACAL CYCLE: Saraiel, Chadakiel, Tzakmaqiel.
STAGE OF THE JAPANESE TEA CEREMONY: Joy.
TAROT ASPECTS:
 -COURT CARDS: Kings or Princes.
 -SUIT: Swords or Daggers.
 -TRUMP: 0-The Fool.
TASTE: Acidic, sour, sharp.
TETRAGRAMMATON OF LPR: YHVH or JHVH (26).
TONE: E.
WHEEL OF EZEKIEL/THRONE OF REVELATIONS/SACRED ANIMAL: Eagle.
WILLIAM BLAKE'S FOUR WORLDS: Beulah.
WILLIAM BLAKE'S FOUR ZOAS: Luvah.
ZODIACAL TRIPLICITY: ♊ ♎ ♒

# Enochian Watchtower – The Great Tablet of the East & Air

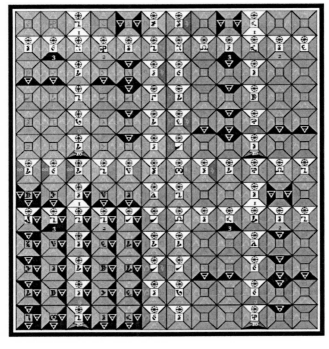

# SOUTH/FIRE

ALCHEMICAL SYMBOL: Sulphur
ANGEL: Aral (232).
ARCHANGEL: Michael (101).
ATU OF THOTH: The Aeon.
AREA OF KNOWLEDGE/DIVINATORY: Passion, ardor, warfare.
BAPHOMET COMPONENT (per Golden Dawn): Lion's tail.
BAPHOMET COMPONENT (Per Levi): Lion's mane and claws.
BODY APPENDAGE: Left Foot.
CARDINAL VIRTUE: Strength.
CHERUBIM OF THE ARK OF THE COVENANT: Lion.
CHIEF DAKINI OF TIBETAN BUDDHISM: Ratna.
CHINESE CORRESPONDENCES PER GODWIN: South, red, bird.
COLOR: Red.
COLOR SCALE: King (brilliance, soft blue, crimson, deep violet, orange, clear pink rose, amber, violet-purple, indigo, yellow, bright pale yellow, blue, emerald green, scarlet, red-orange, orange, amber, greenish-yellow, yellowish-green, violet, emerald green, deep blue, green-blue, blue, indigo, scarlet, violet, ultra-violet, crimson, orange, glowing scarlet-orange, indigo, citrine/olive/russet black/white merging, gray, lavender).
COMPONENT OF THE FIAT FORMULA: I.
COMPONENT OF THE INRI FORMULA: N.
DEMON PRINCE: Samael (131).
DEMON KING: Paimon (837).
DIRECTIONAL EXPRESSION OF ELEMENTAL WEAPONS: Warrior (sword, spear, helmet, shield).
EGYPTIAN GOD: Celurus.
ELEMENTAL ASPECTS:
 -COMPONENTS: Heat & dryness.
 -ATTRIBUTION PER HEBREW LETTER: Shin.
 -KING: Djin.
 -RACE: Salamanders.
 -WEAPON: Wand.

ELEMENT PER LAKOTA SIOUX SHAMANISM: Fire.
ENOCHIAN ASPECTS:
 -DIVINE NAME: OIP TEA PDOCE.
 -GREAT WORD: BITOM.
 -SUPREME ELEMENTAL ANGEL: OHOOOHATAN.
 -TALISMAN: Fire.
 -WATCHTOWER: Fire Tablet.
EVANGELIST/GOSPEL: Mark.
FINGER: Ring.
FOUR GREAT GUARDIANS OF TIBETAN BUDDHISM: Virudhakka.
GENII OF ZODIACAL CYCLE: Sataaran, Sagham, Vhnori.
GENIUS OF THE QLIPPHOTH: Shalicu (500).
GOETIC DEMON KING: Goap (810, 90).
GOETIC GREATER RULER /ELEMENTAL KING: Goap.
GOLDEN DAWN ASPECTS:
 -ADMISSION BADGE: 10 & 12 Square Calvary Cross, Pyramid of the Four Elements.
-COMPONENT OF LVX FORMULA AND SIGN: v, Typhon, the Trident.
-GRADE: Philosophus.
-LORD OF PATH: 27, 28, 29.
-MYSTIC NUMBER: 28.
-PASSWORD: Kaph Cheth.
-SEPHIROTH: Netzach.
-SIGN: the goddess Thoum-Aesh-Neith.
-TITLE: Pharos Illuminans.
GORIN NO SHO CHAPTER: Book of Fire.
GNOSTIC WORLD: Pleroma.
GREAT DIVINE NAME: YHVH Tzaboath (525).
GREEK GOD: Hephaistos.
HEBREW DIRECTION: Darom (810).
HEBREW ELEMENT: Asch or Esh (301).
HINDU TATTVA/COLOR/SHAPE: Tejas, red, triangle.
HUMOR: Choler.
INFERNAL RIVER: Phelgethon.
JUNG'S FOUR MENTAL FUNCTIONS: Feeling.
KERUB OF THE BENEDICTINE OMNIA OPERA: Kerub of Fire, lion.
LETTER OF THE TETRAGRAMMATON: Yod or Jod.

LEVI'S FOURFOLD REVELATION:  First Advent.
LEVI'S FOUR WORDS OF THE MAGUS:  To Will.
LEVI'S FOUR MANIFESTED PHENOMENA OF THE ASTRAL LIGHT:  Electricity.
LEVI'S FOUR MEDIEVAL PHYSIOLOGY OF TEMPERAMENTS:  Sanguine.
LEVI'S FOUR PHILOSOPHICAL IDEAS:  Action.
LEVI'S FOUR PHILOSOPHICAL OPERATIONS OF THE MIND:  Negation.
MOLECULAR ACTION:  Expansion.
NATURAL PRINCIPLE:  Heat.
NAVAJO SACRED FOOD:  Tobacco.
PATH ON THE TREE OF LIFE:  31st Path between Yod and Malkuth.
QABALISTIC WORLD:  Atziluth (537).
QUALITIES OF THE WARRIOR PER SUN TZU:  Destructive as fire.
RIVER OF EDEN:  Pison (1096).
RITUALISTIC MAGICKAL PRINCIPLE:  Consecration.
RULER:  Seraph (1300, 580).
SCENT:  Frankincense.
SENSE:  Sight.
SPHINX (per Golden Dawn):  Lion's mane.
SPHINX (per Levi):  Lion's mane and claws.
SPIRITS OF ZODIACAL CYCLE:  Sarahiel, Seratiel, Saritaiel.
STAGE OF THE JAPANESE TEA CEREMONY:  Gladness.
TAROT ASPECTS:
 -COURT CARDS:  Knights.
 -SUIT:  Wand or Scepters.
 -TRUMP:  20-Judgment.
TASTE:  Spicy, hot and pungent.
TETRAGRAMMATON OF LPR:  ADNI (65).
TONE:  C.
WHEEL OF EZEKIEL/THRONE OF REVELATIONS/HOLY ANIMAL:  Leo the lion.
WILLIAM BLAKE'S FOUR WORLDS:  Eden.
WILLIAM BLAKE'S FOUR ZOAS:  Urizen.
ZODIACAL TRIPLICITY:  ♈ ♌ ♐

# Enochian Watchtower – The Great Tablet of the South & Fire

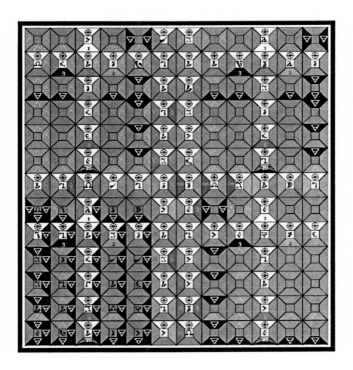

# WEST/WATER

ALCHEMICAL SYMBOL: Mercury.

ANGEL: Taliahad (58).

ARCHANGEL: Gabriel (246).

ATU OF THOTH: The Hanged Man.

AREA OF KNOWLEDGE/DIVINATORY: Poetic, familial, feminine spiritual.

BAPHOMET COMPONENT (per Golden Dawn): Eagle's wings.

BAPHOMET COMPONENT (Per Levi): Women's breasts.

BODY APPENDAGE: Left hand.

CARDINAL VIRTUE: Prudence.

CHERUBIM OF THE ARK OF THE COVENANT: Child.

CHIEF DAKINI OF TIBETAN BUDDHISM: Padma.

CHINESE CORRESPONDENCES PER GODWIN: North, black, turquoise.

COLOR: Blue.

COLOR SCALE: Queen (white brilliance, gray, black, blue, scarlet red, yellow-gold, emerald, orange, violet, citrine/olive/russet/black quadrature, sky blue, purple, silver, sky blue, red, deep indigo, pale mauve, maroon, deep purple, slate gray, blue, blue, sea-green, dull brown, yellow, black, red, sky blue, buff-flecked silver-white, gold-yellow, vermillion, black, amber, deep purple-black, gray-white).

COMPONENT OF THE FIAT FORMULA: A.

COMPONENT OF THE INRI FORMULA: R.

DEMON PRINCE: Azael (108).

DEMON KING: Ariton (926).

DIRECTIONAL EXPRESSION OF ELEMENTAL WEAPONS: Poet (knife, plume, ink cup, papyrus roll).

EGYPTIAN GOD: Horus.

ELEMENTAL ASPECTS:

 -COMPONENTS: Cold and moisture.

 -ATTRIBUTION PER HEBREW LETTER: Mem.

 -KING: Nichsa.

 -RACE: Undines.

 -WEAPON: Cup, goblet, chalice.

ELEMENT PER LAKOTA SIOUX SHAMANISM: Water.
ENOCHIAN ASPECTS:
 -DIVINE NAME: MPH ARSL GAIOL.
 -GREAT WORD: HCOMA.
 -SUPREME ELEMENTAL ANGEL: THAHEBYOBEAATAN.
 -TALISMAN: Water.
 -WATCHTOWER: Water tablet.
EVANGELIST/GOSPEL: John.
FINGER: Index finger.
FOUR GREAT GUARDIANS OF TIBETAN BUDDHISM: Virupaksha.
GENII OF ZODIACAL SIGN: Rahdar, Riehol (?), Rasamasa.
GENIUS OF THE QLIPPHOTH: Malkunofat (307).
GOETIC DEMON KING: Korson (992, 342).
GOETIC GREATER RULER /ELEMENTAL KING: Corson.
GOLDEN DAWN ASPECTS:
 -ADMISSION BADGE: Solid Greek Cubicle cross, Tetrahedron, Greek Cross, Cup of Stolistes.
 -COMPONENT OF LVX FORMULA AND SIGN: L – Isis mourning – the Svastika.
 -GRADE: Practicus.
 -LORD OF PATH: 30, 31, 29.
 -MYSTIC NUMBER: 36.
 -PASSWORD: Eloah.
 -SEPHIROTH: Yod, Jod
 -SIGN: the goddess Auramouth.
 -TITLE: Monocris de Astris.
GORIN NO SHO CHAPTER: Book of Water.
GNOSTIC WORLD: Gnosis.
GREAT DIVINE NAME: Elohim Tzaboath.
GREEK GOD: Poseidon.
HEBREW DIRECTION: Maarab (312).
HEBREW ELEMENT: Maim (650).
HINDU TATTVA/COLOR/SHAPE: Apas/silver/horned crescent moon.
HUMOR: Blood.
INFERNAL RIVER: Styx.
JUNG'S FOUR MENTAL FUNCTIONS: Intuition.
KERUB OF THE BENEDICTINE OMNIA OPERA: Kerub of Water/Eagle.

LETTER OF THE TETRAGRAMMATON: first Heh.

LEVI'S FOURFOLD REVELATION: Antichrist.

LEVI'S FOUR WORDS OF THE MAGUS: To dare.

LEVI'S FOUR MANIFESTED PHENOMENA OF THE ASTRAL LIGHT: Magnetism.

LEVI'S FOUR MEDIEVAL PHYSIOLOGY OF TEMPERAMENTS: Phlegmatic.

LEVI'S FOUR PHILOSOPHICAL IDEAS: Rest.

LEVI'S FOUR PHILOSOPHICAL OPERATIONS OF THE MIND: Discussion.

MOLECULAR ACTION: Contraction.

NATURAL PRINCIPLE: Cold.

NAVAJO SACRED FOOD: Squash.

PATH ON THE TREE OF LIFE: 23rd path between Geburah and Yod.

QABALISTIC WORLD: Briah (218).

QUALITIES OF THE WARRIOR PER SUN TZU: Calm as the forest.

RIVER OF EDEN: Gihon (724, 74).

RITUALISTIC MAGICKAL PRINCIPLE: Purification.

RULER: Tharsis (970).

SCENT: Myrrh.

SENSE: Taste.

SPHINX (per Golden Dawn): Eagle's wings.

SPHINX (per Levi): man's face or woman's breasts.

SPIRITS OF ZODIACAL CYCLE: Phakiel, Sartziel, Vacabiel.

STAGE OF THE JAPANESE TEA CEREMONY: Serenity.

TAROT ASPECTS:

 -COURT CARDS: Queens.

 -SUIT: Cups or chalices.

 -TRUMP: 12th-the Hanged Man.

TASTE: cool, astringent, bitter.

TETRAGRAMMATON OF LPR: EHIH or AHIH (21).

TONE: G sharp.

WHEEL OF EZEKIEL/THRONE OF REVELATIONS/HOLY ANIMAL: Aquarian angel.

WILLIAM BLAKE'S FOUR WORLDS: Generation.

WILLIAM BLAKE'S FOUR ZOAS: Urthona.

ZODIACAL TRIPLICITY: ♋ ♏ ♓

# Enochian Watchtower – The Great Tablet of the West & Water

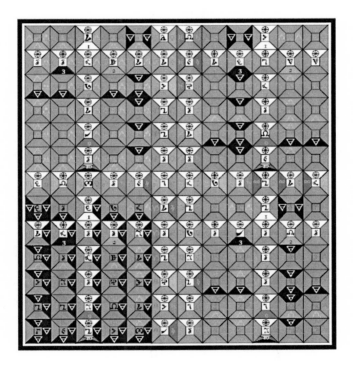

# NORTH/EARTH

ALCHEMICAL SYMBOL: Salt.
ANGEL: Phorlakh (817, 337).
ARCHANGEL: Auriel (248).
ATU OF THOTH: The Universe.
AREA OF KNOWLEDGE/DIVINATORY: nature, maternal, monetary.
BAPHOMET COMPONENT (per Golden Dawn): Bull hooves.
BAPHOMET COMPONENT (Per Levi): Bull hooves, horns.
BODY APPENDAGE: Right foot.
CARDINAL VIRTUE: Temperance.
CHERUBIM OF THE ARK OF THE COVENANT: Bull.
CHIEF DAKINI OF TIBETAN BUDDHISM: Karma.
CHINESE CORRESPONDENCES PER GODWIN: Center, yellow, man.
COLOR: Black, green, citrine, olive, russet.
COLOR SCALE: Empress, knave, or princess (white-flecked gold, white flecked red/blue/yellow, gray-flecked pink, deep azure flecked yellow, red-flecked black, gold amber, olive-flecked gold, yellow-brown flecked white, citrine-flecked azure, black-rayed yellow, emerald-flecked gold, indigo-rayed violet, silver-rayed sky blue, bright rose of series rayed with pale yellow, glowing red, rich brown, reddish gray inclined to mauve, dark greenish-brown, reddish amber, plum, bright blue-rayed yellow, pale green, white-flecked purple like mother of pearl, livid indigo-brown /black beetle, dark vivid blue, cold dark gray/near black, bright red-rayed azure or emerald, white-tinged purple, stone, amber-rayed red, vermillion-flecked crimson and emerald, black-rayed blue, black and yellow, white/red/yellow/blue on outside, gray-flecked gold).
COMPONENT OF THE FIAT FORMULA: T.
COMPONENT OF THE INRI FORMULA: final I.
DEMON PRINCE: Mahazael (83).
DEMON KING: Amaimon (798, 148).
DIRECTIONAL EXPRESSION OF ELEMENTAL WEAPONS: Farmer (scythe, staff, basket, wheel).
EGYPTIAN GOD: Apis.

ELEMENTAL ASPECTS:
 -COMPONENTS: Cold and dryness.
 -ATTRIBUTION PER HEBREW LETTER: Tau.
 -KING: Ghob.
 -RACE: Gnomes.
 -WEAPON: Disk or Pantacle.
ELEMENT PER LAKOTA SIOUX SHAMANISM: Earth.
ENOCHIAN ASPECTS:
 -DIVINE NAME: MOR DIAL HCTAGA.
 -GREAT WORD: NANTA.
 -SUPREME ELEMENTAL ANGEL: THAHAAOTAHE
 -TALISMAN: Earth.
 -WATCHTOWER: Earth Tablet.
EVANGELIST/GOSPEL: Luke.
FINGER: Middle.
FOUR GREAT GUARDIANS OF TIBETAN BUDDHISM: Vaishravana.
GENII OF ZODIACAL SIGN: Bagdal, Iadara, ?.
GENIUS OF THE QLIPPHOTH: ?.
GOETIC DEMON KING: Zimimay (118).
GOETIC GREATER RULER /ELEMENTAL KING: Ziminiar.
GOLDEN DAWN ASPECTS:
 -ADMISSION BADGE: Fylfot Cross.
 -COMPONENT OF LVX FORMULA AND SIGN:  X – Osiris risen – the Pentagram.
 -GRADE: Zelator.
 -LORD OF PATH: ?.
 -MYSTIC NUMBER: 55.
 -PASSWORD: Nun Heh.
 -SEPHIROTH: Malkuth.
 -SIGN: the god Set fighting.
 -TITLE: Pereclinus de Faustus.
GORIN NO SHO CHAPTER: Book of Ground.
GNOSTIC WORLD: Hyle.
GREAT DIVINE NAME: Adonai ha-Aretz (1171).
GREEK GOD: Hestia.
HEBREW DIRECTION: Tzaphon (876, 226).
HEBREW ELEMENT: Aretz or Eretz (1101).
HINDU TATTVA/COLOR/SHAPE: Prithivi/yellow/square.
HUMOR: Melancholy.

INFERNAL RIVER: Acheron.

JUNG'S FOUR MENTAL FUNCTIONS: Sensation.

KERUB OF THE BENEDICTINE OMNIA OPERA: Kerub of earth, bull.

LETTER OF THE TETRAGRAMMATON: final Heh.

LEVI'S FOURFOLD REVELATION: Second Advent.

LEVI'S FOUR WORDS OF THE MAGUS: To keep silent.

LEVI'S FOUR MANIFESTED PHENOMENA OF THE ASTRAL LIGHT: Caloric.

LEVI'S FOUR MEDIEVAL PHYSIOLOGY OF TEMPERAMENTS: Melancholic.

LEVI'S FOUR PHILOSOPHICAL IDEAS: Matter.

LEVI'S FOUR PHILOSOPHICAL OPERATIONS OF THE MIND: Solution.

MOLECULAR ACTION: Cohesion.

NATURAL PRINCIPLE: Bulky.

NAVAJO SACRED FOOD: Corn.

PATH ON THE TREE OF LIFE: the seven Earths corresponding to the Supernal Sephira.

QABALISTIC WORLD: Assiah (385).

QUALITIES OF THE WARRIOR PER SUN TZU: Steady as the mountains.

RIVER OF EDEN: Phrath or Euphrates (680).

RITUALISTIC MAGICKAL PRINCIPLE: Manifestation.

RULER: Kerub (228).

SCENT: Storax.

SENSE: Touch.

SPHINX (per Golden Dawn): Bull Hooves.

SPHINX (per Levi): Bull hooves.

SPIRITS OF ZODIACAL CYCLE: Araziel, Schaltiel, Semaqiel.

STAGE OF THE JAPANESE TEA CEREMONY: Madness.

TAROT ASPECTS:
  -COURT CARDS: Pages, knaves, or princesses.
  -SUIT: Disks, coins, or pantacles.
  -TRUMP: 21-The World.

TASTE: Sweet.

TETRAGRAMMATON OF LPR: AGLA (35).

TONE: A.

WHEEL OF EZEKIEL/THRONE OF REVELATIONS/HOLY ANIMAL: Taurus the Bull.

WILLIAM BLAKE'S FOUR WORLDS: Ulro.
WILLIAM BLAKE'S FOUR ZOAS: Tharmas.
ZODIACAL TRIPLICITY: ♉ ♍ ♑

## Enochian Watchtower – The Great Tablet of the North & Earth

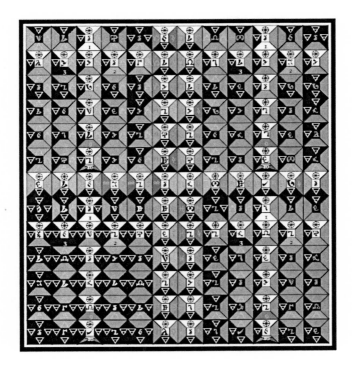

Mike Benjamin

## Enochian Elemental Sigils or Talismans

AIR                    FIRE

EARTH                WATER

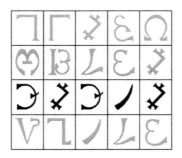

**Enochian Tablet of Union (The Four Great Words)**

300

## The Hindu Tattvas

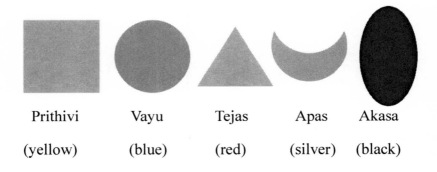

| Prithivi | Vayu | Tejas | Apas | Akasa |
|----------|------|-------|------|-------|
| (yellow) | (blue) | (red) | (silver) | (black) |

## Kanji of the 5 Taoist Elements

| Metal | Wood | Water | Fire | Earth |
|-------|------|-------|------|-------|

301

Mike Benjamin

## Golden Dawn Admission Badges

### Air

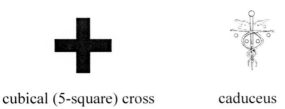

cubical (5-square) cross      caduceus

### Fire

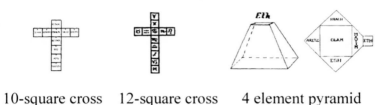

10-square cross   12-square cross   4 element pyramid

### Water

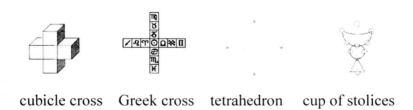

cubicle cross   Greek cross   tetrahedron   cup of stolices

### Earth

fylfot cross

# Appendix B – Associative Charts of Interior Stars/Chakras: From the Hermetic, Buddhist, and Hindu Systems

Explanatory Note: The following charts and accompanying illustrations are a slight example of the correspondences drawn between the subtle energy systems representative of the Hermetic, Buddhist, and Hindu systems. The student should note that in the Hermetic system (representative of Western Magick, Alchemy, and Astrology), what are known as Chakras or Lotuses in the Orient are called by the name Interior Star (or Planet) in Occidental esotericism, but the meanings are identical. Such terms denote the subtle energy wheels, or focal points, that are found through the human organism in ascending scale.

While this work is not meant as a treatise explaining the many meanings behind the Interior Stars/Chakras, these charts will assist the student in gaining a rudimentary understanding of this system as worked within the LPR and other energetic practices, whether Magick, Yoga, or Tai Chi. It must be understood that, depending on the system referenced, different numbers of points will be given and differing meanings as well. The Buddhist system utilized herein only acknowledges five Chakras, while the standard Hindu Yogic system utilized acknowledges seven. However, differing systems (even within Yoga) inconsistently name nine, some thirteen, and some even dozens of different Chakras. The Qabalistic system, based upon the Tree of Life, uses the Sephiroth and is thus in possession of ten energy zones. The Taoist system, generally speaking, only names three, which it calls Dan Tiens.

The student should not become confused with this apparent discrepancy between systems. They are but theoretical frameworks from which to gain understanding and by which one may work on a subtle energetic level. Each system holds validity in its own way and within its own paradigm. They are but different maps of the same territory. Just as some cartographic maps may outline roads, while others geographic topography, and others may illustrate weather patterns or

Mike Benjamin

climate, so do each of the subtle energy models detail a special view not necessarily related in the others. To argue one as being correct and others wrong misses the point of such diversion in theories as each is legitimate in its own right, within its own parameters and worldview.

While these Interior Stars or Chakras do reflect occult knowledge and cause effects upon the one able to unlock and utilize their powers, it must be noted that these models likewise reflect a developmental scale of being that is not mysterious or esoteric at all. For example, we quote an analysis of this fact as related by the philosophical genius Ken Wilber (1996), founder of Integral Methodological Pluralism (or Integralism for short) in his monumental work *Up From Eden – A Transpersonal View of Human Evolution*. Under an illustration of the 7-Step Kundalini Chakra model (as used herein) he states:

> The locations of the Chakra centers themselves are not merely symbolic, but actual. The first (i.e. anal) chakra represents matter (as in faecal matter), the second, sex (genitals), the third, gut reactions (emotions, power, vitality), the fourth, love and belongingness (heart), the fifth, discursive intellect (voice box), the sixth, higher mental psychic powers (neocortex), the seventh, at and beyond the brain itself, transcendence. There is precisely nothing "occult" or mysterious about their locations. (p. 38).

While he argues that there is nothing occult about *the locations* of these Chakras, the student should not misunderstand that this means there is nothing occult about their powers, their development, or their usage. We remind the reader that "occult" simply means secret or hidden, and such practices involving the Chakras are in fact, indubitably so, as competent instruction in such energy work must be sought out and is obviously not found in public schools, on TV, or at the neighborhood block party. For an important introduction into the Chakra theory and its relation to homo sapien evolution, we refer aspirants to Wilber's book mentioned above (especially Part I – Chapter 1 and Part IV – Chapter 11).

As a final note, in the following charts at the top of each page the name of the Interior Star (or Planet) is given along with its Astrological sign. These are laid out in alphabetical order, and are not listed in the ascending scale as found in the human organism. The position of these points is provided in the charts and can thus be cross-referenced with the accompanying illustrations.

## INTERIOR STAR/PLANET: Jupiter.

♃

ANGEL: Sachiel.
ALCHEMCIAL METAL: Tin.
BODILY AREA OF INFLUENCE:  Coccygeal and sacral spine, iliac arteries and veins, sciatic nerves, femur, hips, thighs, feet, toes.
BALANCED EFFECTS UPON SELF:  Manners, charity, lover of the outdoors, ceremonial, religious, law and order.
BUDDHA ASPECT & FAMILY: Quality; Ratna.
BUDDHIST ANIMAL & ELEMENT: Horse; earth.
BUDDHIST BIJA: SWA.
BUDDHIST CHAKRA LOCATION, MEANING, # OF SPOKES, COLOR, & DIRECTION:  Navel; Transmutation; 64; yellow; South.
BUDDHIST POISON & WISDOM: Pride; equalizing.
BUDDHIST SKANDHA: Feelings.
COLOR: Violet.
DYHANI BUDDHA: Ratnasambhava.
EFFECTS WHEN IN OVER-ABUNDANCE:    Pompous, materialistic, over-conservative.
EFFECTS WHEN IN UNDER-ABUNDANCE: Poor circulation, impure blood.
HEBREW LETTER: Kaph.
HEBREW PLANET: Tzedek.
HINDU ANIMAL: Ram.
HINDU BIJA: RAM.

HINDU CHAKRA, PETAL #, COLOR, LETTERS, & EFFECTS: Manipura; 10, gray raincloud-colored petals with blue letters; (DAM, DHAM, NAM, TAM, THAM, DAM, DHAM, NAM, PAM, PHAM); health & vigor, creativity.

HINDU DEITY: Rudra, Vishnu.

HINDU # OF RAYS AND ELEMENT: 62, fire.

HINDU SAKTI: Lakini, Laksmi.

HINDU YANTRA: Agni mandala.

INTELLIGENCE: Iophiel.

MUSICAL NOTE: A-sharp, B-flat.

PHYSICAL LOCATION: Epigastric ganglion, solar plexus, behind stomach.

PHYSIOLOGICAL PROCESSES OF INFLUENCE: Stomach, sympathetic nervous system, pancreas.

QUALITIES: Record of cosmic involution and evolution.

SEPHIROTH: Tiphareth.

SPIRIT: Hismael.

STONE: Sapphire.

TAROT KEY OF MAJOR ARCANA: 10-Wheel of Fortune.

TYPE OF AWARENESS: Sight.

VIRTUES: Justice.

## INTERIOR STAR/PLANET: Mars.

ANGEL: Zamael.

ALCHEMCIAL METAL: Iron.

BODILY AREA OF INFLUENCE: Prostatic ganglion, mesenteric plexuses, adrenals.

BALANCED EFFECTS UPON SELF: Active power, leadership, teaching skills, healing skills, forward looking.

BUDDHA ASPECT & FAMILY: Activity; Karma.

BUDDHIST ANIMAL & ELEMENT: Shang bird; air.

BUDDHIST BIJA: HA.

BUDHIST CHAKRA LOCATION, MEANING, # OF SPOKES, COLOR, & DIRECTION: Genitals; happiness; 32; green; North.

BUDDHIST POISON & WISDOM: Jealousy; all-accomplishing.
BUDDHIST SKANDHA: Concepts.
COLOR: Red.
DYHANI BUDDHA: Amoghasiddi.
EFFECTS WHEN IN OVER-ABUNDANCE: Animal desires, temper, cruelty.
EFFECTS WHEN IN UNDER-ABUNDANCE: Follower, weakness.
HEBREW LETTER: Peh.
HEBREW PLANET: Madim.
HINDU ANIMAL: Makara (mythic crocodile-fish that eats everything).
HINDU BIJA: VAM.
HINDU CHAKRA, PETAL #, COLOR, LETTERS, & EFFECTS: Svadisthana; 6; vermillion petals with lightening-like letters; (VA, BHA, MA, YA, RA, LA); freedom from lust, anger, greed, & sloth.
HINDU DEITY: Hari Vishnu.
HINDU # OF RAYS & ELEMENT: 52, water.
HINDU SAKTI: Rakini.
HINDU YANTRA: White crescent.
INTELLIGENCE: Graphiel.
MUSICAL NOTE: C-natural.
PHYSICAL LOCATION: Between spine and navel.
PHYSIOLOGICAL PROCESSES OF INFLUENCE: Motor centers, reproductive organs, entropic breakdown of cells.
PSYCHOLOGICAL PROCESSES OF INFLUENCE: Desires, impulses, aggression.
QUALITIES: Energy, strength, courage, activity, incitation.
SEPHIROTH: Yesod.
SPIRIT: Bartzabel.
STONE: Diamond.
TAROT KEY OF MAJOR ARCANA: 16-the Tower.
TYPE OF AWARENESS: Taste.
VIRTUES: Strength.

## INTERIOR STAR/PLANET: Mercury.

ANGEL: Raphael.
ALCHEMCIAL METAL: Mercury/quicksilver.
BODILY AREA OF INFLUENCE:   Pineal gland, brain sand, upper intestines, chyle.
BALANCED EFFECTS UPON SELF:   Even of temperament, tranquility, serenity.
BUDDHA ASPECT & FAMILY: Body; Buddha.
BUDDHIST ANIMAL & ELEMENT: Lion; space.
BUDDHIST BIJA: OM.
BUDDHIST CHAKRA LOCATION, MEANING, # OF SPOKES, COLOR, & DIRECTION: Head; bliss; 32; white; center.
BUDDHIST POISON & WISDOM:   Ignorance; absolute wisdom.
BUDDHIST SKANDHA: Forms.
COLOR: Yellow.
DYHANI BUDDHA: Vairocana.
EFFECTS WHEN IN OVER-ABUNDANCE: Indecision, lack of action.
EFFECTS WHEN IN UNDER-ABUNDANCE:   Over activity, mental depression.
HEBREW LETTER: Beth.
HEBREW PLANET: Kokab.
HINDU BIJA: Beyond sound but including all sound.
HINDU CHAKRA, PETAL #, COLOR, & EFFECTS: Sahasrara; thousand petals with the light of a thousand suns; freedom from time and space.
HINDU DEITY: Brahman (the union of Shiva/Shakti, Purusha/Prakriti, Hari/Hara).
HINDU # OF RAYS & ELEMENT:   Total luminosity, Nityananda.
HINDU SAKTI: Nirvana Sakti.
HINDU YANTRA: Beyond form; Mahabindu of the void.

INTELLIGENCE: Triel.
MUSICAL NOTE: E.
PHYSICAL LOCATION: Pineal gland & 18" above the skull.
PHYSIOLOGICAL PROCESSES OF INFLUENCE: Assimilation of chyle by the lacteals.
PSYCHOLOGICAL PROCESSES OF INFLUENCE: Mental alertness, discrimination, emotional balance.
QUALITIES: Higher brain functions, establishment of the Ahben or Philosopher's Stone – the Yogi's gem.
SEPHIROTH: Kether.
SPIRIT: Taphthartharath.
STONE: Agate.
TAROT KEY OF MAJOR ARCANA: 1-Magician.
TYPE OF AWARENESS: Liberation.
VIRTUES: Prudence.

**INTERIOR STAR/PLANET:** Moon/Luna.

ANGEL: Gabriel.
ALCHEMCIAL METAL: Silver.
BODILY AREA OF INFLUENCE: Skeleton, stomach, breasts, esophagus, thoracic duct, liver, lower lungs, neck, palate, larynx, tonsils, lower jaw, ears, atlas, cervical vertebrae, carotid artery, jugular vein.
COLOR: Blue.
EFFECTS WHEN IN OVER-ABUNDANCE: Over-sensitive, co-dependent, idle visions, digestive troubles.
EFFECTS WHEN IN UNDER-ABUNDANCE: Cancer, poor memory, insensibility, temper.
HEBREW LETTER: Gimel.
HEBREW PLANET: Levanah.
HINDU ANIMAL: Unknown.
HINDU BIJA: OM
HINDU CHAKRA, PETAL #, COLOR, & EFFECTS: Ajna; two white petals with white letters (KSAM, HAM); uninterrupted bliss – witnessing all as one presence.

HINDU DEITY: Paramasiva (Sambhu).
HINDU # OF RAYS & ELEMENT: 64; mind.
HINDU SAKTI: Hakini.
HINDU YANTRA: Circle with golden inverted triangle, crescent, & bindu.
INTELLIGENCE: Malkah be Tarashisim ve-ad Ruachoth Schechalim.
MUSICAL NOTE: G-sharp, A-flat.
PHYSICAL LOCATION: Pituitary body, root of nose, sella turcica.
PHYSIOLOGICAL PROCESSES OF INFLUENCE: Respiration rate, sleep cycle, cell system coordination.
PSYCHOLOGICAL PROCESSES OF INFLUENCE: Emotions, psychic rhythms, memory.
QUALITIES: Bodily rhythms, connective activity of cells, telepathy.
SEPHIROTH: Chokmah.
SPIRIT: Schad Barschemoth ha-Shartathan.
STONE: Crystal.
TAROT KEY OF MAJOR ARCANA: 2-High Priestess.
TYPE OF AWARENESS: Consciousness.
VIRTUES: Hope.

## INTERIOR STAR/PLANET: Saturn

ANGEL: Cassiel.
ALCHEMCIAL METAL: Lead.
BODILY AREA OF INFLUENCE: Skin, sweat glands, knees, ankles, kidneys, lumbar spine, bones, vasomotor system.
BALANCED EFFECTS UPON SELF: Poise, deliberation, concentration.
COLOR: Blue-violet (indigo).
EFFECTS WHEN IN OVER-ABUNDANCE: Fear, waste retention.

EFFECTS WHEN IN UNDER-ABUNDANCE: Weak bones, rashes, eccentricity, pipe dreams.
HEBREW LETTER: Tau.
HEBREW PLANET: Shabbathai.
HINDU ANIMAL: Elephant king with seven trunks and black collar.
HINDU BIJA: LAM.
HINDU CHAKRA, PETAL #, COLOR, & EFFECTS: Muladhara; four blood red petals with gold letters (VA 'SA, SA, SA); freedom from disease and fear, mastery of learning and power of speech, spirit filled with great gladness.
HINDU DEITY: Brahma (child).
HINDU # OF RAYS & ELEMENT: 56; earth.
HINDU SAKTI: Dakini.
HINDU YANTRA: Yellow square.
INTELLIGENCE: Agiel.
MUSICAL NOTE: A-natural.
PHYSICAL LOCATION: Sacral plexus near base of spine.
QUALITIES: Waste excretion, life reproduction, Kundalini.
SEPHIROTH: Malkuth.
SPIRIT: Zazel.
STONE: Onyx.
TAROT KEY OF MAJOR ARCANA: 21-the World.
TYPE OF AWARENESS: Smell.
VIRTUES: Temperance.

**INTERIOR STAR/PLANET: Sun/Sol.**

ANGEL: Michael.
ALCHEMCIAL METAL: Gold.
BODILY AREA OF INFLUENCE: Cardiac ganglion.
BALANCED EFFECTS UPON SELF: Strong, vital health.
BUDDHA ASPECT & FAMILY: Mind; Vajra.
BUDDHIST ANIMAL & ELEMENT: Elephant; water.
BUDDHIST BIJA: HUM.

BUDDHIST CHAKRA LOCATION, MEANING, # OF SPOKES, COLOR, & DIRECTION:  Heart; Phenomena; 8; blue; East.
BUDDHIST POISON & WISDOM:  Anger; mirror-like.
BUDDHIST SKANDHA:  Consciousness.
COLOR:  Orange.
DYHANI BUDDHA:  Akshobyha.
EFFECTS WHEN IN OVER-ABUNDANCE:  Feverish, domineering, ambitious, displaying, wasteful.
EFFECTS WHEN IN UNDER-ABUNDANCE:  Poor health, physical depression.
HEBREW LETTER:  Resh.
HEBREW PLANET:  Shemesh.
HINDU ANIMAL:  Black antelope.
HINDU BIJA:  YAM.
HINDU CHAKRA, PETAL #, COLOR, LETTERS, & EFFECTS:  Anahata; remaining qualities the same as the Manipura/Jupiter/Tiphareth.
HINDU DEITY:  Isa.
HINDU # OF RAYS & ELEMENT:  54, Air.
HINDU SAKTI:  Kakini.
HINDU YANTRA:  Shatkona, interlocking triangles, 6-pointed star.
INTELLIGENCE:  Nakhiel.
MUSICAL NOTE:  D-natural.
PHYSICAL LOCATION:  Above and behind heart.
PHYSIOLOGICAL PROCESSES OF INFLUENCE:  Heart.
PSYCHOLOGICAL PROCESSES OF INFLUENCE:  Aspirations, pride, frankness, generosity, humaneness, firmness, honor.
QUALITIES:  Entrance point of Qi/Prana, voice of the silence.
SEPHIROTH:  Tiphareth.
SPIRIT:  Sorath.
STONE:  Ruby.
TAROT KEY OF MAJOR ARCANA:  19-the Sun.
TYPE OF AWARENESS:  Touch.
VIRTUES:  Faith.

**INTERIOR STAR/PLANET:** Venus.

ANGEL: Hanael.
ALCHEMCIAL METAL: Copper.
BODILY AREA OF INFLUENCE: Kidneys, lumbar, skin.
BALANCED EFFECTS UPON SELF:  Good taste, love of beauty, lighter enjoyments. Propensity for dancing, music, poetry.
BUDDHA ASPECT & FAMILY: Speech; Padma.
BUDDHIST ANIMAL & ELEMENT:  Peacock; fire.
BUDDHIST BIJA:  AH.
BUDDHIST CHAKRA LOCATION, MEANING, # OF SPOKES, COLOR & DIRECTION:  Throat; enjoyment; 16; red; West.
BUDDHIST POISON & WISDOM:  Ignorance; discriminating.
BUDDHIST SKANDHA:  Perceptions.
CHAKRA:  Visuddha.
COLOR:  Green.
DYHANI BUDDHA:  Amitabha.
EFFECTS WHEN IN OVER-ABUNDANCE:  Emotional excess, mere amusement & sensation seeking.
EFFECTS WHEN IN UNDER-ABUNDANCE:  Diminished mental & emotional powers.
HEBREW LETTER:  Daleth.
HEBREW PLANET:  Nogah.
HINDU ANIMAL:  Snow white 7-trunked elephant.
HINDU BIJA:  HAM.
HINDU CHAKRA, PETAL #, COLOR, LETTERS, & EFFECTS: Visuddha; sixteen smoky purple petals with crimson letters (A, A, I, I, U, U, R, R, L, L, E, AI, O, AU, AM, AH); serenity, longevity, equanimity.
HINDU DEITY:  Sadasiva.
HINDU # OF RAYS & ELEMENT:  72; space.
HINDU SAKTI:  Gauri.
HINDU YANTRA:  Circle.

INTELLIGENCE: Hagiel.
MUSICAL NOTE: F-sharp, G-flat.
PHYSICAL LOCATION: Throat, thyroid & parathyroid glands.
PHYSIOLOGICAL PROCESSES OF INFLUENCE: Touch.
PSYCHOLOGICAL PROCESSES OF INFLUENCE: Strong emotion and sensitivity.
QUALITIES: Grace, symmetry, artistry, creativity, imagination.
SEPHIROTH: Binah.
SPIRIT: Kedemel.
STONE: Emerald.
TAROT KEY OF MAJOR ARCANA: 3-Empress.
TYPE OF AWARENESS: Hearing.
VIRTUES: Charity.

## The Hermetic Interior Star System

## The Yogic 7-Chakra System

# The Qabalistic Tree of Life Superimposed Upon the Human Frame to Show the Sephira as Chakras

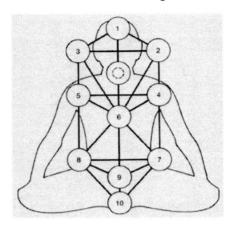

# The Hermetic Caduceus as Emblematic of the Chakras

# Appendix C – Correspondence Chart of the Dhyani Buddhas

Element: space/ether/spirit/void/water/earth/fire/air

| Buddha | Vairochana | Akshobhya | Ratnasambhava | Amitabha | Amoghasiddhi |
|---|---|---|---|---|---|
| Meaning | "He Who Is Like the Sun" or "The Radiating One." | "Imperturbable" or "Immovable" or "Unshakeable." | "The Jewel-born One" or "Origin of Jewels." | "Infinite" or "Immeasurable Light" or "Splendor." | "Almighty Conqueror" or "He Who Unerringly Achieves His Goal." |
| Wisdom | "ALL-PERVADING WISDOM OF THE DHARMAKAYA." The Realm of Truth, in which all things exist as they really are. | "MIRRORLIKE WISDOM." Reflects all things calmly and uncritically and reveals their true nature. Changelessness of diamond-like wisdom. | "THE WISDOM OF EQUALITY." Sees all things with divine impartiality and recognizes the divine equality of all beings. | "DISCRIMINATING WISDOM." Discerns all beings separately yet knows every being as an individual expression of the One. | "ALL-ACCOMPLISHING WISDOM, OR WISDOM OF PERFECTED ACTION." Confers perseverance, infallible judgment and unerring action. |
| Poison Cured By Wisdom Type | Ignorance or delusion. | Hatred and anger. | Pride of all origins-spiritual. intellectual and human. | The passions-all cravings, covetousness, greed and lust. | Envy and jealousy. |
| Mudra | DHARMACHAKRA MUDRA Hold hands at the heart level. Right palm faces outward. Left palm inward. Circle is formed w/right hand thumb & index finger. Second circle is formed with left thumb and index finger. | BHUMISPARSA MUDRA The fingertips of the right hand touch the ground or hang over the right knee, with the palm turned inward. | VARADA MUDRA The right palm faces outward and the fingers are directed downward. | DHYANA MUDRA Hands rest in the lap, palms up, with the right hand on top of the left. | ABHAYA MUDRA Right hand is raised to shoulder height with the palm turned outward and fingers upward. |
| Syllable | Om | Hum | Tram | Hrih | Ah |
| Symbol | Wheel | Thunderbolt | Three Jewels | Lotus | Double Thunderbolt |
| Vehicle | Lion | elephant | horse | peacock | garuda (half-man, half-bird) |

# Appendix D – The Hermetic Order of the Golden Dawn Flying Roll No. VIII: A Geometric Way to Draw a Pentagram

by R.A. Gilbert (cited in King, 1997, p. 285).

Let AB be any line of the length required for the distance between the points of Earth and Fire. Bisect AB in 0 and from 0 draw OH perpendicular to AB. Cut off OC to equal AB.

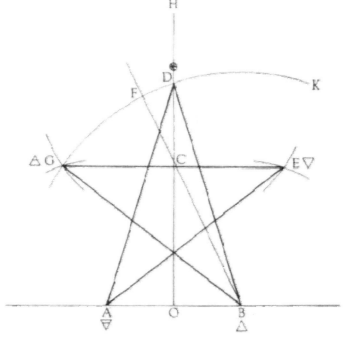

Join B with C and produce the line BC to F making FC to equal OA. From centre B, with radius BF, draw the circle FDK, cutting OH at D. D is then the 'Spirit' angle of the Pentagram. With the centres B and D draw circles with a radius equal to AB, and they cut each other at E which will be the Water angle. In a similar way [i.e. by drawing a circle of radius AB from centre A] find G the Air angle. Join A, B, D, E, and G in the usual way.

# Appendix E – Example of an Artistic Variation on the LPR: Aleister Crowley's Ritual of the Star Ruby

The following ritual is a Thelemic variation on the LPR as authored by Aleister Crowley. Originally taught in the A.A. (the Argentium Astrum or Order of the Silver Star; the Magickal Order he founded along with George Cecil Jones when they both left the Golden Dawn in the early 20th century), it is now perpetuated in the curriculum of the Ordo Templi Orientis (the society headed by Crowley after his A.A. venture) and also within other current Thelemic societies.

It is questionable whether Crowley actually rightfully inherited his status as Frater Superior of the OTO from its founder Theodore Reuss or if he usurped it by default. In the same way, it is equally debatable, according to historical resources, if Grady McMurtry (Hymenaues Alpha) was the rightful successor of Crowley to the same position or whether, as Crowley's own documentation seems to reveal, it was rather Karl Germer. It is even more questionable how the current order head, Bill Breeze (Hymenaues Beta) claims his position as Frater Superior with a clear conscience and without cracking a smile in the mirror. The student is encouraged to study the vast plethora of well-researched material on the historical phenomenon that is the OTO as provided by the impeccable occult anthropologist P.R. Koenig (1996) via his website (www.parareligion.ch/).

Beyond these historical issues, the Star Ruby is an artistically sound variation on the foundational LPR ritual, altered in a much greater form than the one provided by this tome's author. Crowley's is truly beautiful in its incorporation of Greek, Egyptian, and Babylonian components. Once the base form of the LPR is mastered, the student is encouraged to experiment with their own creative variations like this one, as long as what is invented adheres to the basic premise of sound occult correspondences as evidenced in Appendixes A and B.

Readers are also directed to Crowley's poem *The Palace of the World*, contained in his larger work *Temple of the Holy Ghost* (1901), both extant in many online and written sources. This poem proves a highly metaphoric endeavor that both reveals and veils certain insights particular to the LPR, and while paltry in comparison to this present analysis, is worth a quick read.

# The Star Ruby – Liber XXV:

I. Facing East, in the center, draw deep, deep, deep thy breath closing thy mouth with thy right forefinger pressed against thy lower lip. Then dashing down the hand with a great sweep back and out, expelling forcibly thy breath, cry ΑΠΟ ΠΑΝΤΟΣ ΚΑΚΟΔΑΙΜΟΝΟΣ (APO PANTOS KAKODAIMONOS). ["Away, every evil spirit"].

II. The Cross Qabalistic. With the same forefinger touch thy forehead, and say ΣΟΙ (SOI) ["Thine"]. Touch thy member, and say Ω ΦΑΛΛΗ (Ô PhALLE) ["O Phallus"]. Touch thy right shoulder, and say ΙΣΞΥΡΟΣ (ISChUROS) ["the mighty"]. Touch thy left shoulder, and say ΕΥΞΑΡΙΣΤΟΣ (EUChARISTOS) ["the beneficient"]. Then clasp thine hands, locking the fingers, and cry ΙΑΩ (IAÔ). [Isis, Apophis, Osiris].

III. Advance to the East. Imagine strongly a Pentagram, aright, in thy forehead. Drawing the hands to the eyes, fling it forth, making the sign of Horus and roar ΘΕΡΙΟΝ (ThÊRION).

Retire thine hand in the sign of Hoor-paar-Kraat.

Go round to the North and repeat; but say NUIT.

Go round to the West and repeat; but whisper BABALON.

Go round to the South and repeat; but bellow HADIT.

IV. Completing the circle widdershins, retire to the centre and raise thy voice in the Paian, with these words ΙΩ ΠΑΝ (IÔ PAN), with the signs of N.O.X.

V. Extend the arms in the form of a Tau and say low but clear:

PRO MOU YUNGES ["Before me the Iynges,"].

OPISÔ MOU TELETARChAI ["Behind me the Teletarches,"].

EPI DEXIA SUNOChEIS ["on my right hand the Synoches,"].

EPARISTERA DAIMONES ["on my left hand the Daemones,"].

PhLEGEI GAR PERI MOU hO ASTÊR TÔN PENTE ["for about me flames the Star of Five,"].

KAI EN TÊI STÊLÊI hO ASTÊR TÔN hEX hESTÊKE. ["and in the Pillar stands the Star of Six."].

VI. Repeat the Cross Qabalistic, as above (II), and end as thou didst begin (as in I).

# Appendix F – Basic Quaternary Correspondences of Magickal Formulas Inherent to the LPR

The following appendix illustrates a basic diagrammatic scheme of the fundamental formulas intrinsic to the form and function of the LPR. The concluding pages are an extended quotation taken from a letter written by Israel Regardie (1994) and reprinted in the introduction of his monumental *The Golden Dawn*. In this excerpt Dr. Regardie specifically treats the formula of INRI, with all of its complexities, ultimately showing its relation to the formulas of IAO and LVX, so significant in this analysis of the LPR. Note also Regardie's closing sentence, echoing the Buddha who told us to be a light unto ourselves and "Believe not, O brothers. . ." We are also reminded of Levi who similarly admonished the Magickal aspirant: "Be not satisfied by what we tell you; act for yourself." At the end of this appendix are also included illustrations of the Golden Dawn Grade Signs, verbally explained in Regardie's letter.

## Basic Quaternary Formulas Significant to the LPR

### YHVH

YOD     HE     VAU     HE
FIRE   WATER   AIR   EARTH
FATHER  MOTHER  SON  DAUGHTER
YETZILUTH  BRIAH  YETZIRAH  ASSIAH
WANDS   DISKS  SWORDS  CUPS

# INRI

AM   NOUR   RUACH   YEBESHAS
WATER   FIRE   AIR   EARTH
YOD   NUN   RESH   YOD
VIRGO   SCORPIO   SOL   VIRGO
ISIS   APOPHIS   OSIRIS   (I.A.O.)
KHABS   AM   PEHKT
KONX   OM   PAX
LIGHT   IN   EXTENSION   (L.V.X.)

## FIAT LVX

FLATUS   IGNIS   AQUA   TERRA – LIGHT IN EXTENSION

"In the Adeptus Minor Ritual is to be found the analysis of the so-called keyword I.N.R.I. It is found in several places thereafter. Its very frequency should make the student suspect to its importance. Few, however, take time out to apply basic Qabalistic and magical principles to elucidate its meaning. So in order to convey some idea of elementary implications, I have decided to show the student what can be done with these four English letters I.N.R.I. They are, of course, the initials of the Latin phrase "Jesus of Nazareth, King of the Jews." Several other theological meanings to these letters have been given at different periods of history by various groups of people and scholars.

For example, the medieval alchemists suggested that I.N.R.I. meant "Igne Nitrum Raris Invenitum," translated as "shining (or glittering) is rarely found in fire."

The Jesuits in their day interpreted it as "Justum Necare Regis Impius" – "It is just to kill an impious king."

J.S.M. Ward in his book *Freemasonry and the Ancient Gods* gives yet another example:

I.    Yam=Water.
N.    Nour=Fire.
R.    Ruach=Air.
I.    Yebeshas=Earth.

Mike Benjamin

Thus the four letters may be used as Hebrew initials of the four ancient elements.

In the nineteenth century when the Hermetic Order of the Golden Dawn came to be formed, these letters were picked up and integrated into the complex structure of the Order symbolism. To understand the interpretation used by the Order, we need only the most superficial knowledge of the basic attributions given in the Sepher Yetzirah, the Tarot pack of cards, a smattering of Gnosticism and astrology. The first gesture is to convert the four letters into their Hebrew equivalents and then to direct Yetziratic attributions, as follows:

I=Yod=Virgo.
N=Nun=Scorpio.
R=Resh=Sun.
I=Yod=Virgo.

The initial "I," being repetitious, is dropped, only to be picked up again in a later place in order to extend the significance of the meanings derived from the analysis.

This breakdown, though not getting us very far, is nonetheless highly suggestive. Elementary astrology will extend the meaning a little. Virgo represents the virginal side of nature itself. Scorpio is the sign of death and transformation; sex is involved here as well. Sol, the Sun, is the source of light and life to all on earth; it is the centre (sic) of our solar system. All the so-called resurrection gods are known to be solar connected. The Sun was thought to die every winter when vegetation perished and the earth became cold and barren. Every Spring, when the Sun returned, green life was restored to the Earth.

In various of the grade rituals as well as the elementary knowledge lectures of the Order, we find the following which we can add to the data already obtained:

Virgo=Isis – who was nature, the Mother of all things.
Scorpio=Apophis – death, the destroyer.
Sol=Osiris – slain and risen, the Egyptian resurrection and vegetative God.

Here we now begin to get a definite sequence of ideas that proves somewhat meaningful. The simplicity of a natural state of affairs in, shall we say, the Garden of Eden, representing the springtime of mankind, is shattered by the intrusion of the knowledge of Good and Evil, sexual perception. The is due to the intervention of the destroyer Apophis, the Red Dragon, Lucifer, the Lightbearer, who changed all things – by illuminating all things. Thus the Fall – as well as the fall of the year. This is succeeded by the advent of Osiris the resurrection God who is quoted as stating: "This is my body, which I destroy in order that it may be renewed." He is the symbolic prototype of the perfected solar man, who suffered through earthly experience, was glorified by trial, was betrayed and killed, and then rose again to renew all things.

The final analysis off the keyword sums up the formula with the initials Isis, Apophis, Osiris=IAO, the supreme God of the Gnostics. (IAO is pronounced ee-ah-oh!).

Since the Sun is the giver of life and light, the formula must refer to Light as the redeemer. The Order was predicated on the age-old process of bringing Light to the natural man. In other words, it taught a psycho-spiritual technique leading to illumination, to enlightenment. In this connection, one should always remember those beautiful versicles (sic) about the Light in the opening chapter of the Gospel according to St. John.

In the very first or Neophyte Ritual of the Golden Dawn, the candidate is startled to hear the strangely-worded invocation "Khabs Am Pekht. Konx om Pax. Light in Extension." In other words, you may too receive the benediction of the Light, and undergo the mystical experience, the goal of all our work.

"The enlightenment by a ray of the divine light which transforms the psychic nature of many may be an article of faith," says Hans Jonas in his excellent book *The Gnostic Religion*, "but it may also be an experience. . .Annihilation and deification of the person are fused in the spiritual ecstasis which purports to experience the immediate presence of the acosmic essence. In the gnostic context, this transfiguring face-to-face experience is Gnosis in the most exalted sense of the term, since it is knowledge of the unknowable. . .The mystical *gnosis theou* – direct beholding of the divine reality – is itself an earnest of the consummation to come. It is transcendence become immanent; and although prepared for by human acts of self-modification which induce the proper disposition, the event itself is one of divine activity and grace. It is this as much as a 'being known' by God as a 'knowing' him, and in this ultimate mutuality the 'gnosis' is beyond the terms of 'knowledge' properly speaking."

Since this is the basic theme recurrent through all the Golden Dawn rituals and teaching, we would expect to find it repeated and expanded in the analysis of the Keyword of the Adeptus Minor grade. And of course it is there, clearly defined.

The word "light" is translated into LVX, the Latin word for light. A series of physical mimes or gestures are employed by the officiants (sic) to represent the descent of this Light, as well as to summarize the symbolism of the previous findings.

So one Adept or officiant (sic) raises his arm directly in the air above him, while extending his left arm straight outwards (as though to make a left turn when driving a car). This forms by shape the letter "L."

A second Adept raises his arms as though in supplication above his head – the letter "V."

The third adept extends his arms outwards forming a Cross.

All together finally cross their arms on their chests, forming the letter "X."

(A single person may of course perform the identical gestures).

The letters form "LVX" which is now interpreted as the "Light of the Cross."  It is so interpreted because the letters INRI were initially found on the Cross, as well as because LVX means Light. Finally the letters "LVX" themselves are portions of one type or another of the Cross.

$$+ \quad v \quad x$$

A process of repetition is followed in order to synthesize all these variegated ideas and gestures, and to add one more mime to replace the second "I" that was eliminated for being repetitious.

As the "L" sign is being made, the Adept says: "The Sign of the Mourning of Isis."  This expresses the sorrow of Isis on learning that Osiris had been slain by Set or Apophis.

As the "V" sign is made, the Adept says: "The Sign of Apophis and Typhon."  These are other names for Set, the brother and murderer of Osiris, whose body was so mutilated that only the phallus could be found by Isis who had searched all over creation for him.

As the Adept spreads his arms outward from the shoulders forming actively the Cross, he says: "The Sign of Osiris slain." Then crossing one arm over the other on the chest he adds: "And risen. Isis, Apophis, Osiris, IAO."

Thus what started out to be a simple abbreviation of a traditional Latin sentence on the Cross above the head of Jesus, has now evolved by a Qabalistic process of exegesis into a complex series of evocative ideas and symbolic gestures which extend tremendously the root idea. And by knowing these ideas, the gestures may be used practically to aspire to the illumination which it suggests. This is the essential value of the sacramental actions.

The Rosicrucian equivalent of this formula is found in the Fama Fraternitatis, one of the original three classical Rosicrucian documents. Ex Deo Nascimur. In Jesu Morimur. Per spiritus sanctus reviviscimus. "From God are we born. In Christ we die. We are revived by the Holy Spirit."

Nor is this all. If we take "LVX" as symbols of Roman numerals, we have 65. This number, therefore, attains the symbolic equivalent of Light, gnosis and illumination.

The Adeptus Minor obligation imposed on the candidate during the ritual initiation, obligates him, as already demonstrated, to aspire and work and practise (sic) so that by enlightenment he may one day "become more than human." This is the Qabalistic philosophy summarized in the statement that the Adept seeks to unite himself to higher soul, or his higher Self, symbolized again in the Hebrew word Adonai. All the above notions therefore are synthesized in this word Adonai, literally translated "My Lord." Its Hebrew letters are: Aleph Daleth Nun Yod 1 + 4 + 50 + 10 = 65.

This number is also that of LVX Light. Qabalistically the process enables us to perceive a necessary connection between Adonai and the Light, their identity. From here we can move in a variety of exegetical directions.

But enough has been said, I hope, to show the student not to accept superficially any phase of the Rituals and the teachings, but to accept them to the most exacting scrutiny." (Regardie, 1994, pp. 11-14).

Mike Benjamin

# Grade Signs of the Golden Dawn

1. Earth : the god Set fighting.
2. Air : the god Shu supporting the sky.
3. Water : the goddess Auramoth.
4. Fire : the goddess Thoum-aesh-neith.
5. & 6. Spirit : the rending and closing of the veil.

7-re. The L V X signs.
7. + Cabiri: the cross.
8. L In mourning—the Swastika.
9. V Typhon—the Trident.
10. X Osiris risen—the Pentagram.

THE SIGNS OF THE GRADES

328

# Appendix G – Formulation of the Pythagorean Tectractys into the Hexagram

(The following excerpt is taken from *The Portico*, official publication of Dr. Paul Foster Case's (1997) the **Builders of the Adytum**. It is quoted at length due to the significance it holds in our current study of the Cross and its symbolism as related in the LPR, along with its relationship to the hexagram).

"The triad resumed by unity, and with the conception of unity added to that of the triad, produces the first square and perfect number, sourcer (sic) of all numerical combinations, and origin of all forms – the quaternary or tetrad, the tectractys of Pythagoras, whence all is derived. This number produces the cross and the square in geometry. All that exists, whether of good or evil, light or darkness is revealed by the tetrad.

The number Four is the mathematical sign of the Supreme Source of all existence. It represents the One Self, called Parusha by the Hindus, Yaveh by the Hebrews, and recognized by both races as the Lord of all.

Occultists agree that Pythagoras knew the secret of the name Yaveh, and symbolized by the Tectractys, a triangular figure composed of ten dots, which is the geometric basis for many ancient emblems of the Secret Doctrine, including the Swastika and the Pyramid. The swastika is a solar emblem, like the cross worn by the High Priestess (Trump 2). The pyramid typifies the primal fire, or universal radiant energy. Thus the Pythagorean conception of the number Four reminds us that the source of all numerical combinations, and origin of all forms is manifested on earth as the light and heat of the sun.

By joining all points of the Tectractys, a great equilateral triangle may be formed containing nine smaller triangles. Of these only three have sides which form no part of the sides of the great triangle; and the combined length of the lines composing these three triangles is equal to the length of the great triangle. These lines, therefore, might be used to form a triangle of equal area to that of the great triangle. Thus the

Tectractys figure implies two equilateral triangles of equal area; and the length of the lines required to join all the ten dots is exactly the length of the lines required to form a Hexagram, or Shield of David, composed of two triangles of the same area as the great triangle of the Tectractys. . .

The Shield of David is a Hebrew sign for Yahveh; the cross, implied by the number Four, represents Christ. Between these two symbols, long opposed to each other in the field of exoteric religion, stands the Tectractys, based on the four of the cross, yet showing the Ten, which is a prominent number in the Kabbalah, and implying the Hexagram, that summarizes the whole Secret Doctrine of Israel."

# The Tectractys

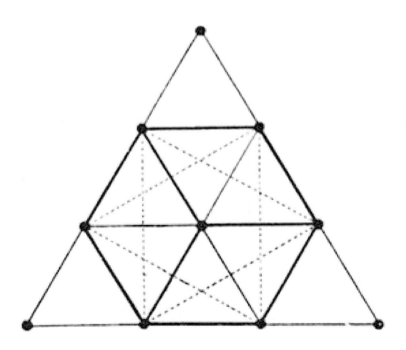

# Appendix H – Ken Wilber's 4 Quadrant Model

The scope of Ken Wilber's Integral school is vastly beyond this examination. However, it should be noted in this exposition of the LPR that Wilber's Integral model is likewise based upon a four-quadrant schematic reminiscent of both the Cross and the comprehensive, holistic applicability of the Universal Mandala's general form. To over-simplify this diagram, Wilber argues that all events tetra-arise in four areas: internal singular; internal plural; external singular; and external plural. As a result, the following chart of Universal evolution is produced. Students are referred to Wilber's (2000) absolutely epic *Sex, Ecology, and Spirituality* for a more-than-thorough explanation of this model and of his consciousness-changing Integral Theory.

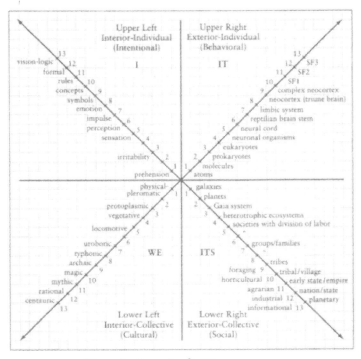

Figure 1. *Four Quadrants.*

# Appendix I – The Emerald Tablet of Hermes

Numerous translations of this text have been produced throughout history, with everyone from Isaac Newton to Madam Blavatsky to Idries Shah producing variations in English. The version quoted below is the official one utilized within BOTA. Also called the *Smaragdine Table*, or *Tabula Smaragdina*, the *Emerald Tablet* is reputed to contain the secret of the *prima materia* and its transmutation. It is regarded as the foundation of the Hermetic arts, especially alchemy. Its authorship is legendarily attributed to Hermes Mercurius Trismegistus, an amalgam of the Greek god Hermes, the Roman Mercury, and the Egyptian Thoth – all messengers of the gods.

Its first known appearance is in an Arabic book written between the sixth and eighth centuries (the *Kitāb sirr al-ḫalīqa - Book of the Secret of Creation and the Art of Nature*). This book is attributed to Balinas (also called Pseudo-Apollonius of Tyana) who tells his readers that he discovered it in a vault below a statue of Hermes in Tyana, where inside on a golden throne an old man held an emerald tablet upon which this work was inscribed. It was then subsequently translated into Latin in the twelfth century by Hugo von Santalla. Its layers of meaning relay various occult secrets including the creation of the Philosopher's Stone, the element system, and the correspondence between the Macrocosm and Microcosm.

# The Emerald Tablet of Hermes Mercurius Trismegistus

True, without falsehood, certain and most true, that which is above is as that which is below, and that which is below is as that which is above, for the performance of the miracles of the One Thing. And as all things are from One, by the mediation of One, so all things have their birth from this One Thing by adaptation. The Sun is its father, the Moon its mother, and the Wind carries it in its belly, its nurse is the Earth. This is the father of all perfection, or consummation of the whole world. Its power is integrating, if it be turned into earth.

Thou shalt separate the earth from the fire, the subtle from the gross, suavely, and with great ingenuity. It ascends from earth to heaven and descends again to earth, and receives the power of the superiors and of the inferiors. So thou hast the glory of the whole world; therefore let all obscurity flee before thee. This is the strong force of all forces, overcoming every subtle and penetrating every solid thing. So the world was created. Hence were all wonderful adaptations, of which this is the manner. Therefore am I called Hermes Trismegistus, having the three parts of the philosophy of the whole world. What I have to tell is completed, concerning the Operation of the Sun.

# Appendix J – The Bodhisattva's Vow

Numerous versions of the Bodhisattva's Vow are extant throughout the history of Buddhism. The one presented here has been poetically adapted from an original found in the *Bodhisattvacaryavatara* authored by Shantideva, a Buddhist monk who taught at the now legendary Nalanda University in India, around the beginning of the 8th century (C.E.). Belonging to the Madyamihka (Middle Path) view of the Mahayana, its ten chapters convey the lessons needed for one to attain Bodhicitta - the enlightened mind.

The Bodhisattva's place in the scheme of evolutionary enlightenment has long been debated within Buddhism. Classically, in some Buddhist views (such as the Theravadan or lesser vehicle school), the Bodhisattva was thought of as preceding a Buddha, being the prior stage, or life before, achieving full awakening. This perspective, however, is now considered erroneous in most Mahayana and Vajrayana systems with the Bodhisattva being placed as a superior type of Buddha, rather than an inferior stage preceding full enlightenment. This is due to the fact that the Bodhisattva willfully chooses not to step off the wheel of Samsara into Nirvana until all other Beings have been liberated from suffering.

I believe it a rightful view that such a Being, having taken this vow and having voluntarily assumed such a noble obligation, and having placed all others altruistically before him or herself, is the supreme condition of fulfillment in true Buddhahood, and rightfully places the Bodhisattva at the vanguard of both Wisdom and Compassion. They are the perfect embodiment of love and sacrifice combined with all-encompassing Kosmic Consciousness, and thus, cannot be considered subordinate to Buddhahood, but rather, a type of fully-succeeded and completely-realized Tathagata. The duty they assume in continuing to return through life, death, and rebirth, over and over again *ad infinitum*, for the benefit of all others, correctly places them beyond the Pratyeka (or lone Buddhas), who are solitary, self-evolved, and non-teaching.

Unlike the Bodhisattvas, Pratyekas take the path of Nirvana upon their physical demise to reside in the unknowable state of the Dharmakaya, never to return physically to the Samsara.

At best, the Pratyekas, while vital to the Universal and evolutionary scheme of things (at least on planet Earth and amongst our homo sapien species), are no more than what Eckhart Tolle (2005) describes as "frequency holders;" at the highest Kosmic scale, no doubt, but still of this sole function nonetheless. As Ken Wilber and others have argued, the Bodhisattvas, on the other hand, in making the choice to come back upon the wheel of metempsychosis again and again for as many eons upon eons as it will take to save all other living Beings – human, animal, plant, deva, demon, genii, asura, preta, naraka, whatever – prove their superiority over Awakened Ones who simply steps off the wheel altogether to just save themselves from suffering. It is thus the Bodhisattva, unlike the Pratyeka, who fully lives by the Tibetan Budddhist injunction of E-MA-HO! (Compassion is to be expressed to all living things).

This may prove a controversial opinion, especially coming from one who neither claims enlightenment nor personally knows any *human* in such a condition. (Just like Tolle, I acknowledge that I have lived with a few Zen Masters – all of them cats!). I do, nevertheless, stand by this assertion and hold that history will prove its soundness as a spiritual hypothesis. I would likewise point out, to this effect, that amongst the Mahayana, especially that of the Tibetans, the Buddha Shakyamuni Himself is not considered a Pratyeka, but rather, as their tradition holds, came back as no less than Padmasambhava for the benefit of all the Earth. Equally, the Buddha's spiritual heir, his cousin Anannda, was said to have returned as the great teacher Nagarjuna, founder of the Mahayana system.

Mike Benjamin

# The Vow of the Bodhisattva

May I be a guard for those without protection,

A guide for those who journey on the road,

For those who wish to cross the water

May I be a boat, a raft, a bridge.

May I be an isle for those who yearn for landfall,

And a lamp for those who long for light;

For those who need a resting place, a bed.

For all those who need help, may I serve them.

May I be a wishing jewel, the vase of plenty,

A word of power, and the supreme remedy.

May I be the tree of miracles,

And for every being, the abundant cow.

Like the great Earth and all the other elements.

Enduring as the sky itself endures,

For the boundless multitude of living Beings

May I be the ground and vessel of their life.

Thus, for every single thing that lives in number

Like the boundless reaches of space and stars

May I be their sustenance and nourishment

Until they pass beyond the bounds of suffering.

# Appendix K – On Transformations: An Hopological Examination of Occult Therianthropy

The power of belief, of the mind's proclivity in perceiving and even creating reality, must not be underestimated. As the eminent Integral philosopher Ken Wilber (2000) has pointed out, the great discovery of post-modern philosophy (echoing Kant) is that the mind not only collects the reality we perceive, it filters, shapes, and structures it as well. The Ayn Rand-esque objectivist viewpoint that there is but a single "true" reality just waiting "out there" for all of us to mutually and equally perceive is now a shattered glass. Our minds not only collect what we see, but interpret how we are able to see it.

Twelve hundred years ago we **knew** that lightening was Thor's angry javelins thrown down to earth from Asgaard for some slight we had paid towards the gods. Two hundred years ago we **knew** that lightening was a form of electricity produced by some partially understood action of weather and storm clouds. Today we **know** lightening is a charged particle phenomenon created through electrical conductivity as a result of the hydrologic cycle's interaction with the atmosphere. Hypothetically speaking, in a few more decades we may come to **know** that lightening is nothing but a morphed neutrino burst resulting from the collective hyper-amplification of anti-matter pulsars leaked at the amber frequency from the 44th dimension. To paraphrase the Master Therion, we are each in our own unique and individual universes due to the unique and individual perspectives we possess as entities, even though it be paradoxically true that we all inhabit the same single Kosmos as well. . .

~

Mike Benjamin

The legend of shape-shifters, human beings with the ability to assume animal form, is a fable extant in every culture of every time period. Whether we look at such myths as a primitive mind's reaction to serial killers, boogeyman stories to scare children, or actual facts reflecting some terrible curse or supernatural disease, is of complete inconsequence to the nature of this treatise. Whether such creatures do exist, or have existed, the author makes no claims to direct knowledge. What is of our concern in this examination is the fact that such creatures were *thought* to have existed, and in some diverse cultures like Haiti, the Sudan, and Romania, are *thought* to exist even to this day. Thus, the reality of many cultures includes these monsters, and to the individuals in these cultures, such a reality is not fantastic but rather commonplace. Whether such a phenomenon is reality or not is inconsequential to this essay. It is, rather, the nature and power of **belief** with which this examination is preoccupied. Let us look then at this interesting phenomenon through our own lens of *hoplological*[117] analysis.

There are four basic types of explanation given to this phenomenon. (While popularly referred to as *lycanthropy*, specifically denoting human to wolf transformation, for our general purposes we will use the formal term of *therianthropy* in reference to any human to animal transformation):

1). By whatever means such a transformation occurs (i.e. Magick, witchcraft, family genealogy, curse, disease, etc.), the transformation is an actual, corporeal change in the subject's anatomical structure. That is, the subject's transformation into an animal occurs on a physical, bodily basis. He or she concretely transforms into the animal in question.

2). The next is not formally a transformation, but rather, is argued as a form of *obsession*. In this theory, the astral consciousness of the subject, their "Body of Light," is made to leave their actual physical body. It is then imposed upon the will and consciousness of an animal, in essence moving the animal's personality or soul aside, so that the subject can temporarily inhabit

---

[117] *"Hoplology"* (derived from the ancient Greek term for a soldier – the hoplite) was coined by the late great martial arts master Donald Draeger denoting the academic study of fighting arts. This essay, while written originally by this tome's author as a martial arts treatise, is reprinted here for its obvious occult application and insights as well.

the animal's body and use it as their own. When the subject removes their astral body from that of the animal's form, the animal supposedly returns to its normal functioning, or in some completely barbaric approaches, its mind is obliterated, or even more tragically, the animal dies.

3). The next explanation is also not a formal transformation, at least not visually to any observer. It is rather a mental/emotional and behavioral transformation through a type of *possession*. This is affected when the essence or spirit of an animal is invoked within the subject in order to partake in that animal's attributes or qualities. A perfect example of this was the ancient Teutonic Berserkers. Berserker means "bear skin" and refers to the fact that these ancient warriors would don the skins of bears or wolves for battle. They would also induce an altered state of consciousness through the use of alcohol and psychedelic plants and/or fungi. These measures were meant to foster an altered state of consciousness, a suspension of disbelief if you will, in which the warrior *believed* he had merged with the animal's skin and thus became that animal spiritually. This, combined with the social pressure of other tribal comrades expressing the same state of mind, would make the Berserker *feel* that he had transformed into an animal and could thus partake of that animal's strength, speed, courage, and ferocity.

4). Lastly, and in antithesis to the first, the subject's transformation into an animal is an illusion induced upon the observer. The transformation is not an actual physical change in the subject, but is rather a "glamour" or hallucination imposed upon whoever is watching. Again, the means by which this is accomplished are differing and have been variably explained as mesmerism, hypnosis, imposed hysteria, Magick, witchcraft, sorcery, voodoo, PSI, suggestion coupled with induced psychedelic psychosis, Neuro-Linguistic Programming, and so forth.

Again, I reiterate, we make no suppositions to the "truth" of any of these above statements. Whether one chooses to believe in any, all, or none of them is inconsequential to this examination. These are but a survey of the explanations given in various historical mythologies, legends, and traditions, East and West, North and South.

What is our concern is the fact that by certain practices one may obtain certain results. We ask for no blind faith, but rather the attitude of a scientist and a skeptic. If the following suggestions prove fruitful to the warrior,[118] then by all means, keep it as a part of your personal arsenal and repertoire. If these suggestions do not, then discard them upon the jump-kick junk-heap of other useless techniques.

Let us examine each of these explanations, and through the tool of adaptation, apply them to our New Warrior[119] purposes. We shall look at numbers one and two first, leaving an analysis of numbers three and four together for the end.

ON PHYSICAL TRANSFORMATIONS - It would be doubtful that even if a person could learn a means to physically transform themselves into an animal form, such a skill would be undesirable for many reasons. One, it would be painful beyond belief for bone and tissue to break down and then reform. It would be an agonizing experience of disintegration and reformation on a cellular level. If accomplished once, I doubt anyone would want to do so again.

However, on a totemistic level, transformation can be a viable aspect of the warrior's development. By totemistic we mean that there are certain animals (by their nature, beauty, qualities, etc.) that we *identify* with. As a result of this identification, we must strive to learn all we can about them through books, direct observation, videos, meditation, and the like. We must strive, therefore, to *emulate* their qualities in ourselves, and in so doing, *share of their nature and of the universe's powers that are reflected in that animal.* Likewise, in identifying with certain animals, we can come to an understanding of other animals whose qualities we are deficient in. We can thus also learn to apply their attributes to ourselves, and in so doing, *strengthen our weaknesses.*

---

[118] Or occultist.

[119] The author's theory or paradigm of the "New Warrior," to over-simplify it for purposes of brevity, denotes a change from the old aeon concept of the warrior. The New Warrior fights altruistically to preserve life and defend the biosphere and not for his or her own selfish, narcissistic, or material ends. The New Warrior does not hunt and practices vegetarianism or veganism to these ends as well, respecting all Sentient Beings as brothers and sisters. The New Warrior defends the weak and does not prostitute his or her skills to the rich or strong.

For example, perhaps I choose a dog as my totem, and meditate upon him to gain a greater sense of love, service, commitment, and loyalty. Perhaps I choose a cat as well to develop more individuality, non-conformity, grace, and stealth. The examples are endless. Ultimately, however, we must understand that the animal doesn't actually imbue us with any quality we don't already possess somewhere within. (As a microcosm, all that Humanity sees out there is already in here, within us – as above so below. . .*tat twam asi* – Thou Art That!). We just may not be as in touch with it as we should be! Thus, the animal acts as a mirror, or a magnifier, showing us another piece of what we already are, bringing a piece of what we could be from the depths of potential to the surface of actuality.

ON OBSESSION – As with physical transformations, it would seem unlikely that even if one could possess another animal's body and mind, why would one want to do this? What would be the beneficent purpose? Why would one wish to thieve the body and being of another? Has not the soul of one who has attained to humanity not traveled long and far through the lives of countless minerals, and plants, and animals to finally attain the summit of Earthly evolution? This would not only be an evolutionary step backwards, but a severe ethical lapse by being willing to partake in an infringement upon that sentient entity's liberty for even a moment. No! Obsession of an animal, or any use thereof for our own selfish benefit or purpose, is not the Way of the New Warrior.

There is perhaps no way to describe such a despicable practice as anything but evil, as it is the ultimate violation of any sentient Being's sole sovereignty. I have been personally privy to one form/lineage of familial Black Wicca in which the women of this clan allegedly utilized feline familiars in such a way. This practice is an abomination and stinks of our species' unique and particular hubris; a delusion played over and over, again and again, throughout humanity's spectrum, from religion to science, superstition to psychology. We seem to falsely believe that because we currently have a position of domination and authority over our fellow Earthlings that somehow we are also justified in exercising this power any way we want for our own selfish ends. Such a belief is at the heart of our own impending apocalypse. As the core of the New Warrior ethos we must come to understand that **they who possess power likewise and equally hold the responsibility to wield that power for the collective benefit of ALL who are affected by that exercise.**[120]

However, the essence of this "obsession" principle can be transformed, sublimated to a higher end, put to a positive and worthy use. Instead of wishing to obsess an animal and take possession of its form, we must instead learn to gain a feeling of complete and total empathy for the animal. We must (in a way akin to obsession, without its inherent exploitative premise) learn how to "live in the animal's skin." We must achieve a sense of empathy, of sympathy, of universal compassion for that animal so that we may have a grace, a glimpse of feeling for how it feels, of seeing as it sees, in order that we can more deeply understand the hardship and the suffering that this mutually sentient Being endures; to appreciate the joy and the life that this fellow creature participates in with us and with all of creation, with all of Divinity. Remember that Shakyamuni, the Tathagata, as part and parcel of his awakening under the Bodhi tree, remembering all of His past lives throughout the evolution of consciousness, saw himself as plants, as amphibians, as fish and insects, as birds and mammals. . .he remembered through a comprehensive *sammasati* all that he had been, the lives and struggles, adversity and deaths of all the forms he had taken through the wheel of *samsara* up to that point. It is this vision that is credited with transforming Siddartha Guatama's consciousness into that of a Buddha's perfect love and absolute compassion towards all Beings.

Even though such a complete vision and universal understanding like that gained by the Buddha may elude us, this practice can still gain the practitioner a valuable insight, even though partial and perhaps paltry when compared to the Buddha's. Nevertheless, through this practice we can gain a visceral comprehension and emotive identification with the animal's plight, with their internal feelings and environmental condition; and in so doing we facilitate a greater concern, a deeper love for

---

[120] This is but reflective of the Basic Moral Intuition (BMI) which espouses that we must live in such a way to foster the greatest amount of good for the greatest number of Beings.

all of Gaia and Her biosphere, for all of the Beings with which we share this gorgeous green and blue Eden.[121] In so doing, the New Warrior strives to be a better steward of this Earth, to be a defender of conservation, a protector of ecology. He or she vows to defend this planet's life and all of its wonderful biodiversity of Beings, from grass to giraffes, from tigers to trees, from kangaroos to kelp, from fish to bees, and all else above, below, and in between!

The days of humanity's attempted domination over Nature and animals for our own selfish greed, for our own insatiable consumptive desires, for our own leisure and ease, MUST BE OVER IF WE (AND MOST OF OUR FELLOW PLANETARY BRETHREN) ARE TO SURVIVE AS VIABLE SPECIES, ARE TO SURVIVE AS FAMILY TOGETHER ON THIS SPINNING BALL, OUR ONLY HOME IN THIS VAST UNIVERSE. We must come to understand that being truly "Pro-Life" (as so many fundamentalist Christians and Catholics mistakenly preach and *think* they are) must mean ALL OF LIFE, ALL OF THE BIOSPHERE, not just a priority on humanity's place and position in this world. Pro-Life must come to mean more than just "pro-human fetus" if we as a species are to survive. Now is a time in which we must shed our old ignorances, a time in which we must grow to be more than human, or we shall, in fact, grow no more. The future will be one of stagnation, reversion, decay, and demise if we do not, individually and collectively, consciously and actively, evolve ourselves into more than the terra-rapists we have so sadly become.

We now possess a much greater understanding of the interconnectedness of all things on Earth and in the universe, of the web of life in which humanity is but a part, of the nested

---

[121] In this vein, the Stoic wisdom of Marcus Aurelius holds particular importance, echoing the Gaia hypothesis that would follow nearly two millennia after him. He writes in his *Meditations,*

> Constantly regard the universe as one living being, having one substance and one soul; and observe how all things have reference to one perception, the perception of this one living being; and how all things act with one movement; and how all things are the cooperating causes of all things which exist; observe too the continuous spinning of the thread and the contexture of the web. (cited in Eliot, 1969, p. 219).

holarchy[122] in which we perch ourselves. We now know that what we do to the Earth and its other inhabitants we likewise do to ourselves. Humanity, like a cancer, is running amuck upon its source; or perhaps more accurately, like a parasite we are destroying the very host upon which our existence depends. And if we, as a species, do not wake up to our role as defenders and preservers of Nature, we will find ourselves in a near future (like the dinosaurs eons ago) lying in a bleak dust as the fossils and bones of an extinct tomorrow.

ON SELF-POSSESSION (OR AURIC THERIANTHROPY FOR COMBAT): Both mysticism and science teach that living forms emit a personal energy signature that is syncretically composed of vibrational frequencies: light, heat, electricity, radiation, and magnetism. It is this energy signature that has been called in both ancient and modern times the "aura." In adult humans the aura extends from the body as a generally egg-like, though oscillating shape, roughly six to ten feet in horizontal diameter, depending upon the physical health and mental-emotional state of the individual.

As a production and emission of our mind-body system, this aura is just as much a part of us as is our denser, cruder, physical body. But, this signature, this emission of our personal energy pattern and internal psycho-spiritual state, is much more fluid and congenial with our external environment and, dialectically, also with other Beings' internal states. Likewise, others' auras are also fluid and congenial, so between us becomes a give and take of subtle energies that most are not consciously aware. With our loved ones we may be more aware that such a give and take is evident, as we can feel, for instance, how another's mood flavors the room. With strangers it may also occasionally arise, as when we instantly and accurately like or dislike someone even though we've done no more than enter their aura's field. This energy is real, and its interplay and our perceptions of it (though ancient and inherent) also compose a new unfolding area of human evolution in both personal communication and social empathy.

---

[122] A term coined by Arthur Koestler and utilized extensively in Ken Wilber's Integralism.

As a vegetarian and practitioner of the *sadhana* (spiritual practice) of *pashu ahimsa* (non-harm to animals) I do not condone the actual donning of animal skins to facilitate the psycho-emotional transformation into an animal as done by the ancient berserkers (outlined above), as this would require the taking of animal's life to accomplish. However, the general outlines of their method, taken into account with the details set forth below in the occult practice known as "assuming god-forms," can be applied for combative usage. In applying this method, a fighter can facilitate a greater sense of courage, ferocity, and strength in themselves through identification with an animal totem.

(By totem, I mean any animal whose physical characteristics and spiritual qualities appeal to you as a person. In regards to combat, we must seek a totem whose qualities are those we wish to intensify for our combative purposes. If we need increased strength, perhaps the bear or moose. For speed and agility, the cougar or snake. For ferocity, maybe the wolf or tiger. For cunning, the fox. Survival intelligence, the crow. . .and so on).

With an animal selected for our totem, we must come to know all we can about it; its habitat, behavior, hunting style, social life, eating preferences, and so on. Once this is done, we can apply the technique of god-form assumption to our animal totem in hopes of gaining the same benefits lauded by the berserker method.

In regards to "assuming god-forms," the following description by Dr. Israel Regardie (2004) on the Hermetic Order of the Golden Dawn's method of this practice deserves careful study. Wherever the good doctor describes this practice in regards to a pagan god, I have simply replaced his direction with the term "totem animal" thus chosen for our focus:

> . . .he should familiarize himself with the shape and form of the (totem animal), the postures in which the (totem animal) is usually portrayed, the gestures customarily employed, and (its) colors. . .With all of these facts in memory, the student should proceed to the more difficult phase of the work which consists of the application of the Imagination and the Will, trained by

345

his former practices. In his working. . .he should endeavor to construct before his mind's eye a perfect image or mask of the (totem animal). The form must stand out boldly and clearly in the vision of the Imagination, gigantic, resplendent, and irradiating. . .These details should then be applied to the simulacrum held firmly in the mind, until it is seen before the living soul as a dynamic image. . .an image in which abides no trace of imperfection. It is a tremendous task of creative imagination, and an arduous one. But day after day it must be continued with ardor and devotion, until the sacred task is consummated, and, complete and glowing, the (animal totem) stands forth…With this image held firmly in the Astral Light, (he) should endeavor to envelop his own form with the shroud of the (animal totem) and then to unite himself with the Form enshrouding him. As (Eliphas) Levi has already been quoted as saying, the Astral body will assume the form of any powerful thought which the mind evokes. This Astral effigy of the (totem animal), previously but an image external to the body…should now be arranged. . .as a figure around his own astral form until they coincide, his own Body of Light being changed and transmuted into the Body of the (totem animal). Only when (he) actually feels the superb influx of spiritual power, the acquisition of the. . .force and energy and spiritual illumination, only when he knows in the intuition of the (totem animal) trance that the identification has been accomplished, is the task of creation complete…Simultaneously with the process of unification with the Body of the (totem animal) it will prove of no little assistance if an invocation is recited. . .chanting praises to the (totem animal), delineating the nature and spiritual qualities of the (totem animal) in speech. . .With the recitation of each point of the invocation. . .a strong realization in thought of the words should be obtained. . .the astral form of the (totem animal) should be seen and actually felt with the senses to emit a refulgence. . .the process of the identification with the Astral Form should be accomplished and realized as vividly as possible. . .By infallible signs within his own consciousness, the quickening of a new life, (he) will. . .know that success does crown his effort. In him, and in his soul, the (totem animal) will seek his eternal dwelling place. Within the heart will be a sanctuary and a serene habitation of a tremendous spiritual force, a...consciousness which throughout all duration will live in him, transforming the child of the earth. . .Within himself latent unfolding spiritual faculties will be felt, and the faint memory of experience gained in time long since past and dead will gradually arise to illuminate the mind and pulse anew in the heart, expanding the horizon of consciousness. (pp. 254-258).

ON INDUCING THERIANTHROPIC ILLUSION OR "GLAMOUR" UPON ANOTHER: It is argued in some systems of occultism that the Will of an individual can in some ways be imposed upon another person at a distance for certain effects. In some systems, one such type of technique is believed to induce upon the observer the illusion that the other individual has been transformed into an animal form. While the benefits to such a technique would be obvious in combat (i.e. scaring the living tar out of your opponent), the very nature of such a technique is, in significant ways, in antithesis to the ethos of the New Warrior.

Such a technique infringes on the other individual by imposing an outright falsity, a lie, upon their awareness. Even though this "other" be an "enemy," we must always be of great care that our methods do not infringe upon the very nature of liberty itself, which is grounded in free-thought. Any action taken that restricts, lessens, or obfuscates another's right to mental clarity is one that stinks of mind control and Black

Magick and should be considered anathema to every New Warrior. It is the New Warrior who must strive to shine light upon the darkness, to bring understanding where there is ignorance, and truth where there is error. To affect such a method upon another (designed to instigate a temporary state of hallucination and unreality) is a violation of that individual's sovereign liberty, even if they be a foe. No, this is not our Way, and its usage should be relegated to the trash heap of unethical, dare we say (though so un-Advaitic!) "evil" practices that must be avoided.

# Conclusions

As exemplified throughout the Asian martial arts, from kung-fu to karate to silat, animals have long been a source of inspiration and knowledge for those masters and practitioners with the ears to hear and the eyes to see. Likewise, in the realm of myth and Magick, animals have been the inspiration for the development of both insightful revelations on one hand and sheer misapprehensions and abuses on the other. In the realm of occult *therianthropy* this dichotomy is most apparent. Practices or rituals, like those outlined above, that prove spiritually maladapted or overtly and morally wrong can be changed (as with the slight modifications listed above) to instead prove fruitful for the facilitation of benevolence, for the manifestation of compassion, and for the gaining of knowledge. As the ancient Masters of both East and West knew (from Pythagoras to Bodhidharma), animals are a well-spring and source, as well as a channel, of Nature's Divine beauty, grace, beneficence, love, fecundity, and power. As such, animals are to be revered and respected for their intrinsic, not utilitarian, worth. They are to be viewed and loved as no less than the sentient family members with whom we share one home, a common mother, and an identical fate.

# Banishing Epilogue Poem

### Evolution

God
sat forever

silent
and still

nothing all
and emptiness

beginningless sleeping
chaos

endless
awakening light

infinite dragon devouring
its birth of starlit tail.

And God said to Itself,
*"Go out and play."*

And so It did
to become
the million million changing things

that forgot Itself

simply

to remember.

# References

Albertus, F. (1974). *The alchemist's handbook*. York Beach, ME: Samuel Weiser.

Andrews, G. (Ed.) (1997). *Drugs and magic*. Lilbum, GA: IllumiNet Press.

Avalon, A. (1974). *The serpent power*. New York, NY: Dover .

Bates, M. (1960). *The forest and the sea*. Alexandria, VA: Time-Life Books.

Birch, C. & Cobb, J. (1981). *The liberation of life*. Cambridge, UK: Cambridge University Press.

Berry, T. (1990). *The dream of the earth*. San Francisco, CA: Sierra Club Books.

Berry, T. (1999). *The great work – Our way into the future*. New York, NY: Bell Tower.

Berry, T. & Swimme, B. (1994). *The universe story*. New York, NY: Harper Collins.

Blake, W. (1995). *Selected poems*. New York, NY: Gramercy Books.

Blakney, R. (Trans.) (1941). *Meister Eckhart: A modern translation*. New York, NY: Harper and Row.

Blavatsky, H.P. (1976). *Isis unveiled*. Wheaton, IL: Theosophical Publishing House.

Blavatsky, H.P. (1977). *The secret doctrine*. Wheaton, IL: Theosophical Publishing House.

Brennan, T. (2013). Stream of consciousness. http://blog.gaiam.com/quotes/authors/sriaurobindo/45931.

Brooke, T. (1988). *Avatar of night*. Eugene, OR: Harvest House .

Builders of the Adytum, (1963). *Adytum news, Vol. 4* (#3, July-September). Los Angeles, CA.

Burroughs, W. (2012). *Junky*. Greenwich, NY: Grove Press.

Byck, R. (Ed.) (1975). *The cocaine papers – Sigmund Freud*. New York, NY: New American Library.

Campbell, J. (1949). *The hero with one thousand faces*. New York, NY: MJF Books.

Carson, R. (1964). *Silent spring*. New York, NY: Crest Books.

Carus, P. (2008). *The gospel of Buddha*. Kila, MT: Kessinger .

Case, P. F. (1985). *The true and invisible Rosicrucian order.* (4th ed.) York Beach, ME: Samuel Weiser.

Case, P.F. (1989). *Highlights of tarot.* (14th ed.) Burbank, CA: Candlelight Press.

Case, P. F. (1989). *The book of tokens.* (14th ed.) Los Angeles, CA: Builders of the Adytum.

Case, P.F. (1997). The secret doctrine of the tarot, chapter VI. *The Portico, Vol. V* (#2), 1-19. Los Angeles, CA.

Cavendish, R. (1983). *The black arts.* New York, NY: Perigee Books.

Chesteron, G.K. (1955). *The everlasting man.* New York, NY: Dodd, Mead, and Co.

Chopra, D. (1995). *The way of the wizard.* New York, NY: Harmony Books.

Clausen, H. (1976). *Clausen's commentaries on morals and dogma.* San Diego, CA: Neyenesch.

Colquhoun, E. (1975). *The sword of wisdom.* New York, NY: Putnam and Sons.

Crowley, A. (1970). *Magick in theory and practice.* New York, NY: Castle Books.

Crowley, A. (1976). *The book of the law.* York Beach, ME: Samuel Weiser.

Crowley, A. (1991). *Eight lectures on yoga.* Phoenix, AZ: New Falcon Publications.

Crowley, A. (1993). *777 and other qabalistic writings.* York Beach, ME: Samuel Weiser.

Crowley, A. (1994). *Magick without tears.* Phoenix, AZ: New Falcon Publications.

Crowley, A. (1995). *The book of Thoth.* York Beach, ME: Samuel Weiser.

Crowley, A. (1996). *Book four.* York Beach, ME: Samuel Weiser.

Crowley, A. (1996). *The book of lies.* York Beach, ME: Samuel Weiser.

David-Neel, A. (1971). *Magic and mystery in Tibet.* New York, NY: Dover .

De Chardin, P.T. (1964). *The future of man.* New York, NY: Harper Collins.

Denning, M. & Phillips, O. (1991). *Foundations of high magick, Vol. I.* St. Paul, MN: Llewellyn.

Dyer, W. (1999). *Manifest your destiny*. New York, NY: Harper Paperbacks.

Eliot, C. (Ed.) (1969). *Plato, Epictetus, Marcus Aurelius*. New York, NY: Collier & Son.

Elk, W. B. (1991). *Black Elk speaks*. New York, NY: Harper Collins.

Evanz-Wentz, W.Y. (Ed.) (1968). *The Tibetan book of the great liberation*. Oxford, UK: Oxford University Press Paperback.

Evanz-Wentz, W.Y. (Ed.) (1971). *The Tibetan book of the dead*. (2nd ed.) Oxford, UK: Oxford University Press Paperback.

Flowers, S.E. (1995). *Hermetic magick*. York Beach, ME: Samuel Weiser.

Frazer, J. G. (1951). *The golden bough – A study in magic and religion – one volume abridged edition*. New York, NY: Macmillan.

Gardner, G. (1991). *Witchcraft today*. New York, NY: Magickal Childe Publishing.

George, L. (1995). *Alternative realities*. New York, NY: Facts on File.

Godwin, D. (1994). *Godwin's cabalistic encyclopedia*. St. Paul, MN: Llewellyn .

Godwin, J., Chanel, C., & Deveney, J. (1995). *The Hermetic brotherhood of Luxor*. York Beach, ME: Samuel Weiser.

Harris, V. (Trans.) (1974). *The book of five rings*. Woodstock, NY: The Overlook Press.

Huxley, A. (1932). *Brave new world*. London, UK: Chatto and Windus.

Huxley, A. (1970). *The perennial philosophy*. New York, NY: Harper and Row.

Incognito, M. (1949). *The secret doctrine of the Rosicrucians*. Chicago, IL: Occult Press.

International Vegetarian Union (2012). Henry David Thoreau. www.IVU.org. http://www.ivu.org.history/usa19/thoreau.html.

Jacobi, J. (Ed.) (1988). *Paracelsus – Selected writings*. Princeton, NJ: Princeton University Press.

Jung, C.G. (1970). *Analytical psychology, its theory and practice*. New York, NY: Vintage Books.

King, F. (1997). *Ritual magic of the golden dawn*. Rochester, NY: Destiny Books.

Koenig, P.R. (1996). The Ordo Templi Orientis phenomenon. http://www.parareligion.ch/.

Kon, F. (2000). Vegetarian quotes. http://choices.cs.uiuc.edu/~f-kon/vegetarian.html.

Layton, B. (Ed.) (1987). *The Gnostic scriptures*. New York, NY: Doubleday.

Levi, E. (1996). *Paradoxes of the highest science*. Kila, MT: Kessinger.

Levi, E. & Waite, A.E. (Trans.) (1910). *Transcendental magic, its doctrine and ritual*. Chicago, IL: Occult Publishing House.

Levi, E. & Waite, A. E. (Trans.) (1996). *The history of magic*. Kila, MT: Kessinger .

Levi, E & Waite, A.E. (Trans.) (2010). *Threshold of magical science*. Kila, MT: Kessinger.

Levi, E. & Wescott, W.W. (Ed.) (1996) *The magical ritual of the sanctum regnum*. Kila, MT: Kessinger .

Linscott, A. (Ed.) (1959). *Selected poems and letters of Emily Dickinson*. Garden City, KS: International Collector's Library.

Lovecraft, H.P. (1965). *Dagon and other macabre tales*. Sauk City, WI: Arkham House.

Lovret, F. (1987). *The way and the power – Secrets of Japanese strategy*. Boulder, CO: Paladin Press.

MacGregor-Mathers, S.L. (Trans.) (1975). *The sacred magic of Abra-Melin the mage*. New York, NY: Dover.

MacGregor-Mathers, S.L. (Trans.) (1989). *The key of Solomon the king*. York Beach, ME: Samuel Weiser.

Mackey, A. & Clegg, R. (1929). *Mackey's revised encyclopedia of Freemasonry, vol. II*. Chicago, IL: Masonic History Company.

Maharshi, Ramana (2008). *Who am I?*(24th ed.) Tiruvannamalai, IN: Sri Ramanasramam.

Maugham, S. (2003). *The razor's edge*. New York, NY: Vintage Books.

Osho (1974). *The book of secrets*. New York, NY: St. Martin's Griffin.

Ouspensky, P.D. (1970). *Tertium organum*. New York, NY: Vintage Books.

Pessoa, F. & Zenith, R. (Trans.) (2002). *The book of disquiet.* New York, NY: Penguin Group.

Philosophers of Nature (1997). *The Stone,* (Issue #23, Nov.-Dec.). Wheaton, IL.

Ratti, O. & Westbrook, A. (1973). *Secrets of the samurai – The martial arts of feudal Japan.* Rutland, VT: Charles E. Tuttle.

Regan, T. (1983). *The case for animal right.* Berkeley, CA: University of California .

Regardie, I. (1994). *The golden dawn.* (6th ed.) St. Paul, MN: Llewellyn.

Regardie, I. (2004). *The tree of life.* (3rd ed.) St. Paul, MN: Llewellyn.

Reymond, L. (1983). *Letters from A Baul – Life within life.* Calcutta, IN: Sri Aurobindo Pathamandir Publishing.

Richardson, R. (Ed.) (1990). *Ralph Waldo Emerson – Selected essays, lectures, and poems.* New York, NY: Bantam.

Scholem, G. (1965). *On the kabbalah and its symbolism.* New York, NY: Schocken Books.

Scholem, G. (1974). *Major trends in Jewish mysticism.* New York, NY: Schocken Books.

Scholem, G. (1975). *On the mystical shape of the Godhead.* New York, NY: Schocken Books.

Scholem, G. (1977). *The Zohar.* New York, NY: Schocken Books.

Spence, L. (1960). *An encyclopedia of occultism.* Secaucus, NJ: Citadel Press.

Summers, M. (1991). *The vampire.* New York, NY: Dorset Press.

Summers, M. (1996). *The Werewolf.* Hyde Park, IL: University Press.

Thoreau, H. D. (1980). *Walden and civil disobedience.* New York, NY: New American Library.

Tolle, E. (1999). *The power of now.* Novato, CA: New World Library.

Tolle, E. (2005). *A new earth.* New York, NY: Penguin Group.

Unger, Merrill (1973) *Demons in the world today.* Carol Stream, IL: Tyndale House.

Waite, A. E. (1995). *The pictorial key to the tarot.* New York, NY: Barnes and Noble.

Wilber, K. (1996). *Up from Eden.* Wheaton, IL: Quest Books.

Wilber, K. (1996). *The atman project.* (2nd ed.) Wheaton, IL: Quest Books.

Wilber, K. (2000). *Sex, ecology, and spirituality – The spirit of evolution.* Boston, MA: Shambhala .

Yang, J. M. (1989). *Advanced Yang style tai chi ch'uan, Vol. I.* Jamaica Plain, MA: YMAA Publication Center.

Yates, F. (1996). *The Rosicrucian enlightenment.* New York, NY: Barnes and Noble .

# Author's Bio

Born October 18th, 1969, Michael Benjamin is a lifelong resident of Rockford, Illinois. He earned his B.A. in History with a minor in Southeast Asian Studies from Northern Illinois University in 1992. Since graduating he has spent over twenty years as a social worker with mentally ill adults, juvenile delinquents, and foster children in addition to writing on the occult and teaching martial arts.

Mr. Benjamin began his martial arts training in 1980 in Okinawan *Shorei-Ryu Karate* under "Bad" Brad Hefton, who would go on to become the PKA World Heavy-Weight Kick Boxing champion. In his teens Mr. Benjamin trained in *Kobudo* and *Kenjutsu* under *Soke* Rodney Sacharnoski, Grandmaster of the world renowned **Juko-Kai Kokusei Remmei Martial Arts Federation**, earning the award of outstanding sword student of the year in 1988. He would then go on to train under *Sigung* Michael Knipprath in *Kang-Nei-Chin Ch'ung Kuo Ch'uan Shaolin Kung-Fu* earning the rank of 4th degree black sash. Under *Sigung* Knipprath he would also earn his *Yondan* (4th degree black belt) in *Shorei Goju Kempo Karate*. To this day, Mr. Benjamin remains the *Sigung's* senior student. With *Sigung* Knipprath's blessing, Mr. Benjamin opened his own *kwoon/dojo* in 2000 to teach his own curriculum of martial arts which he still runs today. (His website can be seen at **www.closequarterskempo.com**). Through the 1990's he was also privileged to have trained under the late great Grandmaster of *Modern Arnis*, Professor Remy Presas. In 2012, Mr. Benjamin earned his Level 5 – Full Instructor's license in *Natural Spirit International* under its Grandmaster, world renowned weapons designer and video producer *Datu* Kelly S. Worden, the longtime official hand-to-hand combat instructor for the First Special Forces Group/Green Berets of Ft. Lewis, Washington. Mr. Benjamin remains the sole Illinois instructor-affiliate for *Datu* Worden and is one of fewer than two dozen men ranked as such in the world. In 2014 Mr. Benjamin also became the first video author from Illinois with the legendary tactical publisher Paladin Press of Boulder, Colorado.

Mr. Benjamin began creatively writing at the age of ten with a poem he authored about death. He has since published two collections of poetry; *The Wind of Seasons* (1994) and *Crowsongs* (1998). He is the only martial artist in the Midwest whose articles have appeared in the legendary magazines *Inside Kung-Fu, Black Belt,* and *Blade.* He has also worked as the official hoplologist for Kelly Worden's **Natural Spirit International Combative Arts Association** assisting in the production of articles, newsletters, and training modules. Mr. Benjamin's article, *"Core Principles of the Worden Defense System"* is the opening essay in *Datu* Worden's official hand-to-hand combat manual for the U.S. Army's First Special Forces Group. Mr. Benjamin's work has also appeared in numerous other genres and mediums, ranging from an anti-dog fighting campaign with the Humane Society of Chicago, to newspapers, to poetry anthologies, to *The Lantern* (the official journal of the **Builders of the Adytum**).

Raised as a youth in the False Church of Roman Catholicism, Mr. Benjamin discarded exoteric papal, fundamentalist, and protestant misinterpretations of the Christos' message by his teens. He became an avid student of Aleister Crowley for almost three decades, spending a few years in the O.T.O. before rejecting that system as erroneous as well. (He remains, however, one of the few people in the world with verbatim copies of Aleister Crowley's complete and unpublished initiation rites for all of the OTO levels). In 1996 he achieved his 32nd degree (Sublime Prince of the Royal Secret) in Scottish Rite Freemasonry. He spent twelve years as a formal intitiate in Paul Foster Case's **BOTA** studying and practicing that Golden Dawn-based system of Hermeticism, Qabalah, Tarot, and Alchemy (and still endorses the total spiritual validity and Magickal legitimacy of that organization). He has also extensively studied the systems of Gardnerian and familial forms of Wicca, Gurdjieff's Fourth Way, Ramana Mahrashi's *Nan Yar*, the *Vigyan Bhairav Tantra* of Shiva, and Taoist Qigong. He now considers himself a practicing *Mahayana Buddhist* focusing particularly upon its *Ch'an/Zen, Madhyamika, Nyingma, Kargyutpa, Vajrayana,* and *Dzogchen* branches. Through those teachings he has achieved the meditative state known in Tibetan Buddhism as the "near black attainment" but, admittedly, has not yet accomplished the "pure clear light." He furthermore espouses that Eckhart Tolle and Ken Wilber are living Bodhisattva-Buddhas whose work *must be studied and practiced if humanity is to evolve and survive* beyond its current aggressive-narcissistic evolutionary level. Despite these details, for those who know, Mr. Benjamin also emphatically asserts that his cairnstone will be shaped in the form of a **cross and a rose**.

A strict vegetarian, animal rights advocate, and feral cat caregiver, Mr. Benjamin lives with his soul-mate Donna and their many beloved felines in a modest home on Keith Creek.

CPSIA information can be obtained
at www.ICGtesting.com
Printed in the USA
FFOW02n1654290514
5652FF